Žižek Now

Theory Now

Series Editor: Ryan Bishop

Virilio Now John Armitage
Baudrillard Now Ryan Bishop
Žižek Now Jamil Khader and Molly Anne Rothenberg

Žižek Now

Current Perspectives in Žižek Studies

EDITED BY
JAMIL KHADER AND MOLLY ANNE ROTHENBERG

polity

Copyright © Jamil Khader and Molly Anne Rothenberg 2013

The right of Jamil Khader and Molly Anne Rothenberg to be identified as Authors of this
Work has been asserted in accordance with the UK Copyright, Designs and Patents Act
1988.

First published in 2013 by Polity Press

Polity Press
65 Bridge Street
Cambridge CB2 1UR, UK

Polity Press
350 Main Street
Malden, MA 02148, USA

ISBN-13: 978-0-7456-5370-9 (hardback)
ISBN-13: 978-0-7456-5371-6 (paperback)

A catalogue record for this book is available from the British Library.

Typeset in 11 on 13 pt Bembo
by Toppan Best-set Premedia Limited
Printed and bound in Great Britain by the MPG Printgroup

The publisher has used its best endeavors to ensure that the URLs for external websites
referred to in this book are correct and active at the time of going to press. However,
the publisher has no responsibility for the websites and can make no guarantee that a site
will remain live or that the content is or will remain appropriate.

Every effort has been made to trace all copyright holders, but if any have been inadvertently
overlooked the publisher will be pleased to include any necessary credits in any subsequent
reprint or edition.

For further information on Polity, visit our website: www.politybooks.com

Contents

Acknowledgments

The editors wish to extend their sincere thanks to all the contributors to this volume for their commitment to the success of this project. In particular, they would like to thank Slavoj Žižek for his support of and collaboration on this project. The editors also gratefully acknowledge the expert assistance of the staff at Polity, especially Andrea Drugan, Lauren Mulholland, and Susan Beer.

Both of us would like to thank our families for making this project possible. Jonathan Riley has provided much-needed and appreciated support, good humor, and expertise to Molly.

Jamil would like to thank his wife, Marie B. Velez, and three daughters, Jamila M., Alana J., and Salma L., for their unconditional love, encouragement, and patience with him through the endless hours he spent working on this project, especially when Žižek's ideas on everything contemporary became the main topic of discussion around the dinner table or on family trips.

At Stetson University, Jamil would like to thank the outgoing Dean of the College of Arts and Sciences, Dr Grady Ballenger, and various colleagues, especially Karen Kaivola and John Pearson, for their encouragement and support for his work. He would like also to acknowledge the assistance of Susan Connell Derryberry and Cathy Ervin at the Dupont-Ball library at Stetson University. Part of the research for his chapter in this book was supported by a summer grant from Stetson University. Molly thanks her colleagues at Tulane University, especially

Dean Carole Haber, whose encouragement of her scholarship during her time as chair was particularly welcome. She also gratefully acknowledges support from the fund for her Weiss Presidential Fellowship at Tulane. Both editors thank Engram Wilkinson for his research assistance.

Notes on Contributors

BRUNO BOSTEELS is Professor of Romance Studies at Cornell University. He is the author of *Alain Badiou, une trajectoire polémique* (La Fabrique, 2009); *Badiou and Politics* (Duke University Press, 2011); *The Actuality of Communism* (Verso, 2011); and *Marx and Freud in Latin America: Politics, Psychoanalysis, and Religion in Times of Terror* (Verso, 2012). He is also the author of dozens of articles on modern Latin American literature and culture, and on contemporary European philosophy and political theory.

VERENA ANDERMATT CONLEY is Long-Term Visiting Professor of Literature and Comparative Literature and of Romance Languages and Literatures at Harvard, where she teaches courses on Parisian cityscapes, transformations of space in contemporary culture, the city, technology, existential literature, and cultural theory. Her recent books include: *Spatial Ecologies: Urban Sites, State and World-Space in French Critical Theory* (Liverpool University Press, 2012); *Littérature, Politique et communisme: Lire "Les Lettres françaises," 1942–72* (New York: Lang, 2005); *The War with the Beavers: Learning to be Wild in the North Woods* (Minnesota, 2003; 2005); and *Ecopolitics: The Environment in Poststructuralist Thought* (Routledge, 1997). She is also the editor of *Rethinking Technologies* (Minnesota, 1993; 1997).

ADRIAN JOHNSTON is a Professor in the Department of Philosophy at the University of New Mexico at Albuquerque and an Assistant Teaching Analyst at the Emory Psychoanalytic Institute in Atlanta. He is the author of *Time Driven: Metapsychology and the Splitting of the Drive* (2005); *Žižek's Ontology: A Transcendental Materialist Theory of Subjectivity* (2008); and *Badiou, Žižek, and Political Transformations: The Cadence of Change* (2009); all published by Northwestern University Press. He has three books scheduled for publication over the course of the next year: *Self and Emotional Life: Merging Philosophy, Psychoanalysis, and Neurobiology* (co-authored with Catherine Malabou and forthcoming from Columbia University Press); *Adventures in Transcendental Materialism: Dialogues with Contemporary Thinkers* (Edinburgh University Press); and *The Outcome of Contemporary French Philosophy: Prolegomena to Any Future Materialism, Volume One* (the first installment of a trilogy forthcoming from Northwestern University Press). With Todd McGowan and Slavoj Žižek, he is a co-editor of the book series *Diaeresis* at Northwestern University Press.

JAMIL KHADER is Professor of English and Director of the Gender Studies Program at Stetson University. He is the author of *Cartographies of Transnational Feminisms: Geography, Culture, Identity, Politics* (Lexington, 2012) and numerous publications on transnational feminisms, supernatural fiction, and literary theory that have appeared in various national and international literary journals including, among others: *Ariel, Feminist Studies, College Literature; MELUS; The Journal of the Fantastic in the Arts; The Journal of Postcolonial Writing; The Journal of Commonwealth and Postcolonial Studies; The Journal of Homosexuality*; and other collections.

TODD McGOWAN teaches critical theory and film at the University of Vermont. His books include: *Out of Time: Desire in Atemporal Cinema* (University of Minnesota Press, 2011); *The Real Gaze: Film Theory after Lacan* (State University of New York Press, 2007); and with Paul Eisenstein, *Rupture: On the Emergence of the Political* (Northwestern University Press, 2012).

IAN PARKER was co-founder and is co-director (with Erica Burman) of the Discourse Unit (www.discourseunit.com). He is a member of the *Asylum: Magazine for Democratic Psychiatry* collective, and a practicing psychoanalyst in Manchester. His research and writing intersects with psychoanalysis and critical theory. He is a member of the Centre for Freudian Analysis and Research, the London Society of the New Lacanian School and the College of Psychoanalysts, UK. His books include: *Revolution in Psychology: Alienation to Emancipation* (Pluto, 2007); and *Lacanian Psychoanalysis: Revolutions in Subjectivity* (Routledge, 2011).

JOSHUA RAMEY is Visiting Assistant Professor at Haverford College. His work covers issues in contemporary continental philosophy, aesthetics, and philosophy of religion. He is the author of *The Hermetic Deleuze: Philosophy and Spiritual Ordeal* (Duke University Press, 2012). He has also published work on figures such as Žižek, Adorno, Warhol, Cronenberg, Deleuze, Badiou, and Rancière in such journals as *Angelaki, Discourse, SubStance*, and *Political Theology*.

MOLLY ANNE ROTHENBERG is Professor of English at Tulane University and a practicing adult psychoanalyst. Her publications include: *The Excessive Subject: A New Theory of Social Change* (Polity 2009); and *Perversion and the Social Relation* (Duke University Press 2003, co-edited with Slavoj Žižek and Dennis Foster). Her work has appeared in *Critical Inquiry, PMLA, ELH*, and the *Journal of the American Psychoanalytic Association*, among others. A chapter on Jacques Rancière's work is forthcoming in *Modernism and Theory* (Routledge), edited by Jean-Michel Rabaté. At present, she is working on a book manuscript that highlights the reactionary positions implicit in diasporic identifications.

ERIK VOGT is Gwendolyn Miles Smith Professor for Philosophy at Trinity College (USA), as well as Dozent for Philosophy at University of Vienna (Austria). He is the author and (co-)editor of fourteen books and has translated six books by Žižek into German. His most recent publications include: *Slavoj Žižek und die Gegenwartsphilosophie* (Vienna – Berlin: Turia + Kant, 2011); *Monstrosity in Literature, Psychoanalysis, and Philosophy*, ed. with G. Unterthurner (Vienna – Berlin: Turia + Kant, 2012); *Antirassismus – Antikolonialismus – Politiken der Emanzipation: Zur Aktualität von Jean-Paul Sartre und Frantz Fanon* (Vienna – Berlin: 2012, Turia + Kant, forthcoming).

SLAVOJ ŽIŽEK is a Hegelian philosopher, Lacanian psychoanalyst, and Communist social analyst. He is a researcher at the Institute of Humanities, Birkbeck College, University of London. His latest publications include: *Less Than Nothing* and *The Year of Dreaming Dangerously* (both London: Verso Books 2012).

Part One

Part One

Introduction
Žižek Now or Never: Ideological Critique and the Nothingness of Being

Jamil Khader

Arguably the most prolific and widely read philosopher of our time, Slavoj Žižek has made significant interventions in many disciplines of the human and natural sciences. Appropriating Lacanian psychoanalysis as a privileged conceptual fulcrum to reload German idealism (Hegel) through Marxism and, more recently, Christianity, Žižek has written extensively (and in several languages) on a dizzying array of topics that include global capitalism, psychoanalysis, opera, totalitarianism, cognitive science, racism, human rights, religion, new media, popular culture, cinema, love, ethics, environmentalism, New Age philosophy, and politics. His interdisciplinary *oeuvre* juxtaposes diverse fields and disciplines in many surprising ways, regularly springing unexpected twists and reversals on the reader. He not only subjects these disciplines to an ideological metacritique of the nature of knowledge itself, but also engages these disciplines through a parallax view, the "confrontation of two closely linked perspectives between which no neutral common ground is possible" (Žižek 2006: 4). For Žižek, rubbing these disciplines against each other does not produce a totalizing synthesis of opposites but rather allows for articulating the gaps within and between these fields through the Hegelian method of negative dialectics that clears a space for elaborating new responses to the underlying antagonism.

Who is this Žižek? What is his work all about? What are the broader theoretical trajectories that frame his work? How can his popular appeal as a philosopher and public intellectual be explained? Slavoj Žižek was born on March 21, 1949 in Ljubljana, Slovenia, the northernmost republic in the Socialist Federal Republic of Yugoslavia, and grew up under the rule of Marshal Josip Broz Tito, who served as president from 1953 to 1980. Although he was a founding member of the Cominform, Tito defied Soviet hegemony and developed an independent path to socialism, while also suppressing particularistic national sentiments in the name of a unified Yugoslavia. The relative cultural freedom in Tito's "second Yugoslavia" has been credited with having an everlasting impact on Žižek's intellectual development and career, allowing him to define his position on the margins of dominant national culture, in critical distance from and resistance to the party line and its institutions or any other mainstream orthodoxy.[1] In this semi-liberal environment, Žižek developed an obsession with and an appreciation for Western cultural commodities, particularly Hollywood films and detective fiction written in English, over and against cultural and literary products in his own country, which he considered to be either Communist or nationalist propaganda. Nonetheless, as Ian Parker notes in his contribution to this volume, living in "the times of lies" that characterized the regime left its indelible mark on Žižek's thought, which was "intimately linked to sarcastic and then increasingly open opposition, a politics of ideology critique that was smart enough not to believe that it spoke in the name of any unmediated authentic reality under the surface." After abandoning his teenage idea of directing films, as he says in a recent interview with the *Telegraph*, Žižek realized by the age of seventeen that he wanted to be a philosopher. He thus obtained an undergraduate degree in philosophy and sociology in 1971, and a Master of Arts in philosophy in 1975 from the University of Ljubljana, writing a 400-page thesis on French structuralism, which the authorities deemed to be ideologically suspicious, costing him a teaching position he was promised at the university. In fact, as Žižek recalls in a conversation with Glyn Daly, he "had to write a special supplement because the first version was rejected for not being Marxist enough" (Daly 2004: 31).

For the next two years, Žižek served in the Yugoslav army and translated German philosophy to support his wife and son, until 1977, when he took up a "humiliating job," as he states in the film *Žižek!*, at the Central Committee of the League of Slovene Communists. In these years, Žižek founded, with Mladen Dolar and Renata Salecl, who became his second wife, the Society for Theoretical Psychoanalysis in Ljubljana, served on the editorial board of a journal called Problemi, and published a book series called Analecta. In 1979 Žižek took a job as Researcher at the University of Ljubljana's Institute for Sociology, where he "had the freedom to develop [his] own ideas" in philosophy and Lacanian psychoanalysis and earned his first Doctor of Arts degree in philosophy · in 1981, writing his dissertation on German Idealism. In the same year, he traveled to Paris for the first time where he met Lacan's son-in-law, Jacques-Alain Miller, who invited Žižek and Dolar to attend an exclusive thirty-student seminar on Lacan at the École de la Cause Freudienne, analyzed him, and secured a teaching fellowship for him as visiting professor at the Department of Psychoanalysis at the Université Paris-VIII. Four years later, Žižek successfully defended his second doctoral dissertation, a Lacanian reading of Hegel, Marx, and Kripke, with Miller, but the latter refused to publish Žižek's dissertation in his own publishing house, forcing Žižek to publish it outside mainstream Lacanian circles.

Meanwhile, Žižek became more involved in the oppositional democratic politics back in Slovenia, writing for the radical youth magazine *Mladina*, publicly resigning from the Communist party in protest at the trial of journalists associated with that magazine, cofounding the Liberal Democratic Party, and running as its candidate in the first multi-party presidential elections in the country in 1990, but narrowly missing office. He served as the Ambassador of Science for the republic of Slovenia in 1991, and continues to serve as an informal advisor to the Slovenian government. Žižek is currently a Professor in the Department of Philosophy at the University of Ljubljana, the International Director of the Birkbeck Institute for the Humanities in London, a returning faculty member of the European Graduate School, and since 1991 he has also held visiting positions at different universities in the US and the UK. He also serves on the editorial board of the Analecta series in Slovenia, and helped establish two series, Wo es war for Norton, and SIC for Duke University Press, in German and English.

Žižek burst onto the intellectual scene in Western Europe and North America in 1989 with the publication of his first book in English, *The Sublime Object of Ideology*, in a series edited by the Argentinean philosopher Ernesto Laclau and Chantal Mouffe. In his psychoanalytic examination of human agency and ideology, Žižek combined his pioneering reading of Freud and Marx with his Lacanian analysis of ideological fantasy, his encyclopedic knowledge of popular culture, his non-standard approach to Hegel, and his Hegelian reading of Christianity. The effects of this dazzlingly eclectic text were unprecedented, and the fact that Žižek was at the time a virtually unknown author, at least among English-speaking audiences, added to the intriguing appeal of the book among the general public. Moreover, Laclau's preface to the book almost instantly secured Žižek's international reputation within leftist circles worldwide.

Indeed, the book resonated deeply with many readers around the world who were committed to the possibility of reinvigorating both the radical core of revolutionary politics and the relevance of philosophy for politically engaged readers.

Since the publication of *The Sublime Object of Ideology* in 1989, Žižek has published over fifty books, edited several collections, and published numerous articles. He has also written books in German, French, and Slovene, and many of his works have also been translated into twenty different languages. Žižek's increasingly expanding *oeuvre* can be divided into four main categories. First, introductions to Lacan through popular culture and everyday examples, as seen in *Looking Awry: An Introduction to Jaques Lacan through Popular Culture* (1991); *Enjoy Your Symptom: Jacques Lacan in Hollywood and Out* (1992); and more recently *How to Read Lacan* (2006). Second, theoretical works that intertwine philosophy and psychoanalysis to develop a critique of ideological fantasy and a political theory of agency and subjectivity: this category includes books such as *The Sublime Object of Ideology* (1989); *For They Know Not What They Do: Enjoyment as a Political Factor* (1991); *Tarrying with the Negative: Kant, Hegel, and the Critique of Ideology* (1993); *The Metastasis of Enjoyment* (1994); *The Indivisible Remainder: An Essay on Schelling and Related Matters* (1996); *The Abyss of Freedom* (1997); *The Plague of Fantasies* (1997); *The Ticklish Subject: The Absent Centre of Political Ontology* (1999); *The Fright of Real Tears* (2001); *On Belief* (2001); *Did Somebody Say Totalitarianism* (2001); *Organs without Bodies* (2004); *The Parallax View* (2006); and *Living in the End Times* (2010). Third, writings that address current political and social events such as *Welcome to the Desert of the Real!: Five Essays on September 11 and Related Dates* (2002); *Iraq: The Borrowed Kettle* (2004); *Violence: Six Sideways Reflections* (2008); *In Defense of Lost Causes* (2008); and *First as Tragedy, Then as Farce* (2009). And fourth, works that appropriate the radical atheist core of Christianity including: *The Fragile Absolute* (2000); *The Puppet and the Dwarf* (2003); and *The Monstrosity of Christ* (2009). His most recent tome is titled, *Less Than Nothing: Hegel and the Shadow of Dialectical Materialism* (2012), in which he presents his own unique interpretation of Hegel and calls for the return to a Hegelianism that exceeds Hegel's accomplishments and repeats, to paraphrase his typical phrase, what in Hegel that is more than Hegel himself.

This prolific output, its political undercurrents and advocacy of anticapitalist struggle, has put Žižek in the spotlight of international media. He has thus been the subject of a documentary called *Žižek! The Movie* (2005) by Astra Taylor; he was also featured, together with seven other professors at American universities, in her film, *Examined Life*. There are also two films featuring formal presentations by Žižek – *The Reality of the Virtual* (2004) by Ben Wright and *The Pervert's Guide to Cinema* (2006) by Sophie Fiennes. Žižek has also been a regular guest on Al Jazeera TV in English and the BBC, and he has maintained a tireless speaking schedule around the world. No wonder, then, that critics have dubbed him the "giant of Ljubljana" and the "most formidable philosophical mind of his generation" (Harpham 2003: 504) and that he is usually referred to in the popular media as the "Elvis Presley of cultural theory" and an "intellectual rock star."

But his increasingly expanding work, international fame, and charismatic presence have also been the source of consternation and concern for Žižek. For one, his tendency to use humor in his lectures has endeared him to the public outside the realm of academic audiences; but it also gives some critics reason to trivialize and dismiss his work as entertainment, with some even going so far as to describe him as a "comedian."[2] Žižek himself laments in Taylor's *Žižek!: The Movie* how for some "making me popular is a defense against taking me seriously." Furthermore, because of the speed with which he writes and publishes, almost a monograph per year, and as a result of his idiosyncratic recursive writing style, some critics have expressed concerns that Žižek's work is unsystematic, repetitive, and contradictory. These critics miss the point, for as Ian Parker argues in this volume that despite his appropriation of Lacan to reload Hegel through Marxism, Žižek insists that such a theoretical elaboration "should be open, negative, and indeterminate." Laclau's preface to *The Sublime Object of Ideology*, moreover, inadvertently helped to define, for better or worse, some of the popular myths about Žižek's writings among the general readership. About the book itself, for example, Laclau writes:

> It is certainly not a book in the classical sense; that is to say, a systematic structure in which an argument is developed according to a pre-determined plan. Nor is it a collection of essays, each of which constitutes a finished product and whose 'unity' with the rest is merely the result of its thematic discussion of a common problem. It is rather a series of theoretical interventions which shed mutual light on each other, not in terms of the progression of an argument, but in terms of what we could call the reiteration of the latter in different discursive contexts. (*Žižek* 1989: xii)

The fact that Žižek continues to revisit and elaborate on the main issues he raised in his first book in English testifies precisely to the systematic nature of his work. Furthermore, Žižek's engagement with fleeting political and social events cannot be properly understood without situating his arguments in the context of the general trajectories and presuppositions of his theoretical writings. Indeed, Žižek's philosophical edifice, which he has been building and refining book by book, in dialogue and debate with many intellectuals, critics, and philosophers from all over the world, remains narrowly focused in its theoretical framework and concerns.

Although his work has been the subject of many volumes of searching criticism and commentary, to date there has been no assessment of its value for the development of the human and natural sciences. Addressing this lack, *Žižek Now* seeks to explore the utility and far-ranging implications of Žižek's thought to various disciplines and provide an evaluation of the difference his work makes or promises to make in different fields. The volume offers chapters on quantum physics and Žižek's transcendentalist materialist theory of the subject, Hegel's absolute, materialist Christianity, postcolonial violence, eco-politics, ceremonial acts, and the postcolonial revolutionary subject. The contributors chart broad trajectories in Žižek's work, showcasing the innovations that his work has inaugurated, mapping continuities and departures in it, and relating it to broader theoretical trends in these fields. While some of these authors use his theoretical framework as a tool for engaging his work in its own terms (McGowan, Bosteels, and Ramey), others assess Žižek's position on a recurrent theme in his *oeuvre* either in the context of the current debates in these fields or in dialogue with prominent thinkers in them (Johnston and Conley). Some find in Žižek's work an opportunity to intervene in a field that he does not address (Vogt and Khader). Rather than re-presenting his work as the lone voice in the desert of academe, therefore, this volume engages his work in relation to the hegemonic trends of the postmodern zeitgeist, be it the universalized historicism of cultural studies, the evolutionism of cognitive science, or the hermeneutics of suspicion of literary theory.

Following this Introduction, in the second chapter of Part One of this volume, the renowned Žižekian critic Ian Parker overviews the three major theoretical trends, within which Žižek frames his work namely, Marxism, Lacanian psychoanalysis, and Hegelian dialectics. Although Parker takes issues with Žižek's polemical style, he considers him a "thinker for our times" whose interventions gain special urgency under contemporary conditions of the global capitalist crisis and concomitant forms of global "psychologization," a concept Parker borrows from the recent work of Jan De Vos, who uses it to name the various technologies, by which every aspect of our thoughts and experiences is adapted, co-opted, and reintegrated within capitalist rationality (De Vos 2011). In Parker's view, Žižek utilizes the internal fissures within the three theoretical currents of his work as well as the contradictions among them to make possible not only "another world," but also "another subject," a project that must necessarily stay incomplete. Parker thus argues that Žižek's *oeuvre* remains concerned from beginning to end with the "conditions of impossibility," of negativity and nothingness at the core of social field that not only frustrate any desire for unity or wholeness, but whose contradictions will also "at some point explode and change the symbolic coordinates within which we choose and act." Exploring the ramifications of this nothingness to Žižek's work, Parker concludes by discussing five targets of Žižek's ideological critique – psychologistic assumptions about the integrity of the self, the exhortation to achieve liberation by de-repressing libidinal energy, the calls for an authentic community, the search for the hidden but true meaning, and the celebration of the free play of narrative. His discussion provides a succinct summary of the major themes and issues that the other contributions to this volume elaborate on in their critical engagement with Žižek's multifaceted work.

In Part Two of this collection, Todd McGowan, Bruno Bosteels, and Josh Ramey establish the grounds for understanding Žižek's critical theory of dialectical materialism. Utilizing Žižek's theoretical framework as a tool for engaging his work in its own terms, McGowan, Bosteels, and Ramey provide the starting point for the critical examination of Žižek's appropriation of Lacan to reactualize German Idealism, Marxism, and Christianity, and for assessing the revolutionary potential – and limitations – of Žižek's thought for philosophy, religion, and politics. Todd McGowan takes his start in Žižek's dialectical materialism as grounded in German idealism, but he focuses especially on the "dialectical" dimension of Žižek's thought which is uniquely predicated on Hegel's "hidden political core" as the basis for formulating an anti-utopian emancipatory politics. Hegel's absolute, in particular, allows McGowan to highlight Žižek's complete identification of political struggle with the recognition of the fundamental antagonism as it reveals itself under conditions of global capitalism. The absolute provides Žižek with an insight into "antagonism without escape," since the absolute makes it clear that "there is no possible reconciliation without the acknowledgment of a fundamental self-division that no amount of struggle can ever overcome." McGowan thus examines Žižek's retroversive reading of Hegel as a critic of Marx, for it is only through Hegel, as Žižek sees it, that we can discern "what is in Marx (the revolutionary potential) more than Marx." In particular, the Hegelian theorization of antagonism as the rejection of the oneness of being underwrites Žižek's Hegelian critique of Marx's fatal conviction that the means of production themselves are self-identical, when in fact they are not. In Žižek's hands, moreover, Hegel's absolute radicalizes Marx's revolutionary philosophy, by offering a basis for the politicization of the subject, since political revolution constitutes a "new way of seeing that foregrounds the ubiquity of antagonism and thus of subjectivity." According to Žižek, in short, the political act forces the subject to confront this irreducible antagonism and refuses any attempt at overcoming the structural fact of the antagonism. This is the only way that neo-liberal democracy can be subjectivized, by lashing out at ourselves and at our faith in democracy as the end of history, to allow for the radical interrogation of global capitalism. Hegel, McGowan concludes, "enables Žižek to retain violence (and thus antagonism) within his politics without succumbing to the logic of the gulag."

Bruno Bosteels engages Žižek's writings on religion, interrogating the political limitations of Žižek's materialist defense of Christianity's perverse atheist core – that there is no big Other that can determine the 'objective meaning' of our actions – as a legacy worth fighting for and retrieving in its organized form before it had congealed into an institutionalized ideology. The problem with Žižek's materialist defense of Christianity, Bosteels argues, is that it remains confined within a proper philosophical matrix through the triangulation of Hegel and Lacan by way of Christianity. Žižek's Lacano-Hegelianism, Bosteels charges, "remain strictly speaking at the level of a structural or transcendental discussion of the conditions of possibility of subjectivity as such." What remains missing in Žižek's materialist defense of Christianity is a genealogical or historical materialist investigation that places the "politics of the subject in a permanent tension field between theory and history." To begin filling in this gap in Žižek, Bosteels examines the ways in which his perverse-materialist reading of Christianity revises, and perverts, Marx's and Freud's critiques of religion which are, nonetheless, not a match for the perverse core of Christianity. For Žižek, according to Bosteels, Marx "disavows the fact of human finitude in the name of an absolute subject-object of history," while Freud "acknowledges and names this traumatic dimension of finitude," only to send us "back to a cosmic-pagan battle of life and death, Eros and Thanatos." As an alternative to Žižek's limited philosophical approach, moreover, Bosteels suggests the development of a historical and genealogical agenda, along the lines of the genealogical work of the Argentine Freudo-Marxist León Rozitchner, which can clear a space for exposing the extent to which theorization of political subjectivity remains embedded and inscribed within Christian theology. Through a close reading of Saint Augustine's *Confessions*, Bosteels contends, Rozitchner did not only demonstrate that capitalism would not have developed the way it did without Christianity, but that he also "continues to expand the historical overdeterminations of the subject in the long run." This is the only way, he suggests, that the subject's real transformation can be rendered possible.

In the last chapter of Part Two, Joshua Ramey takes up a specific dimension of Žižek's political philosophy namely, the potential of liturgical-ceremonial forms in sustaining freedom and authentic revolutionary acts. Drawing on the particular modality of virtual temporality that Gilles Deleuze refers to as the "pure past," Ramey articulates how Žižek proposes "the free Act does not so much open a totally new present as retroactively alter the nature of the past, 'retroversively' determining which pasts now matter, or what in the past is now determinative." It is only after the fact, that is, that a truly free Act can be discerned. Although for Žižek the rediscovery of contingency in the past leads to the reconfiguration of history, Ramey still detects an ambiguity in Žižek's understanding of freedom in relation to the ability of the subject to realize her participation in the unfolding of free acts. To activate or realize freedom, therefore, Žižek argues for the importance of liturgical-ceremonial gestures for authentic revolutionary acts as "an encounter with the 'zero-level' of sense." Ramey thus notes that for Žižek "ritual and ceremonial acts seem to offer an immanent model of *continuity* between the transcendental sources of freedom and the shape of concrete historical acts," for the repetition of certain formalities, which cannot simply be wholly arbitrary, realizes the truth of a political movement. Hence, Ramey points out, Žižek has recently affirmed the power of liturgical-ceremonial acts to serve as an authentic dimension of communist culture, foregrounding the ability of liturgical gestures to politicize enjoyment as the "ceremonialization of everyday life." While it is impossible to guarantee a "stable relationship to virtual potencies of emancipation, love or justice," Ramey contends, the source of the revolutionary act and the substance of all ceremony for Žižek can be located in the "fecundity of the virtual itself."

In Part Three of this book, Adrian Johnston, Verena Andermatt Conley, Erik Vogt, and Jamil Khader highlight specific provocations in

Žižek's work that prove fruitful for guiding us to unexpected areas of inquiry in the context of current debates in quantum physics, media studies, ecological studies, and postcolonial studies. The renowned Žižek critic Adrian Johnston examines Žižek's appropriation of quantum physics, in order to reassess his materialist deployments of natural science and to disprove that any theory of the free subject has to offer a thoroughly materialist account. While Johnston believes it is important for Žižek to ground his ontology partially in scientific theory, he criticizes Žižek for failing to offer a cogent transcendentalist materialist theory of the subject, since Žižek is insufficiently careful in moving between the scientific and the ontological. He thus questions Žižek's recourse to quantum physics on general philosophical grounds, stating that the "theoretical form of his extensions of quantum physics as a universal economy *qua* ubiquitous, all-encompassing structural nexus (one capable of covering human subjects, among many other bigger-than-sub-atomic things) is in unsustainable tension with the ontological content he claims to find divulged within this same branch of physics (i.e., being itself as detotalized and inconsistent)." In other words, Žižek risks turning quantum physics into the One-All of a big Other in stark violation of his own ontology. In fidelity to what he refers to as a "Žižekian ontology of an Other-less, barred Real of non-All/not-One material being," Johnston offers an alternative account of subjectivity grounded in biological emergentism, coupled with a Cartwrightian "nomological pluralism."

Verena Andermatt Conley considers the radical as well as the conservative dimensions of Žižek's "eco-chic," questioning Žižek's attitude toward nature and his reliance on outdated rhetorical oppositions in his critique of New Ageism. While she criticizes Žižek for his selective appropriation of ecological debates and for his vague deployment of the term political ecology, Conley finds Žižek's focus on political ecology compelling, since he addresses problems of nature alongside with those of the "part of no part," or the excluded from the global capitalist system by way of an elaboration of the idea of revolutionary-egalitarian justice. She writes, "Considering ecology in the context of the new emancipatory subject, Žižek holds that *contra* the present ideological mystification of ecology – in effect *contra* the limited lessons of a balanced, harmonious nature that many of its new-age adepts impose with righteous sanctimony – a candid view of an ecology that works *against itself* can come about only when we first think the immense emancipatory potential of the urban slum dwellers." The value of Žižek's contribution to environmental studies can thus be attributed not only to his recognition of the world's massive ecological catastrophes, but more importantly to his theorization of the ecology as a collective experience, "even as a rehabilitation of a "communism" cleansed of its capitalist – *and* communist – mystifications, that is, for a worldwide effort to build a *common* that includes a redistribution of resources." Indeed, Conley maintains, for Žižek a true ecology cannot be thought without socialism or even without communism, since ecology coincides with the communist call for a genuine collective experience.

In the last two contributions of Part Three, Erik Vogt and Jamil Khader address the utility of Žižek's thought for postcolonial studies, an area Žižek does not address explicitly but which, in these encounters, offers new vistas of intellectual inquiry in both Žižek studies and postcolonial studies. Erik Vogt stages an encounter between the conceptions of emancipatory universal politics in the work of the Martinique psychoanalyst and revolutionary Frantz Fanon and Žižek, tracing the various parallels and correspondences in their views on the controversial topic of violence that continues to haunt leftist politics in the West. Even though Fanon and Žižek employ distinct theoretical frameworks, Vogt argues, they still "converge in a trenchant critique regarding the perceived dissimulation of the systemic, objective violence central to the capitalist (neo)-colonialist system – a dissimulation that is generated in large part by depoliticizing representations of different manifestations of subjective violence." After all, Žižek himself has advocated a return to the anticolonial "problematic of Frantz Fanon," as a way to foreground the potential inherent in subjective forms of violence to become sites of radical re-politicization of certain socio-political impasses, even though this violence can be manifested in the form self-violence ("self-beating") on the part of Fanon's "wretched of the earth" and Žižek's "part of no part." Vogt also notes that for both Fanon and Žižek, this violence facilitates the emergence of alternative modalities of collective political subjectivization which require the development of specific political organizations that can stabilize proper universal politicization, so as not to revert into mere spontaneous voluntarism. Finally, Vogt argues that both Fanon and Žižek envision a new type of postcolonial humanity that is grounded in the recognition that "the gap in their self-identity is precisely the universal separating them from themselves – the space in which new concepts of humanity have to be worked out."

In the last chapter of Part Three, Jamil Khader argues that we can salvage Žižek's call to repeat Lenin by recuperating an important dimension of Lenin's revolutionary pedagogy, namely, Lenin's mediation of the national question and his increasing faith in the capacity of the subjects of colonial difference to serve as the vanguard of revolutionary internationalism. He thus argues that if Lenin is to be repeated today, "postcoloniality should (retroactively) be considered one of those causal nodes around which a Leninist act is formed," for Lenin's revolutionary politics can be seen as being over-determined in a retroactive endorsement of the postcolonial link that will determine the future of revolutionary internationalism. Nonetheless, Khader takes Žižek to task for obliterating the history of the national liberation movements in the postcolonial world and for foreclosing the possibility of the construction of the postcolonial as the subject of history and revolutionary internationalism. He attributes this missing link in Žižek's revolutionary politics to his understanding of the postcolonial which is fraught with ambivalence as to the status of the postcolonial under contemporary conditions of global capitalism – he considers the postcolonial in terms of either its function as an ideological supplement to global capitalism or its position as capital's excremental remainder. Khader thus concludes that "Žižek's infidelity to this other/ wise Lenin notwithstanding, a genealogy of the position of postcoloniality in Lenin's work can retroactively foreground the exclusion in Žižek's revolutionary politics, clearing a space for its politicization."

In Part Four of this collection, Slavoj Žižek offers an original contribution that responds, directly and indirectly, to the major themes and concerns that were raised in this collection. If Žižek seems to shift his position on some of the issues under consideration in this collection, we should remember that, as he says in an interview, we ought not be afraid to change our positions, since repetitions can reveal new possibilities over time.[3] It is in this new field of (im)possibilities that Žižek's work opens up for us that we should seize this Žižekian moment, now or never.

Notes

1 This biographical sketch of Žižek's life draws on information gleaned from Myers 2003: 6–10, Parker 2004: 11–35, and various interviews, including the ones with Glyn Daly in his *Conversations with Žižek* (Cambridge, UK: Polity, 2004). It is important to note that Myers and Parker take completely opposite views about the ways in which the modern history of Yugoslavia shaped Žižek's intellectual and ideological development.

2 After describing his appearance – his beard, proletarian wardrobe, his accent, and his "accessible absurdity," Rebecca Mead states that Žižek might appear

like a serious leftist intellectual, but that in fact he is more like a "comedian."
See Rebecca Mead, "The Marx Brother: How a Philosopher from Slovenia
became an International Star," *The New Yorker* May 5, 2003: 38. This essay
can also be accessed on Lacanian ink @ http://www.lacan.com/ziny.htm.
3 Interview with Fabien Tarby, quoted in Conley in this volume.

1

Žižek's Sublime Objects Now

Ian Parker

Slavoj Žižek is a radically divisive conceptual activist. Juxtaposition of academic argument in dense difficult explorations of a wide range of philosophical themes with paradoxical funny excursions into popular culture makes his work into something disturbing. It forces his readers to take sides, and to take sides with him or against him. His theoretical activity is always configured as an intervention, and rare moments of descriptive explanatory prose invariably twist rapidly into cutting polemic. He is a thinker for our times even when he is wrong, and he identifies deadlocks even when he cannot break through them. But where does this naming and refusal of reigning categories of thought, of dominant symbolic forms come from, what resources does it borrow and turn against itself, and where is it going now?

There

A first predictable and reductive way of answering such questions would be to trace the trajectory of Žižek himself from being a student of philosophy at the University of Ljubljana, Slovenia in the late 1960s to researcher in social theory, with a master's degree thesis in 1975 on "The Theoretical and Practical Relevance of French Structuralism," a detour through Frankfurt School tradition psychoanalytic theory, and a doctorate in 1981, before arriving in Paris shortly afterwards. His work had already raised suspicions about his political trustworthiness in what was then still part of the Socialist Federal Republic of Yugoslavia, and he had failed, as a consequence of these suspicions, to obtain a permanent academic position in the university.

His time in Paris, with a second doctorate in psychoanalysis in 1986, a brief analysis with Jacques-Alain Miller and a first major book (in French) on Hegel and Lacan, prepared him for a return to Slovenia, where he stood as presidential candidate for the Liberal Democratic Party in 1990. By now his first book in English *The Sublime Object of Ideology* (Žižek 1989) was already starting to make an impact, partly through the patronage of UK-based "post-Marxist" political discourse theorists (Laclau and Mouffe 1985). Insofar as it is possible to look back at his earlier more critical-theoretical psychoanalytic interventions into the work of Lasch (1978) on the "culture of narcissism," for example, we can then see Žižek (1986) anticipating themes that were to erupt into full view in 1989. The first English-language book and a stream of lengthy elaborations of a circuit around Lacan, Hegel, and Marx since have provoked new research questions and, more importantly, mobilized a new generation of academics around questions of political action.

One might say that Žižek is a consummate political operator, rhetorician, and self-publicist, but to arrive at that as an explanation for his popularity now would precisely to be trapped in the ideological forms that he is trying to dismantle. That is, to treat this particular individual as the locus of all the now politically charged lines of argument that we might debate as being "Žižekian" would be to remain bewitched by the figure of the gifted genius, which is surely one of the sublime objects – Lacan's "objet petit a" – that fascinate us, and which we aim to emulate or subject ourselves to in capitalist society. And, when we are not enthralled by such an individual – the individual as such a powerful object and model of self-hood, which operates as an essential part of the machinery of identification – we can then be just as tempted to find the source of all failures of the argument in the faults of this self-same individual. In the logic of admiration and identification that Lacan (2006) described as running along the line of the imaginary, disappointment focused on the one who fails us overlooks where the real failures are. The bare bones of this biographical account of where he is coming from do not do justice to the history which bears him, and us.

So let us take another path – of the kind elaborated in Žižek's reading of Hegel – after this first step which was in error, into something closer to the truth. To do that we have to say something about what is sometimes, just as mistakenly as focusing on the individual, called the "context" for his work (Parker 2004). At that very moment in the 1970s when Žižek was gathering the conceptual resources for his later work, for what some would like to see as the Žižekian system, the political system around him was beginning to rupture. There are two things to note about this process of social decomposition that the Right now glories in as the end of communism marked by the fall of the Berlin Wall.

The first is that Yugoslavia declared itself to be "socialist," even to be from the 1950s a system of democratic "socialist self-management," but was nothing of the sort. The Tito bureaucracy was a form of state-management, and with a little more flexibility and few more cracks in which those who were sceptical could survive and even, to some small extent, organize. However, despite the break with Moscow and the geographical and political location of Yugoslavia as a buffer-zone between the West and Eastern Europe, the regime was still Stalinist in character. The proclaimed unity of the federal republic was the cover for all manner of tactics of divide and rule, including on ethnic and quasi-nationalist grounds, well before the civil wars of the 1990s, and the supposed tolera-tion of dissent was the excuse for insidious monitoring of the population and enforcement of party rule.

Žižek's writings in the 1980s and 1990s are peppered with jokes which speak of what it was like to live in such conditions, of the lies which had to be endorsed in order to survive, especially when one was part of the cultural apparatus, which academic production of social research in the university certainly was. There is another side of this condition of living in a time of lies, of course, which only became evident when the system collapsed and Slovenia was levered out of Yugoslavia by Western European capitalism, to be launched into the maelstrom of neo-liberal capitalism. Out of the frying pan into the fire, the Left opposition to the regime is even now haunted by nostalgia for what actually seemed, in retrospect, not so bad after all, for the way things were then. And it is easy to read Žižek's own scorn for old Stalinist self-management socialism as tinged with regret that things have turned out so badly, and with justifiable rage at how capitalism is now ravaging the whole planet.

The second thing to note about the disintegration of Yugoslavia is that the opposition movement in Slovenia, of which Žižek was a part, even while he was working as a minor functionary in a sub-committee of the party apparatus, was quite distinctive. Different strands of the "dissident" and opposition movement in Eastern Europe were influenced by free-market liberal or socialist ideas, and there were currents of work, includ-ing in other parts of Yugoslavia, that drew on Frankfurt School critical theory. The opposition in Slovenia, on the other hand, and this much is already indicated in the title of Žižek's master's thesis, was very taken with structuralist theory. Althusser's (1971) account of the role of "interpellation" of the subject by ideological state apparatuses and Foucault's (1977) descriptions of disciplinary "self-management" as self-regulation in the service of power seemed ideally suited to what was happening inside Slovenia, and an increasingly popular politics of subversion and "resistance" also drew on the kinds of situationist strategies that accompanied structuralism and so-called "post-structuralism" in France. And then, when things did kick off in the 1970s against the regime, they did so through punk (Simmie and Deklava 1991).

This gives us the conditions of possibility for forms of theory intimately linked to sarcastic and then increasingly open opposition, a politics of ideology-critique that was smart enough not to believe that it spoke in the name of any unmediated authentic reality under the surface. The contradictions in the regime were thus exploded from within, opened up in such a way as to keep them open rather than allow anyone – religious groups, nationalists, old socialists – to close them over again. This contestation of power, in which Žižek was deeply involved as student and as theoretical inspiration, was one which relied on strategies of "overidentification," internally contradictory and paradoxical disruption of the ideological apparatus which pretended to buy into what it corroded, which ate away at what it seemed to be agreeing to. This is the time of Neue Slowenische Kunst (NSK), a more slippery and indeterminate form of opposition than the regime could handle, and as lies of the regime were met by more enjoyable and potent truth through avatars of this opposition movement, we could see a necessarily and always divided critique pitted against a cracked but defensive system (Monroe 2005). And we can see in this the battle lines drawn on which Žižek wrote then, a field of conceptual activism that he still speaks from and to now.

Then

This then provides the setting for the articulation of theoretical resources – from Marxism, psychoanalysis, and Hegelian philosophy – that exploits the internal fractures of each, and works those contradictions against each of the other traditions. There had, of course, been attempts to combine

Marx and Freud in the Frankfurt School tradition, and this also within a broadly Hegelian framework (Adorno and Horkheimer 1979), but it was evident that a seamless combination of the three currents of work was impossible. Impossibility is the name of the game for Žižek; what Kant and then Foucault referred to as "conditions of possibility" for something to be thought, for a theoretical practice and cultural form, and, more importantly, conditions of *impossibility*. This is why there is no unity, wholeness, cosmology, or worldview without contradictions that will not at some point explode and change the symbolic coordinates within which we choose and act. Let us take each resource in turn, and notice what Žižek does with it.

First, Marxism that pretended to be a coherent tradition of work was evidently no such thing. Marxism is the theory and practice of class struggle, which in Žižek's hands becomes the site of a fundamental antagonism in the "symbolic" while also operating as traumatic kernel of the "real" as that which resists and disrupts both the symbolic and "imaginary" understanding of what we each and all are like. Already Žižek indexes this antagonism to the lack of sexual rapport in Lacan's (1988) *Seminar XX*. There is no sexual rapport, and for Žižek there is no overarching common interest or point of agreement that transcends the real of class struggle.

One only had to live during the time of division of the world into capitalist and "socialist" camps and the false choice between the two – a false choice redoubled by the war between different "socialist" states in which Yugoslavia presented itself as exemplifying a "non-aligned" third way – to know that when ruled by "Marxists" it was very likely that the main enemy was at home. The 1917 Russian Revolution had already been usurped by a bureaucratic caste that scandalously claimed to be building "socialism in one country" and then preferred "peaceful coexistence" with the rest of the world, cynically reducing the Communist parties in other countries to being diplomatic pawns of Moscow. This meant that revolutions that overthrew capitalism (including Mao's and Tito's) would occur in spite of, rather than with the help of Stalin's Comintern.

The transformation of Marxism as theory and practice of collective democratic working-class revolution to overthrow capitalism into a worldview that included the sedimentation of dialectics into Stalinist "dialectical materialism" then led to either slavish adherence to this worldview – and there were enough apparatchiks willing to adapt to it – or to suspicion of any formalization as such. Žižek has rather unfairly been accused of taking the former course, his time writing minutes of sub-committee meetings are held up as evidence of this, and he often jokes about sending his own opponents to the Gulag when he takes power. But it is the very stupidity of a form of Marxism operating as if it were a sealed system of thought with which he was concerned. This form of Marxism, put at the service of a bureaucratic apparatus, is what he had to find loopholes and contradictions in then, and that is a target of his writing since.

Suspicion of formalization of Marxism, and the turning of Marxism against itself to unravel its bureaucratic truth claims is accompanied by conceptual analysis of the way the commodity form under capitalism does not conceal anything of the truth, real value under the surface, but is itself empty. The truth rather lies in *unravelling* of the process of concealment by which the commodity pretends to have substance, to have value, and Žižek speaks this truth about the commodity form. We should notice the consequences of this in Žižek's writing, that while his conceptual activism is effectively Marxist, he does not usually call himself a Marxist; instead, he finds other ways of naming what it might be to oppose capitalism, to "repeat Lenin" (Žižek 2002: 310), for example, or to revive the "idea of communism" (Žižek and Douzinas 2002). There is no substantial truth to be found in Marxism, and no substantial truth to be found in "resistance" to capitalism. Žižek demands something quite different, and to get at that he makes use of psychoanalysis.

So, we turn secondly to psychoanalysis, and we find some uncanny parallels in its development as a theoretical system with that of Marxism. Notwithstanding Freud's own rather liberal queasiness about Marxism as such, many psychoanalysts were on the Left before the rise of fascism, and some saw psychoanalysis as a revolutionary force; they saw it as dismantling layers of internalized authority that bound individual subjects to capitalism (e.g., Reich 1975). There are two problems here. One is that the institutional apparatus of psychoanalysis, the International Psychoanalytical Association (IPA) founded by Freud and his followers in 1910 crystalized into a bureaucratic apparatus comparable to the Comintern, and it not only demanded obedience to a formalized version of psychoanalysis, but colluded with an obedient adaptation of individuals to capitalist society. The other problem is that this conformism incites all the more powerfully the fantasy that from under the surface, from within the unconscious, there could well up something of the human subject that could and should find release; it might accompany or even fuel revolution.

It is Lacan (2006) who excoriates both these problems from inside psychoanalysis itself – even before his "excommunication" from the IPA he railed against the adaptation of psychoanalysts and psychoanalysis to US American capitalism, and while there is an existential-romantic aspect to Lacanian psychoanalysis, Lacan opposes humanistic appeals to a pre-existing self that would realize itself in its struggle against oppression and exploitation. The registers of the symbolic, imaginary, and real are each and together necessary for the human subject to speak, comprehend, and act in the world, but Žižek draws out a fundamental lesson from Lacan's work, which is that these registers do not ever seamlessly knit together; the deadlock within and between them mean that the truth is (as Lacan himself notes) only "half said" and appears transiently in "act" rather than as substance. For Žižek (1989), this is a way in to show how for Freud it is the "dreamwork" that is crucial to psychoanalysis – the process of concealment as such that should be the focus of analytic work – rather than the revelation of a real or "latent" meaning as the substantial truth that lies hidden within it. Lacan (2007) points out that what psychoanalysts often think of as "latent" meaning is something they construct to satisfy themselves, and Žižek (1989: 11) points to the significance of Lacan's comment that, given the homology between dream and commodity, it was indeed Marx who "invented" the symptom.

Psychoanalysis is still indeed a theoretical framework to grasp the nature of "interpellation" of subjects by ideology, of identification with those in power and with all other subjects who have been interpellated in thrall to it, and of strategies of "overidentification" that might thwart that process. This is what attracts Žižek to psychoanalysis, and this is the basis on which he defended NSK (Žižek 1993). And it is from within Lacanian psychoanalysis that Žižek excavates the romantic-existentialist heart of the "subject" who speaks the truth as process – the "subject of the enunciation" – against that which masquerades as truth as established knowledge, that which Lacan (1973: 139) calls the "subject of the statement." Lacan provides Žižek with a theoretical system that will refuse the simple nostrums of orthodox Marxism and enable him to read and retrieve what is most valuable in the German idealist tradition.

So, turning to the third theoretical resource, Hegel, we also discover what turns out to be most valuable to Žižek. From Hegel, Žižek is able to retrieve what is most radical about the Western Enlightenment tradition, and work each of the three key elements of Hegelian philosophy, of universality, reflexivity, and negativity against that tradition. What is "universal" is precisely what is singular about the truth of the subject as it speaks of its predicament as human in the symbolic order. The particular mode of "reflexivity" this requires is one that breaks from comforting imaginary relations with others and operates through a fraught dialectical and error-ridden process, ever incomplete. Against the caricature of supposed Hegelian synthesis (at the end of history for some Marxists, for the individual subject for humanists) Žižek emphasizes "negativity" as the perpetual motor of thought and life; it is this negativity that drives what is most important in Marx and Lacan.

If asked to choose at gun point between German idealism and Lacan, Žižek would, he says, choose German idealism (Parker 2008: 3). Hegel is a resource for conceptualizing the formation of subjectivity as always in relation to another subject, and the demand for recognition gives to the "master–slave" dialectic a tragic irresolvable character that will be sutured over in later quasi-Hegelian forms of US–American psychotherapy that promise eventual mutual recognition between the partners in that battle comfortingly reframed as dialogue. However, Hegel, read through Kojève's (1969) lectures in Paris in the 1930s, attended by Lacan and an array of existentialist philosophers, promises no resolution of this tension between master and slave. There is a general lesson too here for what Marxists would like to take from Hegel and turn into their own instrumentalized version of dialectics.

Marxists warranting Soviet State power turned Hegelian dialectics into a developmental narrative of the course of history – from feudalism to capitalism and then to socialism – which was then used by the bureaucracy to judge when things go too far too fast, and psychotherapy turns Hegel's account into one which leads to reconciliation. Žižek, in contrast, insists that his Hegel is the one who always says no, who is the philosopher of negativity. But – and this is what has come to the fore in Žižek's explicit engagement with anti-capitalist politics in recent years – something can come of nothing in impossible ruptures and what Alain Badiou (2007) will call an "event," what Žižek will name an "act." Hegel is thus the negative core of Žižek's work.

Now

When we attempt to knot together these three key strands – and I will not even attempt to specify here which of them might correspond to the symbolic, imaginary and real – we are, and Žižek is, faced with a problem, or series of problems. One name for this problem or knot of problems is the emptiness of the human subject, theorized as "ensemble of social relations" by Marx (1845), as "lack in the Other" by Lacan (2006) and as "night of the world" by Hegel (1805–6). And to that negative definition of what the individual subject is, its nothingness, corresponds the lack of substance in the social that calls forth fantasies of what Laclau (1996: 53), one-time mentor to Žižek, called the impossible "fullness and universality of society."

Around one aspect of this we can then notice Žižek (2000; Žižek and Milbank 2009) from the late 1990s circling with his engagement with theology. Spirituality is an intensely ideological answer to the problem which needs to be addressed, tackled so that no ground is given to the enemy, to the religious fundamentalism that pretends to fill in this emptiness. Around another aspect we see Žižek more recently insistently combating ecological images of the lost balance of nature and our balanced relation with it that would, again, fill in that emptiness with an ideological claim to achieve closed cosmological harmony (Žižek 2010).

The ideological "context" for these arguments, and it is one that gives all the more urgency to Žižek's entreaties not to fill this emptiness now at a time of prolonged political economic crisis, is an intensification of concerns with "psychology," with how the individual subject should be defined and how it might manage itself. Neo-liberal capitalism presents us all once again with questions of interpellation and self-management that the opposition movement inside Slovenia faced before the fall of the Wall, but with a few more twists. Emotional labour, therapeutic self-empowerment, and the turning of subjectivity into manageable adaptable substance have meant that what Žižek (1989) was writing in *The Sublime Object of Ideology* is even more relevant now. One might see the re-elaboration of the arguments in that book in its different extended forms over the next twenty-five years as crucial urgent interventions in and against contemporary global "psychologization" (De Vos 2012).

There are two aspects of this necessary re-activation and deepening of Žižek's arguments about the "sublime object" of ideology in conditions of psychologization and world crisis that we should attend to when reading him now. The first is the role of "psychology" in its various forms – ranging from the most obviously dangerous "forensic" and "psychometric" elements of the discipline to the ostensibly more helpful "community" and "health" domains – as an apparatus of discipline, of adaptation of individuals to capitalist rationality. Psychiatry and psychotherapy as part of the psy-complex flank this disciplinary process as even more unpleasant biomedical instruments of control and invitations to self-responsibility.

The second aspect is the need for different conceptions of the human subject as a counterweight to what is offered in everyday commonsensical reality to us about what our subjectivity is, and the limits to what it could be. Our demand must be that another subject is possible alongside the assertion that another world is possible. This is what Žižek is elaborating: he is elaborating different possibilities for this drawing on Marxism, psychoanalysis, and Hegel at the same time as insisting that such a definition should be open, negative, and indeterminate. This is what draws him at one moment, from back in the late 1980s, to Walter Benjamin (Žižek 1989; 2008), and in more recent times to Alain Badiou (Žižek 1999; Badiou and Žižek 2009). It is possible, now easier in hindsight to see after Žižek's later books, five elements of ideology critique pertaining to the domain of the "psychological" back in *The Sublime Object of Ideology*. These five points will serve to summarize the trajectory I have outlined so far.

First, there is refusal of our sense that there is a substantial individual subject under the surface that can be recognized and released from bondage. Instead, Žižek's return to Hegel claims the negative moment in dialectics, of transformations in subjectivity that are never closed over in a finished totalizing "synthesis." That negative moment is to be discovered and catalysed in times when there is an "act" which disturbs taken-for-granted symbolic coordinates of life under capitalism. This critique of the ideological appeal to each individual's nascent self runs counter to simple humanistic psychology, and it shows how that psychology itself offers a consolation for our suffering which locks us all the more tightly into what we are trying to escape.

Second, there is refusal of the lure of freedom to enjoy that pits itself against social mechanisms that seem to constrain us. Instead, Žižek's mobilization of Lacan's grim account of the superego uncovers the way it works not merely as an agency which forbids but also as that which operates as the obscene underside of the law, as that which incites us to pleasure, to please ourselves. This critique of the ideological motif of the welling up of libidinal energies from the nasty repression that locks them in place shows us that some forms of radical psychoanalytic liberation are as much a problem as the solution.

Third, there is refusal of the idea that we would be happy if we embedded ourselves once again in an authentic substantial community.

Instead, Žižek's attention to the way we are pulled into action by a cause of desire that is always already Freud's "lost object" – Lacan's objet petit a – that never actually existed, that we never actually possessed, provides an account of the fantasy that others have stolen our enjoyment, that they have this object. This critique of any authentic or balanced psychological need shows us how a retroactively constituted sense of community is organized by our attachment to an object that we will only be free from when we have let it go.

Fourth, there is refusal of the lure of underlying meaning or value hidden under the surface, and here Žižek explores the homology between Freud's interpretation of dreams and Marx's analysis of commodities to show that what each prioritizes is the concealment of something or the mystification of relations. This critique of contents that are there waiting to be unearthed sets itself against all forms of depth psychology and against the fiction that the correct interpretation will be the one that unlocks the true meaning.

Fifth, and finally, there is refusal of the recent turn from a search for things underneath language to the supposedly free play of narrative, of language games that trace the ideological horizons of surface reality, the limited reality of life under capitalism. This critique is of deconstructive and postmodern academic and therapeutic trivial pursuits bewitched by the "social construction" of narrative. He is concerned with the way ideology is meshed into the real nature of a particular political-economic system and the way the truth about capitalism must entail a historic break with it, a break with capitalism.

Žižek's work is indeed impossible to stitch together into one coherent account. In that he is true to what he describes, true to the theoretical resources he mines and to the political conclusions he draws. He does not solve all of the contradictions he lays bare, how could he? In Marxist terms, he is the place of self-critique and perpetual re-education. In psychoanalytic terms, his division is the source of inconsistency and re-suturing of some identity to the argument he makes about himself and the nature of the symbolic. In Hegelian terms, he enacts the necessarily negative dialectical and always unfinished trajectory out of where we are stuck today. The incompletion of what it is to be Žižek, that there is no system or master key to unlock it, is also the incompleteness of what it is to be "Žižekian." Such a thing is impossible, and to grasp that impossibility is to be open to what could be different about the world, to be able to start again from nothing.

References

Adorno, Theodor and Horkheimer, Max (1979) *Dialectic of Enlightenment*. London: Verso.

Althusser, Louis (1971) *Lenin and Philosophy, and Other Essays*. London: New Left Books.

Badiou, Alain (2007) *Being and Event*. London: Continuum.

— and Žižek, Slavoj. *Philosophy in the Present*. Cambridge: Polity, 2009.

De Vos, Jan (2012) *Psychologisation in Times of Globalisation*. London: Routledge.

Foucault, Michel (1977) *Discipline and Punish: The Birth of the Prison*. Harmondsworth: Penguin.

Hegel, Georg Wilhelm Friedrich (1805–6) The Philosophy of Spirit (Jena Lectures 1805–6) Part I. Spirit according to its Concept, http://www.marxists.org/reference/archive/hegel/works/jl/ch01a.htm

Kojève, Alexandre (1969) *Introduction to the Reading of Hegel: Lectures on the Phenomenology of Spirit*. New York: Basic Books.

Lacan, Jacques (1973) *The Four Fundamental Concepts of Psycho-Analysis: The Seminar of Jacques Lacan, Book XI*. Harmondsworth: Penguin.

— (1988) *On Feminine Sexuality, The Limits of Love and Knowledge, 1972–1973: Encore, The Seminar of Jacques Lacan, Book XX* (trans. with notes by Bruce Fink). New York: Norton.

— (2006) *Écrits: The First Complete Edition in English* (trans. with notes by Bruce Fink in collaboration with Héloïse Fink and Russell Grigg). New York: Norton.

— (2007) *The Other Side of Psychoanalysis: The Seminar of Jacques Lacan, Book XVII*. New York: Norton.

Laclau, Ernesto (1996) *Emancipation(s)*. London: Verso.

— and Mouffe, Chantal (1985) *Hegemony and Socialist Strategy: Towards a Radical Democratic Politics*. London: Verso.

Lasch, Christopher (1978) *The Culture of Narcissism: American Life in an Age of Diminishing Expectations*. New York: Norton.

Marx, Karl (1845) "Theses on Feuerbach," http://www.marxists.org/archive/marx/works/1845/theses/theses.htm

Monroe, Alexei (2005) *Interrogation Machine: Laibach and the NSK State*. Cambridge, MA: MIT Press.

Parker, Ian (2004) *Slavoj Žižek: A Critical Introduction*. London: Pluto.

— (2008) "Conversation with Slavoj Žižek about *Slavoj Žižek: A Critical Introduction*," *International Journal of Žižek Studies*, 2(3), http://Žižekstudies.org/index.php/ijzs/article/view/148/248.

Reich, Wilhelm (1975) *The Mass Psychology of Fascism*. Harmondsworth: Pelican.

Simmie, James and Dekleva, Joze (eds) (1991) *Yugoslavia in Turmoil: After Self-Management?* Pinter, London and New York.

Žižek, Slavoj (1989) "Pathological Narcissus as a Socially Mandatory Form of Subjectivity," http://www.manifesta.org/manifesta3/catalogue5.htm, 1986.

— *The Sublime Object of Ideology.* London: Verso.

— (1993) "Why are Laibach and NSK not Fascists?" in Inke Arns (ed.) (2003) *IRWINRETROPRINCIP: 1983–2003.* Frankfurt: Revolver (pp. 49–50).

— (1999) *The Ticklish Subject: The Absent Centre of Political Ontology.* London: Verso.

— (2000) *The Fragile Absolute – or, why is the Christian legacy worth fighting for?* London: Verso.

— (ed.) (2002) *Revolution at the Gates: A Selection of Writings from February to October 1917: V. I. Lenin.* London: Verso.

— (2008) *Violence: Six Sideways Reflections.* London: Profile Books.

— (2010) *Living in the End Times.* London: Verso.

— and Douzinas, Costas (2010) *The Idea of Communism.* London: Verso,.

— and Milbank, John (2009) *The Monstrosity of Christ: Paradox or Dialectic?* Boston, MA: MIT Press.

Part Two

2

Hegel as Marxist: Žižek's Revision of German Idealism

Todd McGowan

Absolutely Immanent

The importance of Hegel's thought as a critical tool for the analysis of society has historically created an impossible dilemma for politically oriented theorists. Because Hegel emphatically distances philosophy from practical political efficacy, one must find a way of injecting a political practice into that philosophy without thereby destroying its power as an analytical tool. One solution, made famous by Georg Lukács, involves separating the conservative mature Hegel from his more radical young counterpart.[1] The lack of elegance of this solution outweighs its simplicity: in order to distinguish two versions of Hegel, it must overlook the remarkable continuity that characterizes his philosophy from the *Phenomenology of Spirit* (1807) to the *Philosophy of Right* (1821). The more compelling alternative focuses on the implicit call for political contestation present even in the late works.

The stumbling block in the way of efforts to redeem the politics of Hegel's philosophy is his conception of the absolute, or absolute knowledge. According to Hegel, philosophy arrives at the absolute when it recognizes how thought infuses reality and vice versa. The idea of the absolute reaches its apex in the late *Philosophy of Right* where he notoriously declares, "What is rational is actual and what is actual is rational" (Hegel 1952, 10). So many later philosophers question and even mock this statement because it eliminates the possibility of challenging the ruling order and thus justifies Hegel's support of the Prussian monarchy at the time. The absolute is just this reconciliation of thought with what is actual, and it demands that the philosopher abandon the idea of thought transcending actuality or actuality transcending thought. This reconciliation appears to mark the end of political contestation – and most interpreters of Hegel understand it as the abjuration of politics – since the absolute eliminates any space outside the given reality from which one might contest the political status quo. When he theorizes the absolute, Hegel seems implicitly to become a partisan of the ruling order, and the radical politics of his youth, including his celebration of the French Revolution, no longer has a place.

But, despite avowing the importance of the absolute, Herbert Marcuse and Gillian Rose have made the case for a thoroughly politicized Hegel from beginning to end. For both of them, what constitutes his political dimension lies in the demand for realizing in the world the advances that thought has already conceived. Here, Hegel's conception of the absolute, or the grasp of the rationality of the real, forces us to struggle to realize fully this rationality. In this sense, the absolute does not imply the abandonment of politics but rather the necessity of it. As Rose puts it, "The overall intention of Hegel's thought is to make a different ethical life possible by providing insight into the displacement of actuality in those dominant philosophies which are assimilated to and reinforce bourgeois law and bourgeois property relations. This is why Hegel's thought has no social import if the absolute cannot be thought" (Rose 1981: 208).[2] According to this way of approaching Hegel's thought, the absolute, the seemingly ultimate retreat from political contestation, functions as an indirect political imperative.

Slavoj Žižek's importance as a reader of Hegel stems from his ability to avoid both the dichotomization that occurs in Lukács and the sense of a political imperative that Rose imagines, and yet to sustain Hegel's importance as a political thinker. In fact, the fundamental idea animating Slavoj Žižek's prodigious theoretical output is not a new version of psychoanalytic Marxism but a reconception of Hegel's philosophy as the basis for politics. Like Marcuse and Rose, but in a new way, Žižek aims at a rereading of Hegel's philosophy that uncovers its hidden political core. Contra Rose's conception of the Hegelian absolute as a practical imperative to realize what thought has already foreseen, Žižek accepts the absolute as the recognition of an endpoint. The achievement of the absolute implies the closed nature of the social process: the apparent openness of the future is nothing but an illusion, blinding us to the irreducibility of antagonism. No matter how much progress society makes, no matter how advanced technological forces become, no social order can overcome the structural fact of antagonism. Absolute knowledge consists in this recognition of closure that renders antagonism inescapable. Antagonism is at once the barrier to society's full realization of itself or achievement of self-identity and its very condition of possibility. To recognize the absolute is to recognize that the barrier to self-identity is also what propels one toward it.

The idea that the recognition of the absolute is in fact a recognition of the inescapability of antagonism has clear roots in Hegel's work, even if earlier commentators have not highlighted these roots.[3] At the end of *The Phenomenology of Spirit*, Hegel discusses absolute knowledge, not as knowledge without limit (as the term suggests), but as knowledge of limit as constitutive for knowledge and for the subject. He writes, "The self-knowing Spirit knows not only itself but also the negative of itself, or its limit" (Hegel 1977: 492). Here, Hegel makes clear that the absolute isn't a triumph over antagonism, or a moment of complete transcendence, but the recognition of antagonism's inevitability. All prior modes of thought hold out hope for escape, which is why they fall into contradiction with themselves and thereby advance Hegel's dialectic toward the absolute. The absolute doesn't succumb to contradiction because it adopts contradiction as its defining principle as thought recognizes the contradictory or antagonistic nature of being itself.

Žižek's interpretation of Hegel's absolute does not eliminate the idea of reconciliation in the way that someone like Jacques Derrida or Jean-Luc Nancy might.[4] Instead, reconciliation becomes associated with a changed perspective on antagonism. Rather than being an obstacle to overcome, antagonism emerges as the form of one's being. As Žižek puts it in *For They Know Not What They Do* (implicitly his book on Hegel's *Logic*), " 'reconciliation' does not convey any miraculous healing of the wound of scission, it consists solely in a reversal of perspective by means of which we perceive how the scission is in itself already reconciliation" (Žižek 1991a: 78). The absolute entails a reconciliation that transforms the valence of antagonism so that the subject can see its necessity and even its fecundity. Though Hegel has often symbolized the philosophical conquest of division and contradiction, Žižek takes up Hegel's banner because he grasps that Hegel is *the* philosopher who correctly theorizes the antagonism of being itself.

But being's lack of identity with itself is not simply a postulate of Hegel's philosophy. We have, on the contrary, undeniable proof for the contradictory status of being – our capacity for speaking. If being were identical with itself, if A=A without remainder, then no one could say so. A world of pure immanence is a world of silence. Language emerges out of a gap in the world where self-identity breaks down, and speech attempts to wrestle with this divide. The existence of a speaking and desiring being testifies to a contradiction at the heart of being. If there are, as Kant has shown, antinomies of pure reason, points at which reason contradicts itself, there must be antinomies of pure being, or points at which being contradicts itself. Otherwise, the antinomies of pure reason could never arise because the oneness or self-identity of being would prevent this from happening. Kant errs through his "excess of tenderness for the things of the world. The blemish of contradiction, it seems, could not be allowed to mar the essence of the world; but there could be no objection to the thinking Reason, to the essence of mind" (Hegel 1975: 77). In contrast to Kant, Hegel sees in the contradiction of reason a direct link to contradiction within being. Without this link, it would be impossible to explain – and Kant doesn't attempt to do so – the ontological derivation of reason's fall into antagonism.

The hidden political core of Hegel's philosophy lies in its destruction of every avenue of escape from the antagonistic or divided structure of being itself. When thought reaches the absolute, it discovers that it can no longer rely on the idea of an outside, which, rather than opening the subject up to another, actually serves to provide an illusory avenue of escape from its own antagonism for the subject. In the *Science of Logic*, Hegel notes, "in its other [the Notion] has *its own* objectivity for its object. All else is error, confusion, opinion, endeavor, caprice and transitoriness; the absolute Idea alone is *being*, imperishable *life*, *self-knowing truth*, and is *all truth*" (Hegel 1969: 824). It is easy to see the difficulty that this idea has created in the history of philosophy after Hegel. One need not be a Karl Popper who identifies Hegel with totalitarian rule in order to find this complete elimination of otherness troubling. But Hegel eliminates otherness in this fashion so that he might cut off the subject's fantasy of escape from its own immanence. The absolute, the point at which the subject assumes its own transcendence, functions for Hegel as the assurance of complete immanence within the social field.

Both Hegel's and Žižek's understanding of immanence differs radically from the typical conception that is associated with Spinoza. Unlike Spinoza (or his contemporary followers like Michael Hardt and Antonio Negri), Hegel does not do away with transcendence altogether. Doing so has the unintended consequence of positing being as whole rather than as divided.[5] Hegel's unique conception of immanence enables him to avoid Spinoza's reduction of being to one, a reduction that theoretically erases the space for political contestation. If being is one, if there is no transcendence within the field of immanence, then all political acts would simply be theater and all transformations would only be apparent. They could never disrupt being's essential self-identity. For Hegel, transcendence is not a realm separate from the field of immanence, but immanence includes transcendence. The transcendent point exists within the field of immanence as a result of this field's failure to coincide with itself. Being is not identical with itself, and transcendence emerges out of this non-identity or contradiction. This contradiction is the source of political change, change that can be revolutionary because there is no oneness to constrain it.

By refusing the oneness of being, we avoid the seduction of self-identical Other and thus must take responsibility for our own political situation. This is why Žižek identifies the absolute with the politicization of the subject: if we have not reached absolute knowledge, we continue to posit perfect self-identity in some form of otherness, and this otherness will always function as a barrier to our political acts. One acts politically when one grasps the social field as a terrain of contestation, not as a terrain of ontological or social givens. With its deflation of the Other, the absolute performs a transformation of the terrain for the subject. The task of theory, as Žižek sees it, lies in making this transformation possible and thus allowing subjects to view themselves as inherently political beings.[6]

This radical transformation is what Hegel is getting at in the preface to *The Phenomenology of Spirit* when he insists that "everything turns on grasping and expressing the True, not only as *Substance*, but equally as *Subject*" (Hegel 1977: 10). Hegel's statement does not imply that all truth is simply perspectival, the product of a subjective account, but rather that being itself is divided in the same way that the speaking subject is. What seems to be substantial or whole is also subject or divided. As a result, we cannot hold onto the idea of an Other that sustains a perfect identity. Every Other – even the seeming harmony of nature – suffers from the same divide that cuts the subject and renders it incapable of a harmonious existence.[7]

In an era that celebrates the encounter with and respect for otherness more than any other value, the demand for Hegel's absolute becomes increasingly exigent. Respect for otherness is not simply a new form of politics that has emerged with the collapse of communism and the decline of the workers' movement, but represents a decisive turn away from politics. Respecting the otherness of the Other necessarily involves granting the wholeness of the Other's identity. In contrast to the divided subject, the Other becomes, according to this conception, self-identical and thereby completely alien to the subject seeking to know it. Panegyrics to the existence of Native Americans before the European invasion of the Americas or to the harmony of the natural world prior to human intervention stem directly from this conception of otherness, and the problem with such an otherwise anodyne conception is its failure to see being as divided and self-identity as impossible. The pre-invasion Native Americans come to represent the purity of self-identical being that the divided subjectivity of Europe corrupted. This represents a toxic political vision because it abandons the terrain of politics altogether. Žižek does not single out multiculturalism so often as the target of his polemics in order to slay a potential leftist rival rather than taking on the real right-wing enemy (as certain critics would have it) but in order to reignite a politics of the Left.[8] If being is identical with itself, political action becomes impossible, and this explains the vehemence and recurrence of Žižek's Hegelian-oriented critiques of multiculturalism.

Žižek's turn to Hegel as a political thinker focuses primarily on this conception of the absolute as the testament to the Other's division. In an elucidation of the absolute, he claims, "The notion of the inaccessible, transcendent Absolute makes sense only in so far as the subject's gaze is already here – in its very notion, the inaccessible Other implies a relation to its own other (the subject)" (Žižek 1991a: 91). In short, the absolute implies an understanding of otherness as itself split, and therefore taking account of the supposed subject of mastery. One thinks of the absolute not in order to envision a rational goal that society must realize, as Gillian Rose and Herbert Marcuse see it, but in order to make clear to oneself the centrality of antagonism in the apparently undivided Other.

A type of thought that halts before the absolute implicitly sustains faith in the self-identity of whatever type of otherness it assumes. Here, the poignancy of Hegel's critique of Kant becomes evident. In the preface to the second edition of the *Critique of Pure Reason*, Kant famously defends his effort to limit the reach of the subject's knowledge in terms of its capacity for faith in God or absolute otherness. He notes, "I had to deny *knowledge* in order to make room for *faith*; and the dogmatism of metaphysics, i.e., the prejudice that without criticism reason can make progress in metaphysics, is the true source of all unbelief conflicting with morality, which unbelief is always very dogmatic" (Kant 1998: 117). Kant critiques reason's tendency to overreach and try to know what falls beyond its bounds, because in doing so it eliminates the possibility for faith and in the process does irreparable harm to our moral being. Morality depends, according to Kant, on a self-identical otherness or on a substance that can lay down the moral law without contradiction. Such a being or position does not exist for Hegel.

Hegel's absolute denies the Kantian limitation on knowledge in order to allow no room for faith of any kind. One cannot have faith in a God of absolute otherness nor in the self-identical otherness of Native Americans living in peace with the natural world nor in the harmony of the natural world itself. Kant's limitation of knowledge makes possible all these versions of faith, but as soon as one conceives the absolute as thinkable, otherness ceases to be absolute and becomes self-divided or subject. Without any faith in the Other on which to rely, the subject must accept the necessity of its own inherent politicization and the irreducibility of antagonism. The antagonism of being creates a world in which the subject must act rather than seeing the self-identical Other as responsible for its condition.

Žižek's attraction to Hegel is inextricable from Hegel's absolute. The absolute provides a path for us to think of antagonism without escape. With the absolute, there is no possible reconciliation without the acknowledgment of a fundamental self-division that no amount of struggle can ever overcome. By revealing that there is no external solution to the antagonism of being, the absolute tells us that we are at the end of history. Once we grasp the absolute, we can no longer hope for relief from the trauma of history, and in this sense, we are at its end. But it is only at the end of history that the real political struggle begins. This is the point when antagonism makes itself manifest as irreducible and when the political battle may be joined.

Retaining the Monarch

Hegel's embrace of constitutional monarchy in the *Philosophy of Right* bespeaks, contrary to the traditional understanding of this gesture, his insistence on political antagonism. This antagonism cannot find an adequate expression in modern parliamentary democracy and thus inevitably subverts the democratic nature of the parliamentary process. Such subversions of democracy are not the exception but the rule: the parliamentary vision of democracy fails to leave a space for the irresolvable nature of antagonism and attempts to reduce antagonism to an agonism in which political actors struggle but ultimately defer to the victor.[9] The problem with this vision of politics, as Hegel implicitly sees it in the *Philosophy of Right*, resides in its refusal to leave a place for what doesn't fit within the political terrain. Or, to put it in other terms, parliamentary democracy creates the impression that political divisions can ultimately find reconciliation through agreeing to disagree, which is the essence of agonism.

Even if we move from the dominant consensus politics to a form of agonistic debate, we will fail to safeguard antagonism, and it will continue to manifest itself in the threatened emergence of fascism, which has an appeal rooted in its open avowal of antagonism. Though Žižek employs antagonism as the basis for leftist politics, it can become fodder for the Right when the Left abandons it. The difference between the leftist and rightist turn to antagonism consists in the promise of a solution. Whereas leftist politics offers antagonism itself as the solution, right-wing politics points to antagonism in order to announce the need for a solution. Antagonism is present for fascism, but it is only present as an obstacle to be overcome in some fashion – through social isolation, deportation, or even murder. For the leftist, in contrast, the enemy is not personalized and thus cannot be killed. It is, instead, nothing but the failure to see the constitutive status of antagonism. In *The Puppet and the Dwarf*, Žižek makes this Hegelian point through a discussion of Christianity. He notes, "We rise again from the Fall not by undoing its effects, but in recognizing the longed-for liberation in the Fall itself" (Žižek 2003b: 86). The misguided Christian (like the fascist) looks for salvation outside of the fall, but the authentic believer (like Žižek's leftist) looks for salvation in the fall itself. Antagonism is central for both the far Right and for Žižek's Hegelian Left, but its role is completely opposed in the two camps.

One reason for the renewed popularity of political philosopher Carl Schmitt, despite his sympathy with Nazism, lies in his insistence on the necessity of sustaining antagonism as the basis for politics as such. As Schmitt puts it in *The Concept of the Political*, "A world in which the possibility of war is utterly eliminated, a completely pacified globe, would be a world without the distinction of friend and enemy and hence a world without politics" (Schmitt 1996: 35). In order to save political contestation and agency, we must constantly be willing to run the risk of war. Though thinkers like Jacques Rancière and Giorgio Agamben bear no resemblance to Schmitt politically, they share his aversion to the disappearance of antagonism and politics. But Schmitt's solution – a situation in which we are permanently confronted by enemies who want to kill us – is clearly unacceptable. Unlike Schmitt, Hegel finds a way to retain antagonism without insisting on the distinction between friend and enemy, the distinction precipitating war.

In the *Philosophy of Right*, Hegel advocates for representative government that centers around a non-representative figure – the monarch. The modern monarch is not like the ancient ruler whose word is identical with law. The modern monarch is not, in short, substantial. Instead, as Hegel conceives this figure, it represents the subjectivity of substance, the split within the state. Only through the monarch does the state reveal the failure of its self-identity. When the monarch enacts the law and proclaims "I will," it subjectivizes the state substance. Hegel insists on its necessity and on this subjective moment (which the ancient world lacked). He notes, "This 'I will' constitutes the great difference between the ancient world and the modern, and in the great edifice of the state it must therefore have its appropriate objective existence. Unfortunately, however, this requirement is regarded as only external and optional" (Hegel 1952: 288).[10] The great error of the modern democracy, according to Hegel, is its belief that it can do without the subjectivizing force of the monarch, that it can become a self-identical substance.

Without the monarch acting as the subject of the substantial state, antagonism loses its visibility, and the people cease to take themselves as political beings. What Jacques Rancière calls "consensus politics" emerges, and consensus, as both Hegel and Rancière agree, represents the abandonment of politics and its replacement by a police state. Rancière notes, "Consensus is the form by which politics is transformed into the police" (Rancière 2010: 100). From a Hegelian perspective, what Rancière fails to think through are the ramifications of his own commitment to complete democracy. The oxymoronic consensus politics emerges out of democracy itself, unless democracy retains a figure, the monarch, who subjectivizes the substantial state. Antagonism disappears in the democratic state, and it subsequently reappears in the form of the fascist leader who reintroduces the distinction between friend and enemy or between us and them. Within a constitutional democracy, antagonism will always make itself felt, and Hegel believes that it is only the retention of the monarch and its subjectivity that can avoid such a path. As long as the monarch remains part of the democratic order, it reveals that order's split from itself and renders impossible any image of oneness or substantiality.

Even when he was in an earlier, more democratic phase of his intellectual trajectory, Žižek was drawn to Hegel's conception of the political necessity of the monarch. Whereas other thinkers indebted to Hegel apologize for the retention of the monarch or dismiss it as the product of Hegel's late turn to conservatism, Žižek views it as an integral development of Hegel's political thought. In *The Sublime Object of Ideology*, Žižek offers a detailed defense of the Hegelian monarch for its philosophical and political necessity. He claims:

> The State without the Monarch would still be a *substantial* order – the Monarch represents the point of its subjectivation – but what precisely is his function? Only "dotting the i's" . . . in a formal gesture of taking upon himself (by putting his signature on them) the decrees proposed to him by his ministers and councillors – or making them an expression of his personal will, of adding the pure form of subjectivity, of "It is our will . . . ," to the objective content of decrees and laws. The Monarch is thus a subject *par excellence*, but only in so far as he limits himself to the purely formal act of subjective decision: as soon as he aims at something more, as soon as he concerns himself with questions of positive content, he crosses the line separating him from his councillors, and the State regresses to the level of Substantiality. (Žižek 1989, 221–2)

Žižek's apology for the monarch stems from his recognition of the dangers that the purely substantial state poses for politics. The monarch testifies to the split necessary for a democratic state, and when we abandon the monarch, we tend to lose the sense of antagonism that revolutionary politics demand.

The great barrier to revolutionary political change, as Žižek sees it, lies not in our collective failure to envision the possibility of escape from oppressive conditions but from the ease with which we can. The failure to grasp the constitutive nature of antagonism leads us to believe that we can overcome it through earning a great deal of money, finding the proper romantic partner, landing the perfect job, achieving a healthy lifestyle, and so on. All these solutions are themselves the problem. The belief in the possibility of becoming substantial in whatever way prevents us from conceiving ourselves as irremediably political beings. Žižek's philosophy – and his affection for the apparently retrograde Hegelian monarch – lies in the revelation that there is no substance not beset by subjectivity, that there is no being without antagonism. In his thought, political revolution doesn't require physical violence or marching in the streets. Instead, it necessitates a new way of seeing that foregrounds the ubiquity of antagonism and thus of subjectivity.[11]

Despite their theoretical divergences, on this point Žižek is proximate to Giorgio Agamben in *The Coming Community*. In this work, Agamben turns to an anecdote about Walter Benjamin when he attempts to imagine political revolution in the form of redemption or what he calls the "Kingdom of the Messiah." According to Agamben, Benjamin once told Ernst Bloch that when the Messiah comes, "Everything will be as it is now, just a little different" (Agamben 1993: 52). In the very next sentence of the book, Agamben makes reference to the idea that "the Absolute is identical to this world," though he never mentions Hegel explicitly (Agamben 1993: 52). The idea that revolutionary political change will create a world that is "just a little different" is firmly within the Hegelian tradition and evinces his sense of the absolute. When one arrives at the absolute, everything remains the same, and yet the absolute introduces the little difference that Benjamin associates with messianic redemption.

The little difference of the absolute is the understanding that there exists no pure substance. While we can accept our own self-division, the great political difficulty consists in accepting the self-division of the Other or the subjectivity of all substance. We want to have faith in an undivided Other – God, nature, religious fundamentalists, different ethnic groups, or whatever – but it is this faith that prevents our accession to the absolute and to Agamben's Kingdom of the Messiah. For Žižek, redemption implies sacrificing the idea of the purity of the Other, just as for Hegel Christianity demands that we accept the idea of God's self-division (which produces Christ on the cross, the point at which God forsakes himself). The political sacrifice that Žižek requires does not involve time, money, or even one's life – all of the sacrifices that we typically associate with political activity – but rather the abandonment of the Other as such.

From Hegelian to More Hegelian

In 1989, Slavoj Žižek made an intellectual splash with his first English-language book, *The Sublime Object of Ideology*. What readers at the time found so fascinating about the book was the renewed legitimacy that it granted to the great figures of Western philosophy after almost a century of theorizing their overcoming or deconstruction. Žižek appeared as an antidote to the tradition inspired by Bergson and Heidegger and running through Deleuze and Derrida. No figure had a more central place in Žižek's study than Hegel. But Žižek also distinguished Jacques Lacan from the grouping of thinkers known in America as post-structuralists. Lacan, as Žižek understood him, belonged in proximity to Hegel rather than to Derrida. This idea came as a revelation to theorists accustomed to grouping Lacan with other French theorists like Derrida, Deleuze, and Foucault. The uniqueness of Žižek's contribution in this book did not end there, however. He also stressed the political dimension of Hegel's and Lacan's thought, a dimension that neither of them had made an explicit priority. (Both Hegel's and Lacan's political pronouncements were extremely limited, in contrast to contemporary thinkers like Fichte, in the case of Hegel, and Sartre, in the case of Lacan.) Hegel and Lacan became, in Žižek's reading, important contributors to a Marxist political project or at least to a Marxist critique of ideology.

Despite the prominence of Hegel in Žižek's early work, he became chiefly known as the foremost exponent of Lacanian theory. Žižek himself contributed to this impression as he publicly identified himself as a Lacanian theorist and referred to Lacan in the subtitle of two early books: *Looking Awry: An Introduction to Jacques Lacan through Popular Culture* and *Enjoy Your Symptom: Jacques Lacan in Hollywood and out.*[12] In an important sense, this identification is not misleading. Žižek's work has a significant debt to Lacanian theory, and he did play the crucial role in disentangling Lacan from other French theorists. But in another way, it places the emphasis of Žižek's thought away from its political foundation, a foundation that he finds in Hegel rather than in Lacan.

In *Tarrying with the Negative* (a work written just after the two works on Lacan mentioned in the above paragraph), Žižek links himself with Hegel by calling for a reversal of the typical practice: we need Hegel to function as a political corrective to Marx, despite unending calls for the reverse procedure. He claims, "Perhaps . . . after more than a century of polemics on the Marxist 'materialist reversal of Hegel,' the time has come to raise the inverse possibility of a Hegelian critique of Marx" (Žižek 1993: 26). Žižek's "Hegelian critique of Marx" focuses on the latter's belief that a reconciliation of subject with substance is possible if only the subject can overcome the alienation produced by inadequate relations of production.

From a Hegelian standpoint, the problem with Marx is not so much that he sees the working class as capable of overcoming its alienation through revolution (though this is one traditional – and certainly Hegelian – critique) but that he views the productive mechanism as independent of the relations of production that form around it. In other words, Marx assumes that the means of production are self-identical while the relations of production are in a state of contradiction – or that the relations of production are responsible for any contradiction whatsoever.[13] Hegel's absolute enables us to understand that the means of production themselves already fail to be self-identical, which is why relations of production come to exist at all. Just as Hegel sees language as the result of a division in being, one can see the development of alienating relations of production as the result of a division in the means of production. Or, to put it back into Hegel's terms, if substance wasn't subject from the beginning, subjectivity could never have emerged. The difficulty is not overcoming the subject's alienation but even recognizing the alienation of substance itself – the fact that substance is already subject.

Marx's fatal assumption, as Žižek sees it, lies in the faith that he has in the means of production, which is akin to a faith in God. Marx assumes that the proletarian revolution will simply let free the means of production previously hampered by capitalist relations of production. This becomes evident in a famous passage from the third volume of *Capital*, where Marx envisions of the possibility of unleashing the productive forces of society from the constraints on production created by capitalism itself. He says there:

> The *true barrier* to capitalist production is *capital itself*. . . . The means – the unrestricted development of the social forces of production – comes into persistent conflict with the restricted end, the valorization of the existing capital. If the capitalist mode of production is therefore a historical means for developing the material powers of production and for creating a corresponding world market, it is at the same time the constant contradiction between this historical task and the social relations of production corresponding to it. (Marx 1981, 358–9)

The key phrase in this passage is "the unrestricted development of the social forces of production." Here, Marx testifies to his faith that substance really is substance rather than subject, or, in other words, that the social forces of production represent a self-identical entity that a proletarian revolution might simply liberate from its capitalist fetters. But contra Marx here, the means of production cannot exist in an unfettered state: the fetters are not just constraining limits but also enabling ones, which Marx's faith in the substantiality of the means of production does not allow him to see.[14]

The entire force of Hegel's insistence on the absolute runs against just such a faith. The social forces of production do not exist independently of capitalist relations of production, which serve as a fetter but also as an engine. Altering the relations of production eliminates the fetter but equally eliminates the engine, and Marx is blind to this inevitability due to his inability to see the subjective nature of what he takes to be substantial. Žižek insists that the great problem for communism is that capitalist relations of production not only constrain the means of production but also drive them. The means of production develop through the restrictions that capitalist relations of production place on them, and removing these restrictions would actually hamper the means of production rather than liberating them. Or, to return to Hegel's terms, the Other (the means of production) already includes the act of the subject (the relations of production). The recognition of this subjectivity of the substantial Other is the absolute. Žižek wants to show how this insight is not just compatible with but can provide the essential core of a Marxist politics.

As Žižek's intellectual path has advanced, he has more overtly identified himself with Marxist politics. Unlike in his early *Sublime Object of Ideology*, he no longer sees democracy as a viable political system, and now straightforwardly calls for a classically Marxist dictatorship of the proletariat. His later works seek to rehabilitate anti-democratic figures who see the necessity of the revolutionary act that violates the representative and electoral process. In *In Defense of Lost Causes* in 2008, Žižek speaks in defense of Martin Heidegger's turn toward Nazism, Michel Foucault's fondness for the Iranian revolution, and Mao's Cultural Revolution. The problem with these would-be revolutionaries was that they didn't take their revolutionary politics far enough, not that they strayed too far from the democratic ideal.

Marxism – the overthrow of capitalism and the installation of communism – requires a more radical step. It must break from any faith in history or in the emancipatory power of economic development. Genuine Marxism, as Žižek sees it, requires putting all theoretical guarantees into question. He claims, "*Nothing* should be accepted as inviolable in this new refoundation, neither the need for economic 'modernization' nor the most sacred liberal and democratic fetishes" (Žižek 2008a: 276). Žižek's critiques of Heidegger, Foucault, and Mao mirror his recent turn away from democracy. Like these intellectuals, democracy bespeaks a refusal to abandon the guarantees of the Other entirely, to accept fully the Other's nonexistence. Žižek has abandoned his previous support for democracy because of his increasing commitment to Marxism.

The intellectual and practical dead end in which the Left today remains stuck results not from its failure to be democratic enough but from its fetishization of democracy. As Žižek notes in *In Defense of Lost Causes*, "What, today, prevents the radical questioning of capitalism itself is precisely *the belief in the democratic form of the struggle against capitalism*" (Žižek 2008a: 183). Democracy is not a political form structured on antagonism but rather a path to its avoidance. Revolutionary political change requires an avowal of antagonism, and this avowal demands the subjectivizing of the democratic form. It has come to serve as a substance for the contemporary Left, as an object in which the Left has complete faith, just as Marx has faith in the means of production.

Faith in democracy is simultaneously faith in the people, a faith that conceives of the people as whole rather than split. The people provides a justification for acts that must occur without justification. It is in this sense that democracy functions as a contemporary ideology. Žižek notes, "the big Other is . . . in the guise of the democratic legitimization/authorization of our acts – in a democracy, my acts are 'covered' as legitimate acts which carry out the will of the majority. In contrast to this logic, the role of emancipatory forces is not to passively 'reflect' the opinion of the majority, but to instigate the working classes to mobilize their forces and thus to *create* a new majority" (Žižek 2008a: 311). Adherence to the principles of democracy limits the extent of the emancipation that might be thought or brought into being because it requires the authorization of the majority. Though this seems like a reasonable limitation, Hegel's philosophy shows – and Žižek emphasizes again and again – that the majority doesn't know what it wants. The emancipatory act creates the majority will that desires it, but this will exists only after the fact, which is why democracy – even a non-parliamentary democracy invested simply in the will of the people – fails to be revolutionary or emancipatory enough.

Democracy lacks any true creative power. Even the creation of democratic values requires a non-democratic act to bring them into being, which we see in the bloodiness of the French Revolution. The advocate of democracy cannot even account for the very democratic values that this advocate espouses. There is thus, according to Žižek, a secret elitism at the basis of all democracy. He claims, "There is no democracy without a hidden, presupposed elitism. Democracy is, by definition, not 'global';

it *has* to be based on values or truths that one cannot select 'democrati-
cally.' In democracy one can fight for truth but not decide what *is* truth"
(Žižek 2003a: 196–7). This fundamental limitation of democracy stems
from its foundation in the idea of the people as an organic whole, as an
Other that really exists. In the lineage of Hegel, Žižek rejects the democratic project as theoretically – and thus practically – unsustainable.

This does not mean that we must, following Hegel, advocate a politics
in which the monarch has a central role. It implies rather that the
advocates of liberty, equality, and fraternity have to avoid seeing the
democratic form as a solution to the problem of antagonism, as a way of
containing antagonism within a formal structure that will limit its disrup-
tiveness. The blind adherence to democracy becomes the path to the
destruction of the values to which the partisans of democracy adhere. In
order to genuinely uphold these values, we can no longer approach
democracy as a substance or as a solution.

Žižek's critique of democracy stems from his reconceptualization of
politics informed by Hegel's philosophy. Though the basis for the reconceptualization exists in his early work, it is only in *The Fragile Absolute*
in 2000 that the contours of Žižek's version of politics would become
clear. In that work, Žižek articulates a politics that aims its weapons not
at the enemy but at oneself. He says, "in a situation of forced choice,
the subject makes the 'crazy' impossible choice of, in a way, *striking at
himself*, at what is most precious to himself. This act, far from amounting
to a case of impotent aggressivity turned against oneself, rather changes
the coordinates of the situation in which the subject finds himself: by
cutting himself loose from the precious object through whose possession
the enemy kept him in check, the subject gains the space of free action"
(Žižek 2000: 150). It is only when we attack ourselves and our most
cherished assumptions – like our faith in democracy – that we change
the world.

Žižek extends this line of thought in his recent discussions of violence, where he laments the failure of the tyrants of the twentieth
century to be violent enough. As he puts it, "If one means by violence
a radical upheaval of the basic social relations, then, crazy and tasteless
as it may sound, the problem with historical monsters who slaughtered
millions was that they were not violent enough" (Žižek 2008b: 217).
True violence is not slaughtering six million Jews but transforming one's
own relationship to the ruling order, an act that Hitler could not accomplish because he could not, in contrast to the hero of David Fincher's
Fight Club (1999), lash out at himself. Žižek notices several other literary

and filmic examples of this self-directed and at the same time emancipatory violence in works like Euripides' *Medea*, Toni Morrison's *Beloved*,
Jan de Bont's *Speed* (1994), and Bryan Singer's *Usual Suspects* (1999), but
his favorite real-world example is that of Freud's act of resistance to
Nazism. In contrast to other Jewish thinkers who responded to the Nazi
caricature of the Jew with empirical refutations, Freud attacked the very
idea of the Jew. By writing *Moses and Monotheism* as Nazi ideology and
power were increasing, Freud sought to deprive Nazism of its enemy.
As Žižek puts it, "by way of an almost masochistic inversion, Freud
targeted Jews themselves and endeavored to prove that their founding
father, Moses, was an Egyptian" (Žižek 1993: 220). One might read
Žižek's critique of democracy in the same way: it is only by ruthlessly
criticizing democracy, by showing that the people don't exist, that one
can struggle against the capitalists and the fundamentalists who would
seek to destroy it.

The violence must be directed to oneself and not only to the political
enemy, because the enemy is never a particular person or group, but
always a certain psychic investment, and no subject is immune to this
investment. The act of violence toward oneself targets one's own psychic
investment in, for instance, capitalist relations of production, and thus
serves as a linchpin for any idea of emancipation. Through his engagement with Hegel and with Hegel's absolute, Žižek comes to think of
politics in terms of violence directed toward oneself. Such violence takes
away the security of a stable Other and thus changes the social field for
everyone. Hegel enables Žižek to retain violence (and thus antagonism)
within his politics without succumbing to the logic of the gulag.[15]

The great irony of Žižek's later thought is that his more vehement
Marxism coincides with a switch in emphasis from Lacan to Hegel.
Though he remains known as perhaps *the* Lacanian philosopher, Žižek
now writes whole books that fail to contain a single citation of Lacan.[16]
Hegel, on the other hand, occupies a more and more central position,
as Žižek himself avows. In an interview entitled "Liberation Hurts,"
Žižek affirms the privileged place that Hegel has in his theorizing. He
says, "ultimately, if I am to choose just one thinker, it's Hegel. He's the
one for me. And here I'm totally and unabashedly naive. He may be a
white, dead, man or whatever the wrong positions are today, but that's
where I stand" (qtd in Rasmussen 2004). This unapologetic embrace of
Hegel stems from the primacy that antagonism has in Hegel's philosophy
and from Hegel's ability to conceptualize antagonism as the ground of
social relations.

This correspondence of a turn to a more militant Marxism, combined with a more expanded role of Hegel in his thought (and a more overt identification with Hegel as his philosophical foundation), suggests that Hegel enables a stringent Marxism. Ironically enough, Hegel's philosophy provides the basis for a more revolutionary Marxism than Marx himself is able to advance. Hegel insists on the irreducibility of antagonism, while Marx centers his entire political project on the belief in its future overcoming. The key to political change lies in making antagonism the foundation of politics.

The universal recognition of antagonism as constitutive is Žižek's political project, and such a project, as he sees it, is identical with authentic communism. It necessitates a society that foregrounds the subject's absolute freedom, while protecting against the constant temptation of wholeness. This type of society is incompatible with any faith in the Other, including that envisioned by capitalism and by socialism as it existed in the twentieth century. Žižek's political project is something genuinely new, despite – or perhaps because of – its grounding in a philosopher of the nineteenth century.

Žižek is an atypical and idiosyncratic figure of the Left not because of his animated speaking style, nor his frequent recourse to the vulgar joke, nor his seamless marrying of high and low culture. One could imagine any of these formal features as the vehicle for a much more traditional leftist politics. What separates Žižek from even his closest political allies (such as Alain Badiou or Jacques Rancière) is his complete identification of political struggle with the recognition of antagonism. This is why he insists that Hegel is "the one for me." Whereas traditional Marxist ideas of politics conceive of practical struggle as the attempt to overcome antagonism as it manifests itself in class society, Žižek locates this political vision within ideology. Ideology tries to convince us that antagonism is not fundamental and constitutive, while politics seeks to affirm its constitutive nature.[17]

Relations of domination exist not because the social order is beset by antagonism but because society works to hide its own antagonistic structure. In the flight from antagonism, subjects find solace in figures of authority who provide the illusion of a foundation that does not exist. When they confront the inescapability of antagonism, however, subjects free themselves from the power of authority and from corresponding relations of domination. The political act, as Žižek sees it, places us face-to-face with antagonism and refuses all paths that promise relief from it.

The end product of Žižek's Hegelian politics is a much less hopeful politics than one typically finds within Marxism. Despite his frequent invocations of the term "Utopia," Žižek's thought is thoroughly anti-utopian. There is no future free of antagonistic struggle, but only a present always enmeshed within that struggle. Žižek makes precisely this point when he notes that the negativity that creates a new order does not disappear, but manifests itself in the form of the new order, whatever that order might be. In *The Parallax View*, he notes, "the new postrevolutionary order does not negate its founding gesture, the explosion of the destructive fury that wipes away the Old; it merely *gives body* to this negativity" (Žižek 2006, 382). Rather than dreaming of a way to surmount antagonism, the task of the political thinker – and this is what makes Hegel the political thinker par excellence – involves tearing down all the false avenues of escape that promise freedom from the alienation that accompanies an antagonistic social structure. For Žižek, as soon as liberation ceases to hurt, it ceases to be liberation.

Notes

1 See Lukács 1976. In her remarkable study *Hegel, Haiti, and Universal History*, Susan Buck-Morss makes a parallel move to that of Lukács in regard to the politics of race in Hegel's thought. She sees in the *Phenomenology* a supporter of the Haitian Revolution and an implicit believer in racial equality, while she condemns the later Hegel of the *Philosophy of History* for a theoretical regression on this question, a regression produced ironically, according to Buck-Morss, by Hegel's reading of the anthropology of the time. The young Hegel was a racial egalitarian because he was insufficiently informed about the racist social science that he would subsequently come to know. For the full account of Hegel's view of the Haitian Revolution and the evolution of his views on race, see Buck-Morss 2009.
2 See also Marcuse 1983.
3 Despite his astuteness as a reader of Hegel, Theodor Adorno articulates the typical reading of absolute knowledge as the triumph of thought over the world that conditions it. He notes, "His thought as a whole is cunning; it hopes to achieve victory over the superior power of the world, about which it has no illusions, by turning this superior power against itself until it turns into something different" (Adorno 1993: 42–3).
4 See, respectively, Derrida 1986 and Nancy 2002. As Nancy defines the absolute, it is the complete absence of reconciliation and the attainment of pure restlessness. He says, "this unrest that *we are* and that we desire (even

as consciousness believes it only wants its self and its objects) is where the proximity of the absolute finds, or happens upon, itself: neither possession, nor incorporation, but proximity as such, imminence and coincidence, like the beat of a rhythm" (Nancy 2002: 79).

5 Alain Badiou traces this problem in the great Spinozist of the twentieth century, Gilles Deleuze. Deleuze proffers a philosophy of immanence in which being is multiple but, as Badiou shows in his study of Deleuze, the insistence on complete immanence doesn't allow being to emerge as multiple. Instead, it remains one, a structure in which differentiations are simply formal. As Badiou points out, "The multiple acceptations of being must be understood as a multiple that is formal, while the One alone is real, and only the real supports the distribution of sense (which is unique)" (Badiou 2000: 25).

6 This is what Žižek is getting at when he explains the task of the intellectual, who is the producer or discoverer of theory. He begins *Tarrying with the Negative* by outlining the task of the intellectual as one of making evident the gap in signification that necessarily renders subjects political beings. According to Žižek, "the duty of the critical intellectual . . . is precisely *to occupy all the time*, even when the new order (the 'new harmony') stabilizes itself and again renders invisible the hole as such, *the place of this hole*, i.e., to maintain a distance toward every Master-Signifier" (Žižek 1993: 2).

7 The vituperatve tone that Žižek adopts when speaking about New Age philosophy or the ecological movement stems from their tendency to posit wholeness in the Other – either in being itself or in the natural world. Doing so depoliticizes the subject, even when one advances this position in the name of a critique of capitalism. Such critiques will never be as revolutionary as they claim to be because they will never access the point – the politicized subject – at which revolutionary change might occur.

8 For a critique of Žižek's tendency to single out multiculturalism and identity politics as the targets for his attacks, see La Berge 2007.

9 This is the version of democracy promulgated by Chantal Mouffe, who is surely the most convincing advocate for a democracy that privileges agonism. Mouffe argues against consensus politics and for an idea of democratic politics that privileges vigorous opposition. As she sees it, consensus politics gives rise to antagonism in the form of far right-wing parties asserting themselves on the political scene, and it is only agonistic debate that can prevent this. She notes, "as a consequence of the blurring of the frontiers between left and right and the absence of an agonistic debate among democratic parties, a confrontation between different political projects, voters did not have the possibility of identifying with a differentiated range of democratic political identities. This created a void that was likely to be occupied by other forms of identifications which could become problematic for the working of the democratic system" (Mouffe 2005: 69).

10 Without the monarch, the people cease to be a state and become once again – or take themselves to be – substantial. Hegel points out, "Taken without its monarch and the articulation of the whole which is the indispensible and direct concomitant of monarchy, the people is a formless mass and no longer a state" (Hegel 1952: 183).

11 Žižek's implicit critique of the great Hegelians of the twentieth century – Alexandre Kojève and Jean-Paul Sartre – is that they limit subjectivity to subjects and refuse Hegel's subjectivization of substance. For Kojève and Sartre, it is only the human subject that suffers from self-division, while the natural world and the world of things is simply being in-itself. In his attempt to systematize Žižek's philosophy, Adrian Johnston makes clear the problem with this position. He notes, "if one maintains that the Real of material being isn't barred (that the body, nature, and the world are organically integrated substances in which the functions of their various constituent elements are coordinated and operate in tandem), then one must either deny the existence of subjectivity (at a minimum, dismissing it as an epiphenomenal residue of physical reality) or regress back into crude versions of the Real-versus-Ideal dichotomy" (Johnston 2008: 107).

12 See Žižek 1991b and Žižek 1992.

13 Ironically enough, the notion that only the relations of production can be responsible for contradiction is also the thesis of committed capitalist Ayn Rand. Despite being political antipodes – for Rand, Marx is the chief enemy – both Rand and Marx view the mode of production as an arena of pure substance and noncontradiction. It is only when one introduces relations of production that contradictions emerge. In Rand's case, this includes any attempts by the state to control economic production, while Marx lays the blame on the capitalist's intercession in the laborer's production of surplus value.

14 Deleuze and Guattari share Marx's fundamental faith in the political possibilities of unchaining the means of production from the relations of production. Doing so would completely unleash the decoded flows that capitalism unleashes on the one hand while attempting to restrain on the other. Thus, they envision, like Marx, capitalism's necessary self-destruction. They claim, "capitalism . . . continually sets and then repels its own limits, but in so doing it gives rise to numerous flows in all directions that escape its axiomatic" (Deleuze and Guattari 1987: 472). Capitalism destroys the limits that it establishes and in doing so creates an unfettered production that would no longer be capitalism. According to Hegel's critique of Marx avant la lettre, such a vision fails to account for the productivity of the limits themselves.

15 The distance between Žižek's politics and that of the gulag manifests itself in one of Žižek's favorite expressions. When confronted with someone who articulates a position with which he disagrees, Žižek will often say, "Five

years in the gulag for you" – or some variation on this. If he subscribed to the logic of the gulag, this joke would become impossible for him.

16 Žižek's turn away from Lacan should not be interpreted as an abandonment of Lacan's thought or of psychoanalysis. His engagement with Lacan in fact continues to provide the basis for his rereading of Hegel.

17 Despite his vehement critique of Louis Althusser, Žižek does largely take up Althusser's definition of ideology as fulfilling a foundational role in obscuring social antagonism. As a result, Žižek rules out the possibility of a struggle between different forms of ideology – between a bourgeois and a proletarian ideology, for instance. The struggle will always be between the proponents of the real antagonism and ideology, while for Althusser it was a struggle between Marxist science and ideology. For an early critique of this position that envisions the possibility of competing ideologies, see Rancière 1974.

References

Adorno, Theodor W. (1993) *Hegel: Three Studies*, trans. Shierry Weber Nicholsen. Cambridge: MIT Press.

Agamben, Giorgio (1993) *The Coming Community*, trans. Michael Hardt. Minneapolis: University of Minnesota Press.

Badiou, Alain (2000) *Deleuze: The Clamor of Being*, trans. Louise Burchill. Minneapolis: University of Minnesota Press.

Buck-Morss, Susan (2009) *Hegel, Haiti, and Universal History*. Pittsburgh: University of Pittsburgh Press.

Deleuze, Gilles, and Félix Guattari (1987) *A Thousand Plateaus: Capitalism and Schizophrenia*, trans. Brian Massumi. Minneapolis: University of Minnesota Press.

Derrida, Jacques (1986) *Glas*, trans. John P. Leavey, Jr. and Richard Rand. Lincoln: University of Nebraska Press.

Hegel, G. W. F. (1952) *Philosophy of Right*, trans. T. M. Knox. London: Oxford University Press.

— (1969) *Science of Logic*, trans. A. V. Miller. Atlantic Highlands, New Jersey: Humanities Press.

— (1975) *Logic: Being Part One of the Encyclopedia of the Philosophical Sciences*, trans. William Wallace. Oxford: Oxford University Press.

— (1977) *The Phenomenology of Spirit*, trans. A. V. Miller. Oxford: Oxford University Press.

Johnston, Adrian (2008) *Žižek's Ontology: A Transcendental Materialist Theory of Subjectivity*. Evanston: Northwestern University Press.

Kant, Immanuel (1998) *The Critique of Pure Reason*, trans. Paul Guyer and Allen W. Wood. Cambridge: Cambridge University Press.

La Berge, Leigh Claire (2007) "The Writing Cure: Slavoj Žižek, Analysand of Modernity." *The Truth of Žižek*, eds Paul Bowman and Richard Stamp. New York: Continuum. 9–26.

Lukács, Georg (1976) *The Young Hegel: Studies in the Relations between Dialectics and Economics*, trans. Rodney Livingstone. Cambridge: MIT P.

Marcuse, Herbert (1983) *Reason and Revolution: Hegel and the Rise of Social Theory*, 2nd edn. Atlantic Highlands, New Jersey: Humanities P.

Marx, Karl (1981) *Capital: A Critique of Political Economy, Volume Three*, trans. David Fernbach. New York: Penguin.

Mouffe, Chantal (2005) *On the Political*. New York: Routledge.

Nancy, Jean-Luc (2002) *Hegel: The Restlessness of the Negative*, trans. Jason Smith and Steven Miller. Minneapolis: University of Minnesota Press.

Rancière, Jacques (1974) "On the Theory of Ideology: Althusser's Politics." *Radical Philosophy* 7: 2–15.

— (2010) *Dissensus: On Politics and Aesthetics*, trans. Steven Corcoran New York: Continuum.

Rasmussen, Eric Dean (2004) "Liberation Hurts: An Interview with Slavoj Žižek." *Electronic Book Review* (July 1): http://www.electronicbookreview. com/thread/endconstruction/desublimation.

Rose, Gillian (1981) *Hegel Contra Sociology*. Atlantic Highlands, New Jersery: Humanities P.

Schmitt, Carl (1996) *The Concept of the Political*, trans. George Schwab. Chicago: University of Chicago Press.

Stavrakakis, Yannis (2007) *The Lacanian Left: Psychoanalysis, Theory, Politics*. Albany: State University of New York Press.

Žižek, Slavoj (1989) *The Sublime Object of Ideology*. New York: Verso.

— (1991a) *For They Know Not What They Do: Enjoyment as a Political Factor*. New York: Verso.

— (1991b) *Looking Awry: An Introduction to Jacques Lacan through Popular Culture*. Cambridge: MIT P.

— (1992) *Enjoy Your Symptom!: Jacques Lacan in Hollywood and out*. New York: Routledge.

— (1993) *Tarrying with the Negative: Kant, Hegel, and the Critique of Ideology*. Durham: Duke University Press.

— (2000) *The Fragile Absolute, or, Why Is the Christian Legacy Worth Fighting For?* New York: Verso.

— (2003a) *Organs without Bodies: On Deleuze and Consequences*. New York: Routledge.

— (2003b) *The Puppet and the Dwarf: The Perverse Core of Christianity*. Cambridge: MIT P.

— (2006) *The Parallax View*. Cambridge: MIT P.

— (2008a) *In Defense of Lost Causes*. New York: Verso.

— (2008b) *Violence: Six Sideways Reflections*. New York: Picador.

3

Žižek and Christianity: Or the Critique of Religion after Marx and Freud

Bruno Bosteels

A Plea for Vulgar Thinking

In a recent review of Paul Ricoeur's book *Memory, History, Forgetting*, Alain Badiou raises an important, if also discomforting, question about the link between contemporary philosophy and Christianity. His charge is not that there would be some conceptual shortcoming or theoretical inconsistency in the book under review, but rather that its author has failed to render explicit the fundamental presupposition behind his call for forgiveness, so that we find only at the last moment what was there from the beginning – namely, the notion of a subject who cannot not be Christian: "Fundamentally, my main criticism bears on what I consider to be not so much hypocrisy as a lack of civility, a lack of civility common to so many Christian proponents of phenomenology: the absurd concealment of the true source of conceptual constructions and philo-sophical polemics."[1] When it comes to Slavoj Žižek, to be sure, no such criticism seems to be in order or even imaginable. This is not to say that Žižek could not be charged – as in fact he has been – with a lack of civility of a different kind, especially in the eyes of genuine religious believers, whatever their creed may well be, but he certainly does not conceal the fact that Christianity is one of the main sources of his ongoing conceptual constructions and philosophical polemics. In fact, for the past decade, from his 2000 book *The Fragile Absolute*, if not already earlier, starting in the mid 1990s with his reading of Schelling's philosophy in *The Indivisible Remainder*, until his recent dialogue with John Milbank in

The Monstrosity of Christ first published in 2009, Žižek has, if anything, been all too insistent on the fundamental importance of Christianity for his peculiar brand of Lacano-Hegelianism.

So then, to ask the question that serves as the subtitle to *The Fragile Absolute*: *why is the Christian legacy still worth fighting for?* Even more, why does Žižek believe that this fight can still (or once again) bring together Christianity and Marxism, as he writes in the opening pages of the same book: "Christianity and Marxism *should* fight on the same side of the barricade against the onslaught of new spiritualisms – the authentic Christian legacy is much too precious to be left to the fundamentalist freaks"[2]? What are Žižek's intentions in making this bold claim again and again in subsequent books, especially at a time when what he himself elsewhere calls "really existing Christianity" seems to be very much alive and kicking, even in the absence of the philosopher's help, for example as part of the ideological agenda for justifying the so-called war on terror in the name of the Christian, or Judeo-Christian, values of the West?

Before coming back in my conclusion to discuss the consequences, whether intentional or not, of this materialist defense of Christianity, and without wanting to sort out all the possible reasons from the author's actual intentions, we can at least enumerate a few basic options. There is first of all the "straightforward" or "honest" reading: Žižek according to this first reading would be a devout Christian who believes that his religion is also worth defending in the domain of dialectical theory and materialist philosophy. Then, there is what I would call the "subversive" or "entrist" reading, which in turn can go two ways: either Žižek is not a straightforward believer so much as he is a genuine materialist philosopher who proposes to latch onto the dominant Western religious ideology in order to subvert it from within; or he is not as straightforward a materialist as he claims to be and really wants to subvert philosophical materialism by smuggling in an element of religious idealism. Finally, we can imagine a "transformative" or "dialectical" combination of all three readings: Žižek is ready to call himself a true Christian only if and when Christianity can be shown to contain from the very beginning the kind of materialist kernel that the first subversive reading prides itself on bringing to the foreground.

Again, in a slightly different formulation closer to the lexicon of psychoanalysis, we can also use the good and the perverse positions together with the two domains of materialism and Christianity. We then obtain the following abstract combinatory of four possible positions: Žižek as a good materialist and also a good Christian; as a good materialist but a perverse Christian; as a perverse materialist but a good Christian; or as both a perverse materialist and a perverse Christian. Obviously, even before going into the details of Žižek's argument, not all of these combinations are equally plausible. Thus, already on purely formal grounds, being a good materialist seems to run directly counter to the possibility of being at the same time a good Christian, since materialism – from ancient atomism to the *Encyclopédie* version of the Enlightenment – supposes the radical debunking of all religious belief: there is no God, only atoms falling and occasionally swerving in the void, as we might conclude with Lucretius; or, with Voltaire, enlightened reason must crush the infamous wretch of superstition! Some measure of perversity, therefore, will be structurally inevitable if Žižek wants to justify his fight for the Christian legacy all the while maintaining his materialist credentials and, even more so, his credentials as a loyal reader of Marx and Freud.

To begin disentangling the dialectic behind this necessary perversion, let us have a closer look at a passage from *The Puppet and the Dwarf*, a book subtitled precisely *The Perverse Core of Christianity*, in which Žižek appears to want to speak as openly and frankly as possible about the place of Christianity in his thinking. Instead of falling for a "soft" or "weak" version of postmodern theology, he argues that what is needed today more than ever is an almost "vulgar" directness to answer the question "Do you really believe or not?" To this question Žižek's answer goes as follows: "My claim here is not merely that I am a materialist through and through, and that the subversive kernel of Christianity is accessible also to a materialist approach; my thesis is much stronger: this kernel is accessible *only* to a materialist approach – and vice-versa: to become a true dialectical materialist, one should go through the Christian experience."[3] In spite of the apparent reversibility of the terms, though, we should notice how there is a profound asymmetry present in this claim, insofar as the affirmation "I am a materialist through and through" on one side is not followed by a comparable affirmation "I am a Christian" on the opposite side. All we obtain is the claim that "one should go through the Christian experience," possibly or presumably so as to come out of this experience and be done with it, in order to become a true materialist. In the end, then, notwithstanding his call for total directness, even Žižek himself does not answer the vulgar question as to whether he really is a believer or not – at least not here.

Later, in *The Monstrosity of Christ*, Žižek rephrases the same question in terms of whether the reference to God in his reading of Christianity is to be taken literally or metaphorically. "Both versions are to be rejected," he argues on this occasion; "it is, of course, not 'literally' (we are materialists, there is no God), but it is also not 'metaphorically' ('God' is not just a metaphor, a mystifying expression, of human passions, desire, ideals, etc.)."[4] Instead, Žižek goes on to suggest, we must come to grips with the fact that there is an intrinsic link *within* Christianity between God and the death of God, figured in Christ on the Cross. As soon as we understand this properly atheist message contained within what for Žižek is the only truly logical monotheism, we are already approaching the perverse core of Christianity. In other words, there is something in Christianity that *justifies* the recourse to God's name in a way that is neither literal nor metaphorical but, rather, conceptually motivated. By contrast, a straightforward materialist debunking of Christianity, as part of a wholesale critique of religion that turns God directly into a man-made product or mass delusion, along the lines of what we can find not only in the works of Marx but also in Freud, would be unable to come to terms with the conceptual motivation of this atheist core of Christianity – with the fact that, just as there is an inhuman core at the heart of humanity, so too this extimate kernel comes to be transposed onto God Himself in the figure of Christ dying and doubting his own Father on the Cross: " 'God' (the divine) is a name for that which in man is not human, for the inhuman core that sustains being-human."[5]

This is why Žižek in *The Monstrosity of Christ* can state even more clearly than in *The Fragile Absolute* how he sees the necessary link between materialism and Christianity. Quoting Jean-Luc Nancy's two propositions: "Only a Christianity which envisages the present possibility of its negation can be relevant today" and "Only an atheism which envisages the reality of its Christian provenance can be relevant today," Žižek agrees by offering the following two paraphrases:

> The first proposition implies that today, Christianity is alive only in materialist (atheist) practices which negate it (the Pauline community of believers, for example, is to be found today in radical political groups, not in churches); the second proposition implies that a true materialism not only asserts that only material reality "really exists," but it has to assume all the consequences of what Lacan called the nonexistence of the big Other, and it is only Christianity that opens up the space for thinking this nonexistence, insofar as it is the religion of a God who dies.[6]

Atheism, which in the process comes to be defined in terms of the death of God as the big Other, would thus be the core content of Christianity.

In what follows, however, I would like to address the extent to which this reading of religion in general and of the Christian religion in particular is possible only at the cost of a highly selective and extremely twisted – properly perverse – reinterpretation of some of Marx and Freud's key materialist insights.

The Atheist Core of Christianity

We might also say that just as, for Marx, there lays a rational kernel within the mystical shell of the Hegelian dialectic, so too for Žižek the dogmatic-institutional shell of Christian belief contains a rational-perverse core. Except that in both cases the point is precisely to avoid the external oppositions of kernel and shell, essence and appearance, inner truth and outward semblance. For Žižek, indeed, the point is always to displace the gap between essence and appearance onto the essence itself. There is not a truer, higher or deeper, essence of Christianity hidden somewhere within the mystical shell of beliefs; Christianity itself already shows that the essence (of God) is *only* its appearing (as God-man or Christ).

Žižek's main thesis about Christianity – the one idea that he keeps repeating in book after book dealing with religion and belief – is actually disarmingly simple and it can be summed up in an often-quoted passage from Chesterton's *Orthodoxy*: "Christianity is the only religion on earth that has felt that omnipotence made God incomplete. Christianity alone has felt that God, to be wholly God, must have been a rebel as well as a king."[7] Doubt, suffering, impotence, and fragility – in one word, finitude – is thus inscribed in a reflexive reversal into the very heart of the Christian God. In Christianity, it is the Absolute that becomes fragile, and not just the finite-mortal creature who is fragile in the face of his infinite-immortal Creator. As Žižek reiterates in *The Monstrosity of Christ*, "In his 'Father, why have you forsaken me?', Christ himself commits what is for a Christian the ultimate sin: he wavers in his Faith. While, in all other religions, there are people who do not believe in God, only in Christianity does God not believe in himself."[8]

If atheism is the truth of monotheism, then for Žižek the only true monotheism is Christianity. As we can read in *The Puppet and the Dwarf*: "This is why Christianity, precisely because of the Trinity, is the only true monotheism: the lesson of the Trinity is that God fully coincides with the gap between God and man, that God *is* this gap – this is Christ, not the God of beyond separated from man by a gap, but the gap as such, the gap which simultaneously separates God from God and man from man."[9] In Christianity, there is thus a double alienation at work, or a double kenosis, not only of man from God but also of God from Himself. Or, to use the more Badiouian-sounding formulation from *The Monstrosity of Christ*: "Insofar as the truly materialist axiom is the assertion of primordial multiplicity, the One which precedes this multiplicity can only be zero itself. No wonder, then, that only in Christianity – as the only truly logical monotheism – does God himself turn momentarily into an atheist."[10]

However, I would argue that the addition of the adverb "momentarily" in the last formulation might turn out to be a crucial concession. What if this momentary atheism quickly gives way once again to the ferocious superego demand of a God who has never really or fully relinquished His power? What if the becoming-finite of God is merely the beginning of an even more terrorizing power of the infinite? After all, the fact that God appears as finite should by no means come as a surprise, nor is it necessarily a radical, atheist or a-theological, core hidden within the mystical shell of institutionalized religiosity. Freud himself, as I will discuss, could help us point this out: how religion depends on human fragility and, thus, how religion is bound sooner or later to figure this fragility even within the Absolute, without for this reason ceasing to be the work of God. Following Freud in *The Future of an Illusion* rather than Lacan in *The Triumph of Religion*, we might as well ask whether a religion without a big Other is still a religion? If not, then why should we continue harping on the nonexistence of the big Other through the example of Christianity which, already as a religion and not only as a really existing institution with its own ideological state apparatuses and so on, cannot be separated from such a reference to a big Other?

Žižek, in other words, reads the self-alienation of God from Himself as a moment of radical doubt and impenetrability. He compares this in psychoanalytical terms, both to one of Freud's formulations that he quotes, among numerous other places, in *On Belief*: "What is incomprehensible within the pre-Christian horizon is the full shattering dimension of this impenetrability of God to Himself, discernible in Christ's 'Father, why did you forsake me?', this Christian version of the Freudian 'Father, can't you see that I am burning?' "[11] and to Lacan's formulation evoked, for example, in *The Puppet and the Dwarf*: "Are we not, in the case of Christian identification, dealing with something similar? In our very failure, we identify with the divine failure, with Christ's confrontation with 'Che vuoi?', with the enigma of the Other's desire ('Why are you doing this to me, Father? What do you want from me?').'[12] Yet what if this cry is not so much the signal of God's total self-abandonment but rather the point at which the fragile, or thrown, human being becomes all the more securely sutured onto religious ideology, precisely, by way of the gap of finitude? Finally, what if it is not so much God the Father who stumbles upon the limit of his omnipotence in Christianity, but Christ who, through his exclamation of doubt on the Cross, assures that impotence serves ideologically to close the gap inherent in God?

We do not even have to phrase these questions in the form of criticisms. Žižek himself is fully aware of the double-edged nature of the identification with failure, which from a reverse perspective can be seen as the recipe for the even greater success of ideological identification. "We are one with God only when God is no longer one with Himself, but abandons Himself, 'internalizes' the radical distance which separates us from Him," Žižek also writes in *The Puppet and the Dwarf*. He continues:

> Our radical experience of separation from God is the very feature which unites us with Him – not in the usual mystical sense that only through such an experience do we open ourselves to the radical Otherness of God, but in a sense similar to the one in which Kant claims that humiliation and pain are the only transcendental feelings: it is preposterous to think that I can identify myself with the divine bliss – only when I experience the infinite pain of separation from God do I share an experience with God Himself (Christ on the Cross).[13]

We may be far removed from the imaginary representations of religion based on divine bliss and awe-inspiring power. Yet, on the other hand, humiliation and pain also come to function as the affective channels for the even more awe-inspiring presence of God qua immanent transcendence within the fragile human body. What unites me with God is the gap that separates God from Himself; but such a logic of separation, far from revealing the atheist core of monotheism, can also be seen as an ever more pernicious incorporation of the human subject into the fold of the Christian God.

Before coming back to this larger question about the double-edged sword of identification, though, we should follow for a few steps longer the progression of Žižek's argument for Christianity as the only true – atheist – monotheism. This argument in fact also includes a frequently reiterated and profusely illustrated minimal historical narrative, first, about the passage from paganism to monotheism, and then, within the mono-theistic so-called religions of the Book, about the passage from Judaism to Christianity – with Islam, as Žižek is the first to admit, evidently presenting an unsolvable "problem" for this by and large orthodox-Hegelian master narrative.

The Only Truly Logical Monotheism?

Obviously, rather than receiving a thick historical or genealogical account, the passages or transitions in question are treated almost exclusively at the conceptual level; they are notional or ideological passages, or shifts at the level of the development of the spirit, as in Hegel, or at the level of the psychic economy of religions, as in Freud or Lacan.

The passage from paganism to the Jewish and Christian tradition, thus, is described in psychoanalytical terms for example as the passage from a view of the immanent fullness of life to a view of human existence based on the contingent encounter of an external element or trauma: "This is the lesson of both psychoanalysis and the Judeo-Christian tradition: the specific human vocation does not rely on the development of man's inherent potentials (on the awakening of the dormant spiritual forces OR of some genetic program); it is triggered by an external traumatic encoun-ter, by the encounter of the Other's desire in its impenetrability."[14] This also means that, with the move from polytheism to monotheism, we actually shift not from the many to the One so much as from pure mul-tiplicity toward the introduction of a gap within the One. "What if, on the contrary, it is polytheism which presupposes the commonly shared (back)ground of the multitude of gods, while it is only monotheism which renders the gap as such, the gap in the Absolute itself, the gap which not only separates (the one) God from Himself, but *is* this God?"[15]

In fact, as we already saw above, only with Christianity does this gap or separation come to be transferred back onto God. This then presupposes an additional shift, within monotheism, from Judaism to Christianity. "At the level of ideology, this shift from external to inherent limitation is accomplished by Christianity. In Judaism, God remains the transcendent irrepresentable Other, i.e., as Hegel was right to empha-size, Judaism is the religion of the Sublime," Žižek writes in *On Belief*. "Christianity, however, renounces this God of Beyond, this Real behind the curtain of the phenomena; it acknowledges that there is NOTHING beyond the appearance – nothing BUT the imperceptible X that changes Christ, this ordinary man, into God. In the ABSOLUTE identity of man and God, the Divine is the pure *Schein* of another dimension that shines through Christ, this miserable creature."[16] The traumatic encounter with the Other's desire, in the passage from Judaism to Christianity, is said to lead to a transposition of this impenetrable Otherness onto God, as an enigma that is in God more than God Himself. Or, to use a formula that is repeated verbatim in both *On Belief* and *The Monstrosity of Christ*: "Judaism remains at the level of the enigma *of* God, while Christianity moves to the enigma *in* God himself."[17]

Žižek on a few occasions acknowledges that this narrative creates an enormous problem in terms of the place of Islam: "No wonder that, to many a Western historian of religion, Islam is a problem – how could it have emerged *after* Christianity, the religion to end all religions?"[18] Žižek's own solution to this problem is thoroughly ambivalent. On the one hand, in *On Belief*, he wonders out loud whether Islam itself might not be the solution, instead of the problem, namely, as a kind of dialectical sublation of both Judaism and Christianity. He quickly moves on, though, to dismiss this possibility with an even more striking and idiosyncratic hypothesis:

> Is, then, Islam a solution? Does Islam not perceive this deadlock of both religions? Does it, consequently, not endeavor to accomplish a kind of "synthesis" of the two? Perhaps, although I am not in a position to pass a competent judgement on it, since from MY (Judeo-Christian) perspective, it appears as if, in this attempted synthesis, Islam ends up with the worst of both worlds. That is to say, the common reproach of Christians to Jews is that their religion is that of a cruel superego, while the common reproach of Jews to Christians is that, unable to endure in pure monotheism, they regress to a mythical narrative (of Christ's martyrdom, etc.) and is it not that, in Islam, we find BOTH, narrative and superego?[19]

Žižek is unlikely to make many friends among Muslims with this combination of common reproaches from the other two monotheisms, now thrown back upon the third. On the other hand, in an endnote to *The Monstrosity of Christ*, as if to compensate for the possible lack of civility entailed by his previous hypothesis, Žižek offers the politically correct counter-hypothesis of Islam as the true monotheism. Now Islam appears not as the worst of both worlds but as the true universal sublation of both Judaism and Christianity:

Even Hegel's logic of triads seems to get stuck in a deadlock here: the triad that offers itself, but that Hegel cannot admit, of course, is that of Judaism-Christianity-Islam: first the immediate/abstract monotheism which, as the price to be paid for its immediate character, has to be embodied in a particular ethnic group (which is why the Jews renounce all proselytism); then Christianity with its trinity; finally Islam, the truly universal monotheism.[20]

Žižek does not further develop this idea, which as he admits would completely upset the Hegelian framework of his reading of Christianity.

My argument with regard to these minimal flashes of historicity in the overarching passage from paganism to monotheism is not that Žižek would be trapped in a form of anti-Semitism by positing the sublation of Judaism as the necessary stepping stone toward the emergence of the Christian-Pauline "New Man."[21] Nor am I concerned with the comparative evaluation of the strengths and weaknesses of each of the three monotheisms, between Judaism, Christianity, and Islam. In fact, what such readings and objections miss in their ideologically motivated adjudication of good or bad points is the crucial extent to which Žižek's take on the passage from Judaism and Christianity – to stick to the only shift about which he does not invoke the excuse of his incompetence – is actually philosophical more so than, or prior to, being theological or historical.

From Kant to Hegel

Žižek indeed toys with quite a large number of philosophical variations on the theme of the passage from Judaism to Christianity. Even within the confines of a single book, for example *On Belief*, we find a Wittgensteinian variation along the lines of the division between saying and showing from the *Tractatus Logico-Philosophicus*: "Christianity involves the distinction between external rule and inner belief (so the question is always: do you REALLY, in the innermost of your heart, believe, or are you just following the dead letter of the law?), while in Judaism, the 'external' rules and practices DIRECTLY ARE the religious belief in its material existence – Jews do not have to DECLARE their belief, they immediately SHOW it in their practice."[22] A few pages later, the above characterization of Christianity is used as a counter-argument against the Levinasian ethics of the Other: "Insofar as the ultimate Other is God

Himself, I should risk the claim that _it is the epochal achievement of Christianity to reduce its Otherness to Sameness:_ God Himself is Man, one of us."[23] Then, promptly, we also obtain a quick Schellingian variation, with an added touch from Lacan: "So, perhaps, the difference between Judaism and Christianity is, to put it in Schelling's terms, the difference between contraction and expansion: Jewish contraction (perseverance, enduring in the status of a remainder) lays the ground for the Christian expansion (love). If Jews assert the Law without superego, Christians assert love as _jouissance_ outside the Law."[24] Schelling, Wittgenstein, Levinas . . . : were we to quote _The Fragile Absolute_ or _The Puppet and the Dwarf_, the list could go on so as to include similar formulations in terms of Badiou's notions of purification and subtraction, or of Lacan's formulae of sexuation.

For Žižek, however, the fundamental philosophical reference for understanding Christianity of course has always been and will always be Hegel – with the passage from Judaism to Christianity then corresponding to the passage from Kant to Hegel, especially as read through the lens of Lacanian psychoanalysis. We thus must come to grasp the inner necessity that links the following three affirmations into a near-perfect syllogism, the first one from _On Belief_: "Christianity is, from its very inception, THE religion of modernity: what the Christian notion of the suspension of the Law aims at is precisely this gap between the domain of moral norms and Faith, the unconditional engagement"; the second, from _The Puppet and the Dwarf_: "Hegel's logic is the (first case of the) _logic of the Real_"; and the third, from _The Monstrosity of Christ_: "Hegel is authentically Christian – for him, the only actuality of Spirit is the actuality of finite life," or again, later in the same book: "Hegel is _the_ Christian philosopher."[25] It is because Hegel is _the_ Christian philosopher that he is also the first truly modern philosopher to present the logic of the Real that we associate more commonly with the work of Lacan. Put differently, Christianity is the vanishing mediator between German idealism and a modern psychoanalytical theory of the subject triggered by the traumatic encounter of the Real.

After comparing the passage from Judaism to Christianity to Badiou's proposal to move from a logic of destruction and purification to one of subtraction and minimal difference, Žižek himself draws the parallel with German idealism:

And is not this shift from purification to subtraction also the shift from Kant to Hegel? From tension between phenomena and Thing to an inconsistency/

gap between phenomena themselves? The standard notion of reality is that of a hard kernel that resists the conceptual grasp – what Hegel does is simply to take this notion of reality more literally: nonconceptual reality is something that emerges when notional self-development gets caught in an inconsistency, and becomes nontransparent to itself. In short, the limit is transposed from exterior to interior: there is Reality because and insofar as the Notion is inconsistent, doesn't coincide with itself. The multiple perspectival inconsistencies between phenomena are not an effect of the impact of the transcendent Thing – on the contrary, this Thing is nothing but the ontologization of the inconsistency between phenomena.[26]

From here, we can actually go on shuttling back and forth between Hegel's logic of the reflexive determination of an external limit and the passage from Judaism to Christianity. Religion, then, serves as an exemplifying illustration of a philosophical problem, just as conversely philosophy can be called upon to explain a religious phenomenon. For example, in *The Puppet and the Dwarf*, Žižek also writes:

In religious terms, this passage from the Impossible-Real One (thing), refracted/reflected in the multitude of its appearances, to the Twosome is the very passage from Judaism to Christianity: the Jewish God is the Real Thing of Beyond, while the divine dimension of Christ is just a tiny grimace, an imperceptible shade, which differentiates him from other (ordinary) humans. Christ is not "sublime" in the sense of an "object elevated to the dignity of a Thing," he is not a stand-in for the impossible Thing-God; he is, rather, "the Thing itself," or, more accurately, "the Thing itself" is nothing but the rupture/break which makes Christ not fully human.[27]

Finally, this reciprocity between Hegel and Christianity is sealed in terms of Lacanian psychoanalysis, inasmuch as the internal reflection of what otherwise appears as an external limit or obstacle is likewise descriptive of the proper function of the Real:

This means that the Real is not external to the Symbolic: the Real is the Symbolic itself in the modality of non-All, lacking an external Limit/ Exception. In this precise sense, the line of separation between the Symbolic and the Real is not only a symbolic gesture par excellence, but the very founding gesture of the Symbolic and to step into the Real does not entail abandoning language, throwing oneself into the abyss of the chaotic Real, but, on the contrary, dropping the very allusion to some external point of reference which eludes the Symbolic.[28]

A first question that one might ask in regard to this triangulation of Hegel and Lacan by way of Christianity is whether the latter is indispensable in order for this entire framing to work as the basic setup behind all of Žižek's philosophy. Is Christianity truly a vanishing mediator or a mediator that is here to stay? Of course, we understand very well how Hegel's philosophy arises historically out of the element of Christianity, but are the logic of the real and the attendant theory of the subject necessarily bound up in this historical complicity as well? Or, alternatively, is there a way out of the triangular cross-referencing of Žižek's Lacano-Hegelianism that would allow us to put Christianity itself in historical perspective? And to begin answering this, should we not consider another, more immediate question, which is to say: to what extent does Žižek in his perverse-materialist reading of Christianity also need to revise, if not also pervert, the well-known insights into religion that can be found in the work of two of the original founding figures behind his materialism, namely, Marx and Freud?

Marx, Freud, and the Critique of Religion

From Freud's take on religion, Žižek in fact borrows only the general subversive move involved in *Moses and Monotheism*. "To deny a people the man whom it praises as the greatest of its sons is not a deed to be undertaken lightheartedly – especially by one belonging to that people," Freud had stated from the outset in what for most readers represents his testament, written in the face of the rising Nazi threat that would force him into exile to London: "No consideration, however, will move me to set aside truth in favour of supposed national interests."[29] Žižek, we could say, seeks to do for Christianity what Freud did for Judaism, that is to say, in an act of seeming betrayal that is actually the only possible ethical act, to take away the very core of religion in the guise of a reliance on some founding authority: "Is not such a betrayal part of every difficult ethical act of decision? One has to betray one's innermost core; as Freud did in *Moses and Monotheism*, where he deprives the Jews of their founding figure."[30] In addition to making Moses into an Egyptian, that is, into someone who is a stranger to the Jews rather than one of their own, Žižek claims that Freud also breaks another taboo by revealing the unwritten, or spectral, history that constitutes the hidden obverse of Judaism, namely, the trauma represented by the very break with polytheism and the passage into monotheism – a violent founding act or event symbolized in the murder of Moses the Egyptian. "The paradox of Judaism is that it maintains fidelity to the founding violent Event precisely by *not* confessing, symbolizing it: this 'repressed' status of the Event is what gives Judaism its unprecedented vitality," Žižek writes in *The Puppet and the Dwarf*. But then this is precisely what the founder of psychoanalysis dares to reveal in his final book: "What Freud endeavors to reconstitute in *Moses and Monotheism* (the story of the murder of Moses, etc.) is such a spectral history that haunts the space of Jewish religion tradition."[31] We can easily understand the appeal of this gesture for Žižek. Does he too not endeavor to reveal the obscene underside of our most cherished ideological presuppositions? No wonder that Žižek prefers *Moses and Monotheism* over other texts such as *The Future of an Illusion* in which Freud calmly reduces religions to being nothing more than mass delusions – the collective equivalent of individual neuroses – which he hopes human progress, through reason and experience, will allow us one day to do without. "Religion would thus be the universal obsessional neurosis of humanity; like the obsessional neurosis of children, it arose out of the Oedipus complex, out of the relation to the father," concludes Freud. "If this view is right, it is to be supposed that a turning-away from religion is bound to occur with the fatal inevitability of a process of growth, and that we find ourselves at this very juncture in the middle of that phase of development."[32]

Even within *Moses and Monotheism*, however, Freud also offers a series of keen insights into matters such as the historical links between monotheism and imperialism, for which the reader will search completely in vain in *The Puppet and the Dwarf* or *The Monstrosity of Christ*. To account for these links Freud even suggests a kind of "reflection theory," more commonly associated with so-called vulgar Marxism. "Egypt had become a world empire. The new imperialism was reflected in the development of certain religious ideas, if not in those of the whole people, yet in those of the governing and intellectually active upper stratum," and among such ideas, that of a unique universal God arose first in Egypt before being taken up by Moses: "In Egypt monotheism had grown – as far as we understand its growth – as an ancillary effect of imperialism; God was the reflection of a Pharaoh autocratically governing a great world Empire."[33] An expanding empire needs a single, easily shared and universalizable God. Surely we would be hard put to find anything similar to even such cursory statements, for example, in the discussion of the passage from polytheism to monotheism in Žižek.

As for *Group Psychology and the Analysis of the Ego*, in which the Church
and the Army are presented as two examples of so-called "artificial
groups," Žižek does not ignore Freud's provocative conclusions but in
a rather convoluted manner seeks to bypass them in the name of
Christianity. On the one hand, he is well aware that there is no point
in pretending to go back to the original form of the primitive Christian
community prior to its collective organization into an artificial group.
This is why Žižek will always approve of Badiou's idea that Christ's
message is as inseparable from Paul's militantism as Marx is from Lenin
– or even Freud from Lacan. Žižek is quick to add, though, that Lenin
is not the same as Stalin, suggesting that similarly the Pauline communities are not quite yet the institutionalized Church. Following the model
of the return to Lenin, the goal of Žižek's writings on religion would
thus be to retrieve a form of Christianity that is *already* organized but *not
yet* institutionalized into an ideological apparatus: "The return to Lenin
is the endeavor to retrieve the unique moment when a thought already
transposes itself into a collective organization, but does not yet fix
itself into an Institution (the established Church, the IPA, the Stalinist
Party-State)."[34]

On the other hand, Žižek also goes one step further so as directly to
attack Freud's interpretive model in texts such as *Totem and Taboo*, by
arguing that the community formed by the Holy Spirit in the Christian
tradition, a community which would be comparable in this regard to the
revolutionary party, is an exception to the model of the crowd or group
based on the interiorized guilt over an originary crime such as the killing
of the primordial father: "Today's political philosophers like to point out
how, *within the domain of mass psychology itself*, psychoanalysis cannot
account for the emergence of the collectives which are not 'crowds'
grounded in primordial crime and guilt or unified under a totalitarian
leader, but united in a shared solidarity."[35] Such would be, precisely, the
case of the authentic Christian community designated by the Holy Spirit:

> The theoretical (and political) interest of this notion of community is that it
> provides the first example of a collective that is not formed and held together
> through the mechanism described by Freud in *Totem and Taboo* and *Moses
> and Monotheism* (the shared guilt for the parricide) – are not further examples
> of this same collective the revolutionary party and the psychoanalytic society?
> "Holy Spirit" designates a new collective held together not by a Master-
> Signifier, but by fidelity to a Cause, by the effort to draw a new line of sepa-
> ration that runs "beyond Good and Evil," that is to say, that runs across and
> suspends the distinctions of the existing social body.[36]

Žižek's reading of Freud on the topic of religion thus turns the model of mass or group psychology back upon itself so as to reveal its supposed inability to deal with the genuine radicalism of Christian groups, capable of organizing a universal community of believers who are loyal to a Cause without relying on the founding consistency of some big Other. Really existing Christianity, or the history of the institutionalized Church, by contrast, can be defined as a series of defense mechanisms against this atheist-materialist core of Christianity. "What happens with institutionalized Christianity is that it wants to have its cake and eat it: the tension between the particular and the universal is lost, the universal frame of the community of believers turns into a kind of protective umbrella of our particular groups, the disruptive aspect of universality is obliterated," we read in *The Monstrosity of Christ*. "We should go even further here: what if the entire history of Christianity, inclusive of (and especially) its Orthodox versions, is structured as a series of defenses against the traumatic apocalyptic core of incarnation/death/resurrection? What if Christianity comes near to this core only at its rare apocalyptic moments?"[37]

A similar combination of highly selective readings, subtle displacements, and clever reversals can be found in Žižek's self-conscious attempt to come to terms with the Marxian critique of religion. Žižek certainly quotes Marx's famous invocation of religion as "the opium of the people," for example, but only in order to refer to what he calls Western Buddhism as opposed to the genuine version of Zen Buddhism. "It is here that we should locate the difference between Zen proper and its Western version: the proper greatness of Zen is that it cannot be reduced to an 'inner journey' into one's 'true Self'; the aim of Zen meditation is, quite on the contrary, a total voiding of the Self, the acceptance that there is no Self, no 'inner truth' to be discovered," and this void, which is the radical core of Buddhism that is similar at least in this regard to the perverse core of Christianity, becomes obfuscated in the wisdom of New Age Westernization. "What Western Buddhism is not ready to accept is thus that the ultimate victim of the 'journey into one's Self' is this Self itself."[38] Žižek, therefore, feels justified to pull out the old Marxist reference to describe the particular fit between contemporary capitalism and Western Buddhism: "One is almost tempted to resuscitate here the old infamous Marxist cliché of religion as the 'opium of the people,' as the imaginary supplement of the terrestrial misery: the 'Western Buddhist' meditative stance is arguably the most efficient way for us, to fully participate in the capitalist dynamic while retaining the appearance of mental sanity."[39]

As for the extraordinarily steady "fit" between capitalism and Christianity, which is at least five centuries old, Žižek is well aware how, long before Max Weber, Marx already described this in one of his economic manuscripts known as *Theories of Surplus Value*:

> The development of capitalist production creates an average level of bourgeois society and therefore an average level of temperament and disposition amongst the most varied peoples. It is as truly cosmopolitan as Christianity. This is why Christianity is likewise the special religion of capital. In both it is only men who count. One man in the abstract is worth just as much or as little as the next man. In the one case, all depends on whether or not he has faith, in the other, on whether or not he has credit.[40]

Similarly, in *Capital*, Marx writes:

> For a society of commodity producers, whose general social relation of production consists in the fact that they treat their products as commodities, hence as values, and in this material form bring their individual, private labours into relation with each other as homogeneous human labour, Christianity with its religious cult of man in the abstract, more particularly in its bourgeois development, i.e., in Protestantism, Deism, etc., is the most fitting form of religion.[41]

Žižek alludes to these and other comparable passages, yet far from elaborating them as inchoate criticisms that are part of a budding Marxist critique of religious ideology and commodity fetishism, he takes them at face value as apt descriptions of the actual functioning, even the epochal greatness, of the figure of Christ in Christianity:

> With regard to the figure of Christ, this reference to the universe of commodities also enables us to reactualize Marx's old idea that Christ is like money among men – ordinary commodities: in the same way money as universal equivalent directly embodies/assumes the excess ("Value") that makes an object a commodity, Christ directly embodies/assumes the excess that makes the human animal a proper human being. In both cases, then, the universal equivalent exchanges/gives itself for all other excesses – in the same way money is the commodity "as such." Christ is man "as such"; in the same way that the universal equivalent has to be a commodity deprived of any use value. Christ has taken over the excess of Sin of ALL men precisely insofar as he was the Pure one, without excess, simplicity itself.[42]

Of Marx's entangled critique not only of Hegel but also of the critique of Hegel by the Young Hegelians such as Bruno Bauer, Žižek does not say a word, at least not in his vast and still-growing corpus of writings on Christianity. We thus miss out on the complexity of what Alberto Toscano in a recent article has called Marx's "critique of the critique of religion," which is never content simply to serve up yet another enlightened argument for the secularization of religion. "Marx has moved beyond the 'eliminativist' programme, which he polemically counterposed to the theological foibles of the young Hegelians, to a historical-materialist incorporation of the religious phenomenon into a theory of the social emergence of different modes of 'real abstraction,'" Toscano convincingly argues. "It is not simply a matter of referring the illusory autonomy and separation of religious representations to a material basis, but of showing the socio-historical necessity and rootedness of the 'phantoms' and 'sublimates' of a *specific* religious form."[43] In Žižek's writings, instead, Marx's take on religion is reduced precisely to the standard reading of dis-alienation of religion into politics, of theology into anthropology, and of God into man – which is a position that, if it might serve to describe Feuerbach or certain Young Hegelians, certainly fails to take into account, let alone develop, the wealth of possibilities opened up in Marx's admittedly cursory mentions of Christianity as *the* religion of capitalism.

Žižek's response to what he labels the Feuerbachian–Marxian logic of dis-alienation is actually quite convoluted. Rephrasing the problem in terms of the Hegelian shift from *positing the presuppositions* to *presupposing the positing*, he claims that the logic of dis-alienation suggests the possibility of a complete humanization of God. "In religious terms, this would amount to the direct (re)appropriation of God by humanity: the mystery of God is man, 'God' is nothing but the reified/substantialized version of human collective activity, and so on," Žižek writes in *The Monstrosity of Christ*. But, he continues to argue, this would mean losing out on the fact of human finitude, which as we know is transposed and integrated – according to the perverse reading summarized above – within the God of Christianity:

> What is missing here is the properly Christian gesture: in order to posit the presupposition (to 'humanize' God, reduce him to an expression/result of human activity), the (human-subjective) *positing itself should be 'presupposed,' located in God as the substantial ground-presupposition of man, as its own*

becoming-human/finite. The reason is the subject's constitutive finitude: the full positing of presuppositions would amount to subject's full retroactive positing/ generation of its presuppositions, i.e., the subject would be absolutized into the full self-origin.[44]

Upon this reading, it is Marx's treatment of religion that would be idealist – presupposing the full self-positing of an absolutized subject – whereas the Hegelian reinterpretation of Christianity – based on the finitude that tears apart the Absolute itself – would be capable of giving us the only properly modern, materialist, and atheist theory of the subject! In fact, in this last regard the reversal of Marx's own argument with regard to Feuerbach is almost perfect. Whereas Marx in his "Theses on Feuerbach" famously argues that an inversion of theology and anthropology is insufficient insofar as it fails to understand the split of the earthly realm that calls for the projection of the heavenly realm in the first place, Žižek opposes both Marx and Feuerbach by claiming that a proper understanding of Christianity forces us to place this split not just in the earthly world of the human subject but also and above all in God.

What is missing from Marxism's account of Christianity according to Žižek, in other words, is an understanding of the overlap between two forms of alienation, or two forms of what in theology is called kenosis, that is, the self-emptying of both man *and* God. "This double kenosis is what the standard Marxist critique of religion as the self-alienation of humanity misses," Žižek concludes in *The Monstrosity of Christ*. And, summarizing a now-familiar argument, he continues:

> For subjectivity to emerge – not as a mere epiphenomenon of the global substantial ontological order, but as essential to Substance itself – the split, negativity, particularization, self-alienation, must be posited as something that takes place in the very heart of the divine Substance, i.e., the move from Substance to Subject must occur within God himself. In short, man's alienation from God (the fact that God appears to him as an inaccessible In-Itself, as a pure transcendent Beyond) must coincide with the alienation of God from himself (whose most poignant expression is, of course, Christ's "Father, why have you forsaken me?" on the Cross).[45]

Marxism, then, does not have a sufficiently materialist theory of the subject, since it is unable to think the genesis of the subject out of the fundamental gap, or ontological deadlock, in the order of substance.

Now, insofar as psychoanalysis is *the* logic of the real of this gap or deadlock, understood as a certain excess of life within ordinary life, and

insofar as the Judeo-Christian tradition is built around a similar acknowledgment of the traumatic effect of this element of excess, we might
expect to see a final positive return to Freud in Žižek's openly perverse
approach to Christianity. For Freud is after all the major theorist of this
strange, excessive, and traumatic dimension of human life, which he calls
the death drive: "The lesson of psychoanalysis is that humans are not
simply alive, but possessed by a strange drive to enjoy life in excess of
the ordinary run of things – and 'death' stands simply and precisely for
the dimension beyond 'ordinary' biological life."[46] And yet, in a final
twist of the plot, Žižek will argue that Freud ultimately gives up on this
fundamental lesson. Indeed, by turning the death drive once again into
an external impulse, or even a separate dimension parallel to the life
instinct, Freudian psychoanalysis becomes marked by a regression, which
furthermore might explain why we end up with a fairly traditional argument for the secularization of religion in the name of progress and
science, for example, in *The Future of an Illusion*.

The dualism of Eros and Thanatos, thus, would be a way of obfuscating the atheist core at the heart of genuine monotheism, which for Žižek
is the radical promise in light of which he believes the Christian legacy
is still worth fighting for. Far from radicalizing this promise, the metaphysical battle of those two opposing principles actually marks not just a
domestication but actually a step back from the epochal achievement of
true monotheism, embodied by Christ on the Cross:

> The apparent "radicalization" is, in effect, a philosophical domestication: the
> break that disrupts the functioning of the universe – its ontological fault, as
> it were, is transformed into one of the two positive cosmic principles, thus
> reestablishing the pacifying, harmonious vision of the universe as the battle-
> field of the two opposing principles. (And the theological implications here
> are also crucial: instead of thinking the subversive deadlock of monotheism
> through to the end, Freud regresses to pagan wisdom.)[47]

The theory of the subject's constitutive finitude, based on the ontological
fault at the heart of the universe's substance, would be maintained only,
or at least in a privileged manner, in Christianity: "The finitude of
humanity, of the human subject (collective or individual), is maintained
here: Christ is the excess which prohibits simple recognition of the collective Subject in Substance, the reduction of Spirit to objective/virtual
entity (presup)posed by humanity."[48] Neither Marx nor Freud, in other
words, is a match for the perverse core of Christianity according to Žižek:

Marx, because he disavows the fact of human finitude in the name of an absolute subject–object of history; and Freud, because even though he acknowledges and names this traumatic dimension of finitude, in order to do so he sends us back to a cosmic-pagan battle of life and death, Eros and Thanatos.

Consequences and Tasks

What conclusions can we draw from Žižek's reading of Christianity? What tasks does this reading prescribe for us? And what are some of its consequences, intended or not?

In *On Belief*, Žižek right from the outset alludes in a slightly enigmatic way to the task that he sets for himself and for his readers: "What Christianity did with regard to the Roman Empire, this global 'multiculturalist' polity, we should do with regard to today's Empire."[49] So what *did* Christianity do to the Roman Empire? Here, the suggestion is that there exists a relation of fundamental discontinuity between the early Christian communities and the power of command of the Roman Empire – a discontinuity that subsequently is repeated in the guise of various moments of subversive dis-identification with the established order, as figures such as Saint Francis propose a radical "unplugging" or "delinking" from the existing social bond. In such moments of messianic or apocalyptic unplugging, the perverse core of Christianity would continue to be preserved intact. The official history of the Roman Church, by contrast, is marked by the set of "rearrangements" and "defenses" implemented in order to contain the subversive threat of these gestures. "Recall the fate of Saint Francis: by insisting on the vow of poverty of the true Christian, by refusing integration into the existing social edifice, he came very close to being excommunicated – he was embraced by the Church only after the necessary 'rearrangements' were made, which flattened this edge that posed a threat to the existing feudal relations."[50]

Put differently, the official Christian Church, or what Žižek calls "really existing Christianity" in analogy with "really existing socialism," excels in a type of perversion that runs completely counter to the genuinely perverse core ascribed to Christianity, which is based on the self-doubt and, ultimately, the death of God. This is why Žižek can speak of "the perverse solution that forms the very core of 'really existing Christianity,'" which consists in the desperate attempt – for example, on behalf of today's neo-conservatives with their call for a return to basic family values – of covering up the nonexistence of the big Other: "Perversion is a double strategy to counteract this nonexistence: an (ultimately deeply conservative, nostalgic) attempt to install the law artificially, *in the desperate hope that we will then take this self-posited limitation* 'seriously,' and, in a complementary way, a no less desperate attempt to codify the very transgression of the Law."[51] But is this line of demarcation between the "genuine" perversion and the "perverse" perversion really so easily drawn? Is there not a risk that, as an unintended side-effect of Žižek's interpretation, all this talk about the "epochal greatness," the "genuine gesture," or the "good news" of Christianity as "the only truly logical monotheism" will simply end up confirming the traditional believers in their beliefs – with the possible exception of those "fundamentalist freaks" who will have felt insulted all along – at least, that is, if they ever even read the work of someone like the giant from Ljubljana?

We could also raise this concluding question in a different way, by inquiring into Žižek's real or likely interlocutors on the topic of Christianity. As we saw, Žižek's own claim is that Christianity contains a subversive atheist core that is worth retrieving. At bottom, accepting this subversive core amounts to abandoning all reliance on an authoritative principle or dogmatic big Other: "The point of Christianity as the religion of atheism is not the vulgar humanist one that the becoming-man-of-God reveals that man is the secret of God (Feuerbach et al.); rather, it attacks the religious hard core that survives even in humanism, even up to Stalinism, with its belief in History as the 'big Other' that decides on the 'objective meaning' of our deeds."[52] And, furthermore, such an abandonment of the reliance on a God-like principle of authority, whether Man or History, coincides with what Žižek, following Lacan, describes as the end of the psychoanalytic cure, when the analysand accepts the inconsistency of the symbolic order, in which lies revealed the nonexistence of the big Other. "Contrary to all appearances, this is what happens in psychoanalysis: the treatment is over when the patient accepts the nonexistence of the big Other," writes Žižek in his conclusion to *The Puppet and the Dwarf*. "The ideal addressee of our speech, the ideal listener, is the psychoanalyst, the very opposite of the Master-figure that guarantees meaning; what happens at the end of the analysis, with the dissolution of transference – that is to say, the fall of the 'subject supposed to know' – is that the patient accepts the absence of such a guarantee."[53]

The question that then immediately arises is not only the one that Žižek himself raises, namely: why speak of this task in the terms of

religion at all? Why not simply adopt the vocabulary of either psychoanalysis or philosophical materialism? "Why this eternal replaying of the
death of God? Why not simply start from the positive materialist premise
and develop it? The only appropriate answer to this is the Hegelian one
– but *not* in the sense of the cheap 'dialectics' according to which a thesis
can deploy itself only through overcoming its opposite. The necessity of
religion is an inner one," Žižek writes in yet another slightly enigmatic
assertion. "A truly logical materialism accepts the basic insight of religion,
its premise that our commonsense reality is not the true one; what it
rejects is the conclusion that, therefore, there must be another, 'higher,'
suprasensible reality. Commonsense realism, positive religion, and materialism thus form a Hegelian triad."[54] The question is also: whom is Žižek
trying to convince by running the materialist argument one more time
through the whole conceptual, even doctrinal, machinery of Christianity?
To what extent is he trying to bring genuine believers to the point
where, inspired by the perverse core of their monotheism, they move
over to the atheist-materialist camp? Or is he rather preaching to the
converted, that is, to fellow materialists who will have but little patience
for his dabbling in matters of theological doctrine?

Here the contrast with Freud is once again potentially illuminating.
After all, the author of *The Future of an Illusion* has himself no illusions
whatsoever about the impact his study may have on the religious convic-
tions of believers: "I myself regard my undertaking as completely harmless
and free of risk," except perhaps for the author's own person and for the
fate of psychoanalysis: " 'Now we see,' they will say, 'where psychoanalysis leads to. The mask has fallen; it leads to a denial of God and of
a moral ideal, as we always suspected' "; but, other than that, Freud adds,
"there is no danger of a devout believer's being overcome by my arguments and deprived of his faith."[55] In fact, Freud foresees a fate for his
text that might also be in store for Žižek's writings on psychoanalysis:
"If the application of the psychoanalytic method makes it possible to find
a new argument against the truths of religion, *tant pis* for religion; but
defenders of religion will by the same right make use of psycho-analysis
in order to give full value to the affective significancy of religious doc-
trines."[56] Similarly, are there not also unintended consequences that
follow from an endeavor such as Žižek's, as can be seen from the fact
that his interlocutors in this debate for the most part have been conservative leftists such as John Milbank, whose brand of socialism Marx no
doubt would have catalogued as "feudal socialism" and who nonetheless

make use of Žižek's ideas to give full affective significancy to his reactionary religious doctrine?

Finally, is there not also a risk in opting for the formal or transcendental explication of the basic Christian gesture properly speaking – the miraculous possibility of a "new beginning" for the newborn subject based upon the acceptance of the "ontological fault" present within God – that is, the risk of ignoring the historical and genealogical dimension of the profound collusion between capitalism and Christianity?

At a minimum, the genealogical investigation that I have in mind would have to address two different issues:

First, there can be no doubt that the religious turn of the past decade or two, of which Žižek is an exemplary and outspoken case in point, also serves as a displaced diagnostic of the experience of radical militancy in the 1960s and 1970s. Even if we stick for the time being to the context of Western Europe, in each of the so-called three religions of the Book, in Judaism with thinkers such as Benny Lévy or Jacob Taubes, in Christianity with Alain Badiou or Giorgio Agamben, and in Islam with Christian Jambet or Guy Lardreau, the invocation of messianic, saintly, or otherwise redemptive–utopian schemes is still waiting to be processed as part of this context of the crisis of Marxism and the ensuing disorientation of the Left.

Second, there is also a long-term project awaiting proper genealogical attention. When Žižek refers back to the time of the Roman Empire, or when Michael Hardt and Toni Negri reinterpet Augustine's two cities in favor of the pure immanence of the earthly city, for example, they are pointing toward a much broader agenda for investigation that is no longer strictly philosophical but also historical. This is the kind of investigation that the Argentine Freudo-Marxist León Rozitchner, who recently passed away, had made is own in the final years of his life. But, contrary to Žižek, Rozitchner believes that for anyone intent upon developing the reasons for why Christianity might be *the* religion of capital, there are still untapped resources present in Marx's work, not only in passages such as the ones quoted above from *Theories of Surplus Value* or *Capital* but also already in some of Marx's early writings, when he allegedly still stood under the influence of the Feuerbachian matrix of dis-alienation.

What Marx proposes to do in that most controversial of texts, "On the Jewish Question," for example, is at least minimally to retrace some of the steps that lead up to the paradoxical accomplishment of the

Christian spirit in the modern secular-capitalist State. The political timeli-
ness of this proposal for the present moment should be obvious enough,
provided that we do not let ourselves be seduced by the simple secularization thesis nor are misled by the accusations of anti-Semitism or Jewish
self-hatred so frequently raised against Marx. But methodologically speaking, too, there are important lessons to be learned from Marx's youthful
text. In addition to developing a Marxist theory of the subject, a contemporary reading of "On the Jewish Question" thus would require that
we also reconstruct a history of the place of Judeo-Christianity in modern
capitalist as well as pre-capitalist forms of subjectivity, along the lines of
what Rozitchner does in his book *La Cosa y la Cruz* (*The Thing and the
Cross*), which offers a close page-by-page reading of Saint Augustine's
Confessions as the quintessential manual of subjection of the individual to
both the Christian religion and the power of command of the Roman
Empire.

Augustine's text in Rozitchner's hands thus becomes the target of an
incursion into hostile territory where a declining Roman empire, making
a common front with the Christian Church in a world-historical juncture
best depicted in Augustine's own subsequent elaboration in *City of God*,
gives rise to sinister subject formations that prepare the onslaught of
capitalism several hundreds of years later. The Christian saint, then, is not
a model; he is the enemy, or at best an anti-model. "In his theological
libidinal economy the saint proposed to us, from the oldest times, the
most productive originary investment to accumulate sacred capital: 'By
hoarding on the flesh you will invest in the spirit,'" Rozitchner
writes, before summing up the bold hypothesis behind his reading of the
Confessions: "The Christian Spirit and Capital have complementary metaphysical premises."[57] Following this hypothesis, we slowly delve into the
visceral depths of the subject so as to locate the place where terror and
the fear of death, from the earliest experiences of the child onward,
become ingrained into the material soul. Far outstripping Max Weber's
hypothesis about the ideological affinity between capitalism and protes-
tantism − Rozitchner thus holds that capitalism simply would not have
been possible without Christianity: "Triumphant capitalism, the quantita-
tive and *infinite* accumulation of wealth in the abstract monetary form,
would not have been possible without the human model of religious
infinity promoted by Christianity, without the imaginary and symbolical
reorganization operated in subjectivity by the new religion of the Roman
Empire."[58] Augustine is *the* model of these profound transformations in
the psychic economy.

As Rozitchner explains in retrospect about the purpose of his investigation in *La Cosa y la Cruz*:

> Thus we told ourselves: If we were to read Augustine and laid bare the fundamental equation of his model of humanity, this "Love" and this "Truth" of the divine word that only the chosen ones get to hear, which calls for the negation of the body and of the life of others as the necessary sacrifice that allows them to situate themselves beyond crime, do we not also, in doing so, lay bare a cultural system that uses death and converts it, secretly, in an inevitable exigency of its political logic? If we take this human model, considered to be the most sublime, and if we show that there, in the exaltation of the most sacred, the commitment to what is most sinister also finds a niche, will we not also, in doing so, have uncovered the obscene mechanism of the Christian religious production? This is the challenge: to understand a model of being human that has produced sixteen centuries of subtle and refined, brutal and merciless subjection.[59]

Rozitchner, however, avoids the temptation of merely becoming enthralled to the revelation of the obscene underside of the law – merely showing or rendering its dark and gutsy entrails, as the death-driven ground of the human condition as such. Not only does he refuse to remain locked in a structural or quasi-transcendental framework but, what is more, he also continues to expand the historical overdeterminations of the subject in the long run. By doing so, he has at least opened up the possibility of its real transformation.

Rozitchner's book on Augustine, which I mention here only by way of illustration of the kind of genealogical labor that I think is worth pursuing, has the enormous virtue of exposing the extent to which the notion of political subjectivity continues to be contaminated by Christian theology:

> This is why we were interested in finding the ground of the political in what is most specifically religious. And we asked ourselves if it is possible that each believer, with the content of the Christian imaginary, and despite the best of intentions, and even if he or she ascribes to the Theology of Liberation, can have a political experience that is *essentially* different from the politics it is fighting against. We ask if the fundamental ground of Christian religion is not *necessarily* the fundament of domination precisely in what is religious in it.[60]

The examples of Badiou, Negri, and Žižek reveal the real difficulty there is in answering the demand for a political experience, including on a subjective level, that would be *essentially* different from the one it combats. All of these thinkers, in fact, remain deeply entangled in the political theology of Christianity – unable to illustrate the militant subject except through the figure of the saint, for example: Saint Paul (Badiou and Žižek) or Saint Francis (Negri and again Žižek).

To sum up: for those who, like Žižek, seek to defend Christianity as a legacy still worth fighting for, or as a lost cause worth defending, such a fight or such a defense requires a materialist reversal whereby what otherwise appears to bask in the light of dogmatic truth all of a sudden shines forth as a fragile absolute, summed up in Christ's exclamation on the Cross. Far from simply betraying a momentary lack of faith, Jesus' cry then highlights the properly revolutionary nature of Christianity. No matter how much we may spice them up with examples drawn from Hegel to Hollywood, though, all such dialectical reformulations and perverse reversals of Christianity in the name of a newborn materialism remain strictly speaking at the level of a structural or transcendental discussion of the conditions of possibility of subjectivity as such. By contrast, what remains to be done would be once more closer to the task of the genealogist or historical materialist who puts the politics of the subject in a permanent tension field between theory and history. "We therefore must reach back from political to religious alienation in order to understand the persistence of the religious within the political," as Rozitchner also writes in his careful commentary about "On the Jewish Question": "We must show that the Christian essence, which 'critical criticism' claims to have overcome, remains and is objectified in the material social relations of the democratic secular State whose terminal form, as Marx demonstrates, are the United States of America. And to show, let us add, how it persists to this very day."[61]

Notes

1 Alain Badiou, "The Subject Supposed to be a Christian," *The Adventure of French Philosophy*, ed. and trans. Bruno Bosteels (New York: Verso, 2012), p. 333.

2 Slavoj Žižek, *The Fragile Absolute – or, Why is the Christian Legacy Worth Fighting For?* (London: Verso, 2000), p. 2.

3 Slavoj Žižek, *The Puppet and the Dwarf: The Perverse Core of Christianity* (Cambridge: MIT Press, 2003), p. 7.

4 Slavoj Žižek and John Milbank, *The Monstrosity of Christ: Paradox or Dialectic?* ed. Creston Davis (Cambridge: MIT Press, 2009), p. 240.
5 Ibid., p. 240.
6 Ibid., p. 287.
7 Žižek, *The Puppet and the Dwarf*, p. 15.
8 Žižek, *The Monstrosity of Christ*, pp. 48–9.
9 Žižek, *The Puppet and the Dwarf*, p. 24.
10 Žižek, *The Monstrosity of Christ*, p. 96.
11 Žižek, *On Belief* (New York: Routledge, 2001), pp. 145–6.
12 Žižek, *The Puppet and the Dwarf*, p. 90.
13 Ibid., p. 91.
14 Žižek, *On Belief*, p. 47.
15 Žižek, *The Puppet and the Dwarf*, p. 25.
16 Žižek, *On Belief*, p. 89.
17 Ibid., p. 145; *The Monstrosity of Christ*, p. 38.
18 Ibid., p. 85.
19 Žižek, *On Belief*, p. 165.
20 Žižek, *The Monstrosity of Christ*, p. 106n125.
21 For a critique of the patriarchy and anti-Judaism behind the association of Christianity with the figure of the "new man" as invoked by both Žižek and Badiou, see Amy Hollywood, "Saint Paul and the New Man," *Critical Inquiry* 35 (2009): 865–76.
22 Žižek, *On Belief*, pp. 128–9.
23 Ibid., p. 138.
24 Ibid., p. 140.
25 Žižek, *On Belief*, p. 150; *The Puppet and the Dwarf*, p. 70; *The Monstrosity of Christ*, pp. 267 and 291. For a deconstructive rejoinder to this "perverse" reading of Christianity *with* Hegel, see John D. Caputo, "The Perversity of the Absolute, the Perverse Core of Hegel, and the Possibility of Radical Theology," in *Hegel and the Infinite: Religion, Politics, and Dialectic*, ed. Slavoj Žižek, Clayton Crockett, and Creston Davis (New York: Columbia University Press, 2011), pp. 47–66.
26 Žižek, *The Puppet and the Dwarf*, p. 66.
27 Ibid., p. 80.
28 Ibid., pp. 69–70.
29 Sigmund Freud, *Moses and Monotheism*, trans. Katherine Jones (New York: Vintage, 1967), p. 3.
30 Žižek, *The Puppet and the Dwarf*, p. 17.
31 Ibid., p. 128.
32 Sigmund Freud, *The Future of an Illusion*, trans. James Strachey (New York: W. W. Norton, 1989), p. 55.
33 Sigmund Freud, *Moses and Monotheism*, pp. 72 and 80.
34 Žižek, *On Belief*, p. 4.

35 Ibid., p. 16.
36 Žižek, *The Puppet and the Dwarf*, p. 130.
37 Žižek, *The Monstrosity of Christ*, pp. 252 and 260.
38 Žižek, *The Puppet and the Dwarf*, p. 39.
39 Žižek, *On Belief*, p. 13.
40 Karl Marx, *Theories of Surplus Value*, vol. 3 (Moscow: Progress Publishers, 1971), p. 448.
41 Karl Marx, *Capital*, vol. I, trans. B. Fowkes (London: Penguin, 1990), p. 172.
42 Žižek, *On Belief*, pp. 99–100.
43 Alberto Toscano, "Beyond Abstraction: Marx and the Critique of the Critique of Religion," *Historical Materialism* 18 (2010): 13, 15.
44 Žižek, *The Monstrosity of Christ*, p. 75.
45 Ibid., p. 59.
46 Žižek, *On Belief*, p. 104.
47 Žižek, *The Puppet and the Dwarf*, p. 71.
48 Žižek, *The Monstrosity of Christ*, p. 76.
49 Žižek, *On Belief*, p. 5.
50 Ibid., p. 8.
51 Žižek, *The Puppet and the Dwarf*, p. 53.
52 Ibid., p. 171.
53 Ibid., p. 170.
54 Žižek, *The Monstrosity of Christ*, p. 240.
55 Freud, *The Future of an Illusion*, p. 45.
56 Ibid., p. 47.
57 León Rozitchner, *La Cosa y la Cruz. Cristianismo y Capitalismo (En torno a las Confesiones de san Agustín)* (Buenos Aires: Losada, 1997), p. 12. The title of this book, *La Cosa y la Cruz*, is a pun on Hegel's famous passage from his *Philosophy of Right* in which he proposes to read the cross or crucifixion itself as the revelation of reason in history: "To recognize reason as the rose in the cross of the present and thereby to enjoy the present, this is the rational insight which reconciles us to the actual, the reconciliation which philosophy affords to those in whom there has once arisen an inner voice bidding them to comprehend, not only to dwell in what is substantive while still retaining subjective freedom, but also to possess individual freedom while standing not in anything particular and accidental but in what exists absolutely." See G. W. F. Hegel, *Philosophy of Right*, trans. T. M. Knox (Oxford: Oxford University Press, 1977), p. 12. Rozitchner substitutes the Freudian Thing (*das Ding* in German, *la Cosa* in Spanish) for Hegel's rose (*la Rosa* in Spanish), in order to investigate via the example of Augustine's *Confessions* to what extent a psychoanalytical approach also means tearing apart the relation of reconciliation with reality promised by Christianity. Žižek's own argument, of course, can be summed up by saying that this tearing apart happens already

within the Christian God, so that Hegel's dictum about the rose and the cross, which Žižek frequently quotes, represents already the highest expression of the perverse core of Christianity.

58 Rozitchner, La Cosa y la Cruz, p. 9. For a more detailed discussion, see Bruno Bosteels, "Are there any Saints Left? León Rozitchner as a Reader of Saint Augustine," Cities of Men, Cities of God: Augustine and Late Secularism, ed. Leo Russ, special issue of Polygraph: An International Journal of Culture and Politics 19–20 (2008): 7–22.

59 Rozitchner, La Cosa y la Cruz, p. 10.

60 Ibid., p. 11.

61 León Rozitchner, "La cuestión cristiana," in Volver a "La cuestión judía," ed. Esteban Vernik (Barcelona: Gedisa, 2011), p. 199. I further discuss Rozitchner's work in Chapters 4 and 5 of Marx and Freud in Latin America: Politics, Psychoanalysis, and Religion in Times of Terror (London: Verso, 2012).

4

Ceremonial Contingencies and the Ambiguous Rites of Freedom

Joshua Ramey

What does freedom mean for Žižek? I begin with a passage from his 2008 work, *In Defense of Lost Causes*. Here Žižek asserts that we are:

> simultaneously less free and more free than we think: we are thoroughly passive, determined by and dependent on the past, but we have the freedom to define the scope of this determination, that is, to (over)determine the past which will determine us . . . "Freedom" is thus inherently retroactive: at its most elementary, it is not a free act which, out of nowhere, starts a new causal link, but a retroactive act of endorsing which link/sequence of necessities will determine me.[1]

The first crucial aspect of freedom, for Žižek, is that it is a relation of the subject not primarily to an open-ended future, but to the *past* – specifically, to a *contingency* proper to the past itself. For Žižek, the past does not determine the present. On the contrary, it is only because there has been a past that there can be a (different) future. That is to say, a truly free act is not a break from, but an assumption of and a transformation of a past. Only in relation to determining causes are we free – any act that was unrelated to the past would be meaningless.

In view of this notion of freedom not as break but as transformation, Žižek distinguishes, throughout his work, between ordinary and extraordinary senses of the term "act." For Žižek (following Lacan), the ordinary sense of "act" relates to the scope of activity and agency as supported by the Symbolic register: the dimension manifest as language, social codes, rituals, habits, and institutional structures that together offer to subjects a more or less clear sense of what is possible, and from within which, as alienated from herself, the subject nevertheless finds herself.[2] Imaginary and fetishistic practices of identification allow the subject to maintain the illusion that there is something natural or organic about her place in the social totality, and that she has some measure of control or agency within the objective, neutral substance of social life. For Lacan, however neces- sary or "natural" a Symbolic register may appear to any subject imbricated within it, all such registers are contingent and ultimately arbitrary arrange- ments that contain potentially traumatic sites of antagonism and discord. This inconsistency in the Symbolic, the Real, is "barred" from subjective experience, and subjectivity is produced with an excess or "extimate" aspect – namely, the contingency of the very entrance of the subject into any Symbolic network.

The variety of neuroses and psychoses is interpreted by psychoanalyti- cal theory (which Žižek follows) as so many attempts to domesticate or to ward off the anxiety incumbent upon our contingent belonging to one another, and indeed the utterly mediated mode in which we relate to ourselves, since we borrow even the meanings we attribute to our own lives from the social totality in which we (do not) find ourselves. While the subject never comes to exist apart from such Symbolic deter- minations, insofar as her actions conform to the coordinates of any given symbolic network, such actions are not, strictly speaking, free. Only actions which break with the Symbolic count as truly free, as Acts, in the Žižekian sense.

That is to say, truly free Acts, for Žižek, produce a change in what it will have been possible for a subject to *be*. But how is such radical change possible? In recent work, Žižek asserts that a change in conditions of possibility is itself conditioned by access to a particular temporality, the "pure past" that Gilles Deleuze identified as *virtual*: a dimension of events that exceeds all temporal unfolding, yet is completely immanent to the historical sequence in question.[3] Following Deleuze, Zizke employs the logic of the virtual to explain the ontology of freedom. For Deleuze, since history is contingent, and time could always have unfolded other- wise, unexplored potentialities in events always already exist or "insist" in the past. Under certain conditions, the past can be retroactively or "retroversely" affected by the way in which the present liberates unexplored potentials in the past itself.[4] As Žižek puts it, "while the pure past is the transcendental condition for our acts, our acts not only create an actual new reality, but also retroactively change this very condi- tion."[5] That is to say, the free Act does not so much open a totally new present as retroactively alter the nature of the past, "retroversively" determining which pasts now matter, or what in the past is now determinative.

It is crucial for Žižek's view, however, that the conditions for actions that retroversely alter the past are not themselves within the conscious control or intentional purview of subjective agency. It is in fact only under certain extraordinary and totally unpredictable conditions that free Acts are possible. The reason for this has to do with the difference between the levels of *Desire* and *Drive* at the heart of subjective experience. Žižek follows Lacan in asserting that desire, as articulated within the Symbolic, manifests as an attempt to cover or fill a lack in the subject constituted by the subject's very entrance into the Symbolic itself. Desire is never for the objects of desire, but for an *objet petit a* that supplements and serves as a fantasmatic ontological support for (and reassurance against the contingency of) desire itself. When subjects access the level of Drive, per se – and *per impossibile*, act from that level – they fully embrace their contingency, momentarily sustaining the object-less character of the drive, which wants nothing but itself. Subjectivity at the level of drive is free subjectivity because it fully assumes its own determination as utterly indeterminate, as conditioned by nothing but the vertigo of empty drive itself, around which *objet petit a* momentarily circulates not as a screen covering lack, but as the lack itself, the cut in the real itself with which the subject temporarily identifies.

As Molly Anne Rothenberg points out, this is the place at which genuine agency (and freedom) appears in Žižek's account. Rothenberg indicates that Žižek's picture of the subject is of an "excessive" subject, one that is constituted by an "extimate" relation to itself. Entrance into any Symbolic order is constituted by a cut or "formal negation": taking one's place within a social network creates an externality (the place one occupies) that is experienced as an emptiness or void one experiences at the heart of oneself (as one's symbolic identity). The negativity that sunders one from oneself constitutes one's existence within a network of social relations. Access to the level of Drive depends on a particular suspension/assumption of this traumatic experience of subjective genesis, normally occluded by fantasy, hysteria, or simply neurosis. The opening onto the level of drive that takes place under the extraordinary conditions of the Act exposes the genesis of subjectivity itself, and simultaneously makes another genesis possible. As Rothenberg puts it:

> The refusal of all Symbolic differences [as in the free Act] puts this equation front and center: the extimate cause not only sets off the subject, producing

the hollow that cradles the subject within the Symbolic, it also produces the empty set, which, in a parallax shift, appears to be embodied or substantialized as the obstacle to the Symbolic itself. This same formal gesture that inscribes the subject in the Symbolic also generates the subject's excess over (and therefore apparently athwart) the Symbolic. Setting off the ontic properties of the subject demonstrates their contingency. By creating an aesthetic distance from what seemed to be the given and inevitable characteristics of the situation, the neosubject sets the state for other coordinates to come into view and into play.[6]

While Rothenberg's account emphasizes the static or formal aspect of subjective genesis, for my purposes I will focus on how Žižek treats dynamic or temporal aspect of this genesis, since it is here, that I find a crucial ambiguity in his view.

Repetition and Contingency

One remarkable aspect of Žižek's conception of freedom is that a truly free act is never unprecedented, but is always bound up with a kind of repetition: to freely act in the present is to revisit and even to radically revise the past. On this point Žižek again follows Deleuze, who, following Bergson, conceptualized the dimension of a pure past whose virtual objects exist or "insist" between various levels or series of historical (and natural) events. For Deleuze the virtual is immanent to lived reality; but in a stronger sense lived temporal experience is immanent to the virtual itself. Variations and versions in historical experience are expressions of pure potencies – pure not because eternal or outside of time, but because the pure past is indefinitely fecund, redolent of more sense than any particular event can encompass. While the virtual does not cause events in the actual, the virtual is the *condition* of novelty, providing the transcendental-genetic elements of repetition insofar as such repetition can alter the sense – both the meaning and direction – of the past itself, and thus change the present by retroactively determining the past.

In *Living in the End Times*, Žižek offers two examples to illustrate this point, one taken from art and one from politics. Edgar Doctorow's novel *Billy Bathgate* was made into a film whose aesthetic merit, Žižek asserts, is nothing compared to the original novel. Žižek avers that, after seeing the film, when one goes on to read the novel, one is disappointed, and thinks to oneself "this is *not* the novel the film evoked as the standard with regard to which it failed."[7] Where is the "real" novel? Where is the work of art superior to the film? Not in the original novel, but in a virtual work, "the true novel whose specter is engendered in the passage from the novel to the film." It is not, Žižek asserts, that the novel is an "open work" subject to multiple versions, but that only in the case of a specific relation between different, ultimately *failed* instances of the same work can a different, better work appear.

This same structure, Žižek thinks, can be applied to thinking the relation between Leninism and Stalinism: it is not that Stalinism betrayed an original Leninism, but that the very failure of Stalinism itself makes it possible to finally see the emancipatory core of Leninism itself, a core which was not even visible to Lenin in his own context. To discover Lenin after Stalin is to disinter a Lenin that literally never was. For Žižek, this structure is the very essence of the Hegelian dialectic of the Absolute, of "absolute knowledge" itself. He writes:

> The eternal absolute is the immobile point of reference around which temporal figurations circulate, their presupposition; however, precisely as such, it is posited by these temporal figurations, since it does not preexist them: it emerges in the gap between the first and the second – in the case of *Billy Bathgate*, between the novel and its repetition in the film.[8]

Novelty, that is to say, is an intra-serial relation between firsts and seconds. The genuinely new is not *sui generis* or unaccountably emergent, but a function of deadlocks that reveal themselves in specific histories, in peculiar series constituted through historical repetition.

But how, precisely, does repetition, and the "absolute" contingency that it expresses, relate to a concept of freedom? The difference a free act makes is, of course, different in each case: the effective truth of freedom is a truth relative to immanent historical circumstances, to the antagonisms constitutive of a social field. But it is nevertheless necessary to ask how, and by what means freedom – the freedom to retroactively alter the absolute taken as pure past – relates to the necessity of repetition. For a kind of nihilism lurks here. If repetition is a matter of sheer historical contingency, then the subject might not seem to be only occasionally, but indeed only arbitrarily free. The freedom *of* the discovery of as-yet-unexplored potentialities might amount to nothing but an abstract freedom *for* nothing but chaos, disorder, or violent rupture.

But Žižek's obsessive attention to historical circumstance and to intimate, even obscene cultural detail is more than ample evidence that he
does not intend to reduce the freedom of the act to the merely arbitrary.
He seems rather to argue that the rediscovery of contingency in the past
somehow renews the possibility of the irruption of the absolute into
historical sequences. For Žižek, because the continuum of history is "all
there is" (he says the virtual is an "actual nothing"), the contingent does
not reduce to the arbitrary, but to the reconfiguration of a *specific* historical sequence, what Alain Badiou calls a "situation." The task of freedom
is to renew *a particular world.* And yet, the process of freedom remains
plagued by an existential and ontological ambiguity that Žižek is still at
pains to clarify. The ambiguity lies in Žižek's conception of freedom in
relation to his assertions regarding whether agents can recognize if, when,
and to what degree they are conscious participants in the unfolding of
free acts. The key ambiguity here is the *location* of the subject's "reflexive
gesture of putting to work the negativity that gave birth to it." Where
– in what temporal duration – does this operation take place?[9]

As Adrian Johnston observes, this is a question that Žižek has been
reluctant to answer, since it might bring him dangerously close to having
to characterize "successful" workings-out or workings-through of negativity as positive glimpses of an organic, substantial totality. Such a teleological perspective would undermine Žižek's Lacanian-inspired resistance
to occupying the position of a "subject supposed to know," and would
rob the subject of the positive task of free creation. It would also violate
Žižek's basic thesis that subjectivity and freedom must *appear as* cosmic
accidents, in order that there be no possible illusion of phantasmatic,
substantial Utopia, let alone enchanted cosmos, toward which our work
in time strives, or in which it ultimately participates. For Žižek, freedom
does not continuously *strive* toward a final resolution of antagonism, but
intermittently *drives*, in a kind of temporary quantum upsurge.

But how coherent is this position? It would seem that, to make sense
of sustained action, whether individual or collective, human subjectivity
would, at the very least, have to be in a position to prepare for, if not
completely recognize, a kind of *portent* or sign of how freedom might
unfold, in time. But as we have seen already, Žižek claims that if, when,
and to what purpose such irruptions occur can only be espied retroactively, through a backwards glance of interpretation. That is to say, we
only recognize after the fact whether, and to what extent, a free act has
occurred, let alone what such free acts aimed at bringing into being. The

problem is, how do we put ourselves in a position to activate or realize freedom, and to, as Badiou puts it "keep going"?

The Lesson of *Parsifal*

Can freedom live by revolt alone? Alain Badiou recently made a series of somewhat surprising remarks on this point. In *Five Lessons on Wagner*, he writes:

> . . . the question as to whether the Crowd declares itself, as Mallarmé puts it, cannot be exclusively recapitulated in collective figures of revolt. The people's declaration, the declaration of the Crowd, somehow cannot be satisfied with anarchic revolt alone. It must put forward, examine and produce its own consistency.[10]

Badiou's remark here is a gloss on Mallarmé's notion that a revolutionary people must practice "intrusion into future ceremonies" (*l'intrusion dans les fêtes futures*). And Badiou here links Mallarmé to Wagner: the people's aspirations, the substance of their hopes and aspirations, must be put into ceremonial, even ritualized form, such as that symbolized by the Grail ritual in Wagner's *Parsifal*. This ceremony produces the consistency of the sacred knighthood – symbolic, for Badiou, of an emancipatory collectivity. In spite of its obvious ideological shortcomings (especially the sexist and inegalitarian exclusion of Kundry from the Grail community) Badiou insists that *Parsifal* is a crucial work of art for our times, since it demonstrates both the necessity and the impossibility (or at least the extreme difficulty) attendant upon ceremonial presentation of the liberated, emancipated, and revolutionary collective. Badiou puts the problem this way:

> If we agree that the subject of *Parsifal* is the great question about the possibility of a new ceremony raised at the end of the nineteenth century – where and how will the new ceremony take place, in which the collectivity will represent itself to itself without transcendence? – if this is indeed the subject of *Parsifal*, then we have to admit that there is a certain indeterminacy between restoration and innovation with respect to the realization of the Idea. I'm not saying that restoration prevails over innovation but rather that there is an undecideability between the two. It is perhaps precisely *this* that is the subject, all

things considered. It is the idea that, concerning the question of the new ceremony, there is no clear distinction between restoration and innovation, or between nostalgia and the creation of something new.[11]

For Badiou, we must have, then, what Wagner hoped to achieve in *Parsifal*: a kind of "sublation of Christianity without transcendence,"[12] – the mass as a sending (*missa*) of the people to itself (rather than to or from a god). Apart from such ceremony, the people cannot sustain the revolutionary effort; revolt alone cannot sustain the work of emancipation. Put somewhat differently, although the *events* inspiring revolutionary action are discontinuous with all precedent, emancipatory work itself cannot be punctual, discontinuous, and for its sustenance must be embodied in an ideal consistency that sustains the event itself, in symbolico-aesthetic form.

Yet Badiou acknowledges that the creation of a modern ceremony, a ceremony without transcendence, is extremely difficult, perhaps impossible. Wagner himself, according to Badiou, did not actually achieve his desired result – the obvious symptom of this failure being that Wagner redoubled the ceremony of *Parsifal* with demands for a ceremonial gathering to attend Parsifal, stipulating that there should be no applause after the first act, etc. *Parsifal* was *not* the ceremony of the masses' self-presentation, and was merely a spectacle attended by the obedient if somewhat befuddled bourgeoisie.[13] But what *Parsifal's* failure demonstrates, for Badiou, is not that such a project should be abandoned, but that a truly modern ceremony, at least for now, is unworkable, and that democracy is the symptom of this failure.[14] We have democracy, with its multiplicity of false rituals (of enjoyment, spectacle, etc.) as so many substitutes for the impossible ceremony of the future. Yet it remains our revolutionary task, Badiou insists, to somehow be present at future ceremonies, to prepare for an event that would "make a ceremony possible."[15]

In his most recent tome, *Living in the End Times*, Slavoj Žižek also argues for the necessity of ritual and spectacle for any emancipatory political activity. For his part, Žižek describes liturgical–ceremonial behavior as an encounter with the "zero-level" of sense, a stammering or stuttering Deleuze once identified with an immanent power of language, captured by certain artists who have the ability to become, as Proust put it, a foreigner in their own tongue, to make the familiar strange.[16] Such a stammering effort to bring the unknown into the known, the invisible into the visible, is for Žižek a problem faced by all revolutions. Žižek writes:

And is this problem of liturgy not also the problem of all revolutionary processes, from the French Revolution with its spectacles to the October Revolution? Why is this liturgy necessary? Precisely because of the precedence of non-sense over sense: the liturgy is the symbolic frame within which the zero-level of sense is articulated. The zero-experience of sense is not the experience of a determinate sense, but the absence of sense, more precisely: the frustrating experience of being sure that something has a sense, but not knowing what it is. *This vague presence of a non-specific sense is sense "as such," sense at its purest* – it is primary, not secondary; in other words all determinate sense comes second, as an attempt to fill in the oppressive presence-absence of the that-ness of sense without its what-ness. This is how we should answer the reproach that "communism" is being used here as a magic word, an empty sign lacking any precise or positive vision of a new society, merely a ritualized token of belonging to a new initiatic community: there is no opposition between liturgy (ceremony) and historical opening; far from being an obstacle to change, liturgy keeps the space for radical change open, insofar as it sustains the signifying non-sense which calls for new inventions of (determinate) sense.[17]

Žižek's claim here, in short, is that it is necessary continuously to repeat certain formalities that, while not directly incarnating the truth of a political movement, nevertheless alone make possible that movement. Ritual and ceremonial acts seem to offer an immanent model of *continuity* between the transcendental sources of freedom and the shape of concrete historical acts. Žižek seems to be claiming that, in basic agreement with Badiou, we can only continue to (re)invent revolution insofar as some dramatic form of the revolutionary act is (re)presented. That is to say, the revolutionary Act has to *appear*, not merely at a transcendental level of "nonsense" *qua* gaps in the Symbolic, but in *deliberate (re)enactments of that very gap* in something like aesthetic or liturgical space-time.

Žižek's devotion to Wagner, and to *Parsifal* in particular, is well known.[18] But his take on *Parsifal*'s relevance is somewhat different from Badiou's. Žižek asserts that the true genius of *Parsifal* lies in its relation to *contingency* – that is to say, in how it ceremonializes the accidental aspects of the drama, incorporating hesitation, near-misses, and mistakes into the ritual structure of the drama itself. Žižek notes that Amfortas' reluctance, and then final acquiescence in performing the ritual at all, as well as Parsifal's arriving just in the nick of time, are crucial elements of the ceremony.[19] But this makes it seem as if a truly authentic ceremony, for Žižek, would be nothing but the "dotting of the *i*" on a series of contingencies. So where, in the end, does Žižek stand? Is there for him, as for Badiou and Mallarmé, an elusive "inner necessity" to the structure of certain ceremonies, such that they might be *constructed* and *continued* so as to embody and sustain free acts, or is, on the contrary, every ceremony a concatenation of events that can only be retroactively affirmed?

The apparent success of liturgical-ceremonial practices in sustaining freedom, revolt or even revolution would entail that the concrete specificities of any actual ceremony cannot be wholly arbitrary. Certain aesthetic formalities must themselves mediate revolutionary mandates. In the case of ceremony, liturgical gestures must anticipate, however dimly, the words and deeds – the transformative Acts – that any such liturgy will have portended or prophesied. "Non-specific" sense *cannot* be arbitrary sense, nor can the "absence of sense" be maintained as the ground of freedom, as Žižek himself is almost led to aver before he stops short and says that the fundamental experience of non-sense is "more precisely . . . being sure something has a sense but not knowing what it is."[20]

But Žižek oddly hesitates, here. In his *In Defense of Lost Causes*, he suggests that the "ritualistic evocation" of sense involves the structure of a "necessary illusion." The illusion is that sense precedes us, that it is "out there," waiting for us. Žižek notes that, along similar lines, Marcel Proust described a particular piece of music that deeply haunted Swann, and struck him "as if the performers not so much played the little phrase as executed the rites necessary for it to appear." This sense that the truth of our investments is "out there," that their true meaning is, as Žižek puts it, "waiting for our call in its virtual presence,"[21] is what Žižek calls a "necessary illusion." But here Žižek is faced with a dilemma: either free acts consist entirely of discontinuous contingencies, and thus all ceremony is illusion, or if ceremony is non-illusory, then there are forms of continuity that not only announce but *embody* freedom, as such. Ceremony, in the latter case, would participate (however minimally) in the substance of utopian life, however minimally or formally construed. But because Žižek is committed to reading the sustaining power of the virtual as an illusion, it remains finally unclear how he can account for the power of particular ceremonial rites to embody the shape of emancipated life.

Nevertheless, at the end of *Living in the End Times*, Žižek affirms ceremony as an authentic dimension of communist culture. He gives a number of examples of both the necessity for, and power of ceremonial-liturgical behavior. In the *Liebestod* duet, of *Tristan* and *Isolde*, the couple's passionate *Lust* can be expressed only when their discourse shifts from intimate conversational address to formal, declamatory modes of speech: the truth of passion is revealed only in the repetition of stylized formulas.[22] Žižek also affirms the liturgical power of the "furniture music" of Eric Satie, since this music lets us *hear the background* of life, thus providing an intense experience of collective intimacy. Likewise Dziga Vertov's *Man With A Movie Camera* arranges a tableau of everyday life, a parataxis that is an ecstatic paean to the joys of life.[23]

What Žižek is arriving at here, with this affirmation of liturgical gestures, is a view that any critique of ideology requires as its necessary supplement not so much the insertion of ourselves into future ceremonies, but some kind of ceremonialization of everyday life. Precisely, this would be a politicization of enjoyment (the opposite of an aestheticized politics). Of course there is always the danger that such enjoyment-in-advance can be co-opted by the status quo. But Žižek is now clearly affirming that practices of *repetition* are crucial to the inception of a future. As he puts it, in *In Defense of Lost Causes*, "Freud's famous motto, 'what we do not remember we are compelled to repeat,' should be turned upside down: *what we are unable to repeat, we are haunted by and are compelled to remember.*"[24] Paradoxically, ceremony is a kind of weapon against memory, against the entrapments of the past. (It is not accidental, in this connection, that so many ceremonies are designed to deal with ancestral guilt, grudges, or stigmas.)

But again, the critical task, for Žižek, is not that of how to be present at future ceremonies, but of how to read, in the very *limitations* of present ceremony, the seeds of future authentic rites. *Parsifal*, for example is limited by the way that it paganizes Christianity, reinscribing the singular Act of the Redemption into a myth of perpetual restoration or Eternal Return. By contrast, the *Ring* cycle, which appears to be a pagan epic, culminates in a truly revolutionary Gospel message – Žižek calls it "the ultimate Paulinian work of art."[25] The key moment of the *Ring*, for Žižek, is the end of the *Götterdammerung*: the gods have departed, and the human community is left alone, thrust into the open field of contingent historical decision.[26] The *Ring* is, for Žižek, the opera that actually succeeds in being a ceremony, as effectively functioning as a ceremony, since it "ceremonially" evacuates the gods, leaving only the human community, the community of the Holy Spirit. For Žižek, the end of the *Götterdammerung* is an image of radical incarnation: the gods dying symbolize the becoming-immanent of God in the community of believers, the moment when God steps into his own picture.[27] The *Ring* thus "knows" the lesson that must be remembered through the failure of

Parsifal. It is the correct ritual which never appears as such, but is retrieved through its "recreation" once the failures of *Parsifal* are recognized.

Ritual Reticence

There is, then, for Žižek, a revolutionary consistency, a continuous source of revolutionary life. The "substance of undead life," and the substance of all ceremony, would derive from as-yet-unrealized contingencies in the past itself. From this perspective, Žižek's penchant for re-writing the endings of his favorite films, novels, and operas is an extremely significant aspect of his thought. It is a revisionism that speaks directly to his view of freedom. In *Living in the End Times*, Žižek concludes with a series of lessons on the importance of being able to think through alternative possible histories of political struggle, as well as through alternative possible *dénouements* for various artworks. He argues, in fact, that his own perspective entails a profound commitment to a kind of science-fictional, what-if style of thinking. This commitment, he insists,

> brings the What-if logic to its self-reflexive reversal. For a radical Marxist, *the actual history that we live is itself a kind of realized alternative history*, the reality we live because, in the past, we failed to seize the moment and act . . . we have to leap back in time, before the fateful decisions were made or before the accidents occurred that generate the state which now seems normal to us, and the way to do so, to render palpable this open moment of decision, is to imagine how, at that point, history might have taken a different turn."[28]

How does Žižek's insistence upon the possibility of radically different histories relate to ceremonial behavior? As we have seen it is paradoxically – and perhaps not with complete coherence – through an affirmation of contingency itself that Žižek seeks to affirm the necessity of ceremony. And yet in general Žižek affirms only something like a Bartleby-style, individual subjective withdrawal from the concrete options open in the present. He seems to aver only certain types of ascetic and individual refusals or withdrawals. But if ceremony is necessary to the repetition involved in freedom, or more precisely, embodies such repetition directly, the future cannot be accessed simply by withdrawing from the times, from the concrete and embodied aspects of the status quo, but must also strategically re-double its formal elements. This is how, for Žižek, the repetition of fascist imagery in the rock band Rammstein manages to introduce a gap between fascist/Nazi imagery and its ideological background, leaving in place only the obscene desire of/in the image itself, a desire that can be exuberantly consummated as a cathartic having of fascism and eating it too. Žižek fully endorses the obscene and orgiastic immersion of the individual in such collective experiences.[29] But this endorsement is a far cry from the suicidal position of Bartleby, and one wonders whether Žižek himself would join in any future celebration.[30]

That is to say, although he seems to affirm certain aspects of ritual practice, Žižek's obsession with a sheerly disruptive view of contingency rests on something like a suicidal affirmation of violence at the ontological level, and cuts against the grain of a sustaining collective formal gesture. But violence can only save us if, at the virtual level, this implies that there are potencies that, while contingent, are not inherently self-destructive or self-undoing. Only in that case can violence be productive and not merely destructive, and only in case there are ceremonial and aesthetic modes of sustaining those potencies in ways that unhook individual obsessions and marshal collective affects, will freedom have a ritual consistency. We should fully grant, against fetishistic and phantasmatic views, that there is no fixed way to guarantee and maintain a stable relationship to virtual potencies of emancipation, love or justice – it is the power of such potencies as virtualities constantly to mutate. But as Žižek himself now avers, there are ritual, liturgical, or more generally "aesthetic" modalities of ceremonial consistency that, while not sacred in and of themselves, create sacred and sustaining *passages* – passages not to the act but to the fecundity of the virtual itself. This is what Žižek seems to increasingly realize, of late, with his turn to affirmations of ceremony and Deleuzian affirmation of the virtual.

But it still seems to me that this turn is in tension with both a strident voluntarism and an ontology of ultimate violence. Affirming the agency of ceremony thwarts voluntarism because it interrupts the interruptive process of refusal or *Versagung*, subordinating refusal to collective affirmations. And ceremonial aesthetics itself points to a dimension of the virtual that, while contingent, is not plagued by internal negativities or self-undoings. If, as Deleuze taught, all relations are external to their terms, then it may be that the rites of freedom, limited as they may be, establish the conditions under which subjects can sustain externalities so as to endure and create through the ordeal of their contingency, rather than suffer from such extimacy through the all too common symptoms of hysteria, paranoia, and psychosis. Žižek seems to see that there are liturgical, ceremonial, and collective aesthetic practices that access this level of health rightly deemed utopian, but remains incoherently committed to an ultimate ontological and existential background at odds with the very future he himself is driven toward.

Notes

1 Slavoj Žižek, *In Defense of Lost Causes* (London: Verso, 2008), p. 314.
2 Ibid., p. 315.
3 Žižek's criticisms of Deleuze are well known – see especially his *Organs without Bodies: On Deleuze and Consequences* (London: Routledge, 2005). What is less discussed are his more recent and generally positive usages of Deleuzian and Bergsonian conceptions of time, as I continue to outline in the rest of this article.
4 Gilles Deleuze, *Difference and Repetition* (trans. Paul Patton. New York: Columbia, 1994), p. 183.
5 Slavoj Žižek, *In Defense of Lost Causes* (London: Verso, 2008), p. 315.
6 Molly Anne Rothenberg, *The Excessive Subject: A New Theory of Social Change* (Cambridge: Polity), p. 185.
7 Slavoj Žižek, *In Defense of Lost Causes* (London: Verso, 2008), p. 322.
8 Slavoj Žižek, *In Defense of Lost Causes* (London: Verso, 2008), p. 324.
9 Rothenberg suggests that it takes place through the cultivation of collective practices that enable groups to entertain what Guattari called "transversal" relations both to themselves and to others. This involves a certain movement of suspending or distancing oneself from the affective charges attending to our extimacy. The closest Žižek comes to Rothenberg's suggestion is in his own affirmations of aesthetico-ritual practice as a potential revolutionary site. But this affirmation, I will argue is plagued by an ambiguity proper to his ontological commitment to a view of the necessity of thinking contingency as violence.
10 Alain Badiou, *Five Lessons on Wagner* (trans. Susan Spitzer. London: Verso, 2011), p. 158.
11 Alain Badiou, *Five Lessons on Wagner* (trans. Susan Spitzer. London: Verso, 2011), p. 156.
12 Ibid., p. 158.
13 Ibid.
14 In terms of *Parsifal* itself, its inner dynamics, for Badiou it is Kundry that is the symptom of the failed ceremony. The fact that she is enigmatic,

unplaceable, at times innocent and at times guilty, at once within and without the utopian male brotherhood of freedom and truth. Badiou suggests that Kundry's very unplaceability might be symptomatic of the very resistance of historical mutability itself to ceremony, to an inherent impossibility of ceremony itself.

15 Alain Badiou, *Five Lessons on Wagner* (trans. Susan Spitzer. London: Verso, 2011), p. 159.

16 Gilles Deleuze, "He Stuttered" (*Essays Critical and Clinical*, trans. Daniel W. Smith and Michael A. Greco. Minneapolis: University of Minnesota Press, 1997, pp. 107–14).

17 Slavoj Žižek, *Living in the End Times* (London: Verso), 2010, p. 378.

18 Not only in *Opera's Second Death* (with Mladen Dolar, London: Routledge, 2002), but in places too numerous to cite, throughout his now-massive *oeuvre*.

19 It is telling that Žižek, sees in the very failure of *Parsifal* the seeds of its positive message, the germ or kernel that can and must be repeated forward. Žižek argues that one could imagine an alternate plot line for *Parsifal*, one in which Parsifal brings Kundry back with him, abolishes the males-only Grail ritual, and restores fertility to the land by renewing the male-female balance. But Žižek also condemns such a "Feuerbachian" resolution as false, or at least incomplete, since *eros*, can only affirm the temporary, punctual power of love against the law, and not the power of *agape* to fully assume and thus fully displace the law. (Slavoj Žižek, "Afterword"; Alain Badiou, *Five Lessons on Wagner* (trans. Susan Spitzer. London: Verso, 2011), p. 222).

20 Žižek's affirmative view of liturgy, and of ceremony comes after a reading of Jameson's *Seeds of Time*, and a Jameson-inspired description of post-revolutionary life as a flourishing of the freaks – a flowering of idiosyncratic, neurotic, and schizophrenic vitalities no longer subordinated to a model of deviance from the sterile vision of psychic health demanded of consumer culture (373–6). Žižek asserts that the flowering of the individual, which Marx himself affirmed – "the freedom of all will be grounded in the freedom of every individual" – can only "thrive against the background of a shared ritual" (377).

21 Slavoj Žižek, *In Defense of Lost Causes* (London: Verso, 2008), p. 314.

22 Slavoj Žižek, *Living in the End Times* (London: Verso, 2010), p. 377.

23 With Vertov, Žižek writes, "there is no tension between the eye and the gaze here, no suspicion or urge to penetrate the deceptive surface in search of the secret truth or essence." Žižek also points to Altman as a recapitulation of Vertov; Altman's apparently dark and pessimistic *Short Cuts* points up the reality of "subliminal reality" as a space of freedom much as Deleuze and Guattari read Kafka as presenting a universe where "the Absence of the "elusive transcendent Center (Castle, Court, God) betrays the Presence of multiple passages and transformations" (ibid.).

24 Slavoj Žižek, *In Defense of Lost Causes* (London: Verso, 2008), p. 321.
25 Slavoj Žižek, "Afterword" Alain Badiou, *Five Lessons on Wagner* (trans. Susan Spitzer London: Verso, 2011), p. 222.
26 Slavoj Žižek, "Afterword" Alain Badiou, *Five Lessons on Wagner* (trans. Susan Spitzer London: Verso, 2011), pp. 224–5.
27 Ibid., p. 225. In keeping with his ontology of freedom, for Žižek this "undead incarnation" appears not as the abundance of supernatural life, but as the excess of Undeath. That which survives the death of the gods is not immortal life, but Undeath, that dimension of subjectivity that cuts against the superego injunction to enjoy. As Žižek puts it, in *Living in the End Times*,

> The standard idealist question, "Is there (eternal) life after death? should be countered by the materialist question, "Is there life before death?" . . . what bothers a materialist is this: am I really alive here and now, or am I just vegetating, as a mere human animal bent on survival? When am I really alive? Precisely when I enact the "undead" drive in me, the "too-much-ness" of life (Eric Santner). And I reach this point when I no longer act directly, but when "it [*es*] —which Christians name the Holy Spirit — acts through me: at this point, I reach the Absolute.

But if the Absolute is simply transcendental negativity, the tearing of the fabric of being from itself, it is nevertheless necessary to ask, *what is this negativity for*? A reference to Christianity makes Žižek's perspective on this question clear.

> There is no guarantee of redemption-through-love: redemption is merely possible. We are thereby in the very core of Christianity: it is God himself who made a Pascalian wager . . . Far from providing the conclusive dot on the *i*, the divine act rather stands for the openness of a new beginning, and it is up to humanity to live up to it, to decide its meaning, to make something of it.

28 Slavoj Žižek, *Living in the End Times* (London: Verso), 2010, p. 87.
29 Ibid. , p. 387.
30 In the end I would argue that what is at issue here is the particular way in which Žižek is haunted by Christianity. His affirmation of Protestant voluntarism is ultimately at odds with his affirmation of catholic formalism. He is in a kind of double cross, attempting to affirm catholic universalism without its substantive view of grace, and to affirm Protestant voluntarism without its hope for ultimate redemption. Whether or not his interest in Christianity is ultimately metaphorical or analogical (Christian structures forming structural analogs for emancipatory processes that can be divorced from Christian particularities), the tension of Žižek's affirmation of rites and rituals remains palpable.

Part Three

5

A Critique of Natural Economy: Quantum Physics with Žižek

Adrian Johnston

This intervention constitutes an additional installment in a debate between Žižek and me, previous installments of which can be found in the journals *Subjectivity* (Žižek 2010a; Johnston 2010) and *La Revue Internationale de Philosophie* (Žižek 2011; Johnston 2012a). Our ongoing discussion, at least as I perceive it, pivots around the question of how to situate materialism, on the one hand, in relation to naturalism and the sciences, on the other hand. Whatever our disagreements, we hold a number of commitments in common, including a fidelity to certain aspects and versions of a robust, ambitious Hegelianism.

Thanks to these common commitments, my criticisms of Žižek tend to be immanent (rather than external) ones. This tendency will continue to prevail here too. At the current juncture of our conversation, I find myself facing Žižek's modified redeployment of his previous appropriations of quantum physics elaborated elsewhere.[1] *Contra* my "transcendental materialist" concern with tying a carefully qualified quasi-naturalist theory of subjectivity partially to life-scientific foundations, he now argues that the physics of the unimaginably small, instead of the biology of comparatively much larger mid-sized beings and processes, can and should play a singularly special anchoring role in relation to a viable account of the subject as conceived at the intersection of German idealist philosophy, Freudian-Lacanian psychoanalysis, and the natural sciences of today.

According to my immanent critique to be laid out below, Žižek's mode of recourse to quantum physics not only is questionable on general philosophical grounds – it also is awkwardly at odds with the distinctive core tenets of his fundamental ontology. The peak of this self-subverting irony is the fact that the theoretical form of his extensions of quantum physics as a universal economy *qua* ubiquitous, all–encompassing structural nexus (one capable of covering human subjects, among many other bigger–than–sub–atomic things) is in unsustainable tension with the ontological content he claims to find divulged within this same branch of physics (i.e., being itself as detotalized and inconsistent). After replying directly to Žižek's newest addition to our back–and–forth, I will return to his earlier uses (and, arguably, abuses) of quantum physics (especially as contained in "Quantum Physics with Lacan") so as to reassess his materialist deployments of natural science in relation to his contemporary positions taken in the context of our still–unfolding debate.

Before problematizing "Quantum Physics with Žižek" then (1996) and now (2011), I will begin by summarizing and commenting on Žižek's most recent response to me (Žižek 2011). Therein, he gets well–and–truly underway thus:

> Today, THE scientific discovery which needs philosophical rethinking is quantum physics – how are we to interpret its ontological implications AND avoid the double trap of superficial pragmatic empiricism and obscurantist idealism ('mind creates reality')? Lenin's *Materialism and Empirio-Criticism* has to be thoroughly rewritten – the first thing to do is to abandon the old naive notion of the existence of fully constituted material reality as the sole true reality outside our minds. This reality is 'all' and, as such, relying on the overlooked exception of its transcendental constitution. The minimal definition of materialism hinges on the admission of a *gap between what Schelling called Existence and Ground of Existence*: prior to fully existent reality, there is a chaotic non-all proto-reality, a pre-ontological virtual fluctuation of not yet fully constituted real. This pre-ontological real is what Badiou calls pure multiplicity, in contrast to the level of appearances, which is the level of reality constituted by the transcendental horizon of a world.

I certainly agree that the past century's worth of advances in theoretical physics demand ample additional intellectual labor on the part of philosophers (especially Continentalists typically averse to the mathematical and the scientific). However, I take issue with the "THE" here, namely, with the assertion that a single sub-branch of the natural sciences enjoys a unique privilege for philosophical reflection of a materialist kind. My objection to this isn't merely a minor complaint resting on nothing more than the underlining of the simple fact that there are many other scientific disciplines and domains besides quantum physics. A contention central to my reply to Žižek in this particular installment of our extended exchange is that his manner of privileging this one science is incompatible with the fundaments of his ontology and corresponding conception of subjectivity.

The second half of the preceding quotation amounts to a restatement by Žižek of his basic ontological *Weltanschauung*. Mixing Schellingian, Lacanian, and Badiouian terms, he speaks of the Real *Grund* of a *Logos*-eluding zero-level presupposed by onto-*logy*, a ground that is, in itself, a detotalized, un-unified jumble of heterogeneous pluralities and proliferations. Incidentally, Badiou would reject Žižek's equation of the "inconsistent multiplicities" of being *qua* being with quantum-physical structures and dynamics; for the former, his set-theoretic ontology of *l'être en tant qu'être* is put forward as different-in-kind from any and every ontic discipline bearing upon determinate beings, including mathematized physics, with its applied (instead of pure) mathematics. However, I am supportive of Žižek's healthy materialist impulse to root his ontology partially in scientific soil.[2] But, I believe that Žižek is insufficiently careful in moving between scientific and ontological dimensions on this occasion.

One of the axioms of Žižek's ontology is a philosophical generalization, an appropriation and redeployment, of Lacan's dictum according to which, "The big Other does not exist" (*Le grand Autre n'existe pas*) (Johnston 2008b 189, 208; Johnston 2012b). Within the most minimal of its strata, being is, for Žižek, the barred Real of a non-All not-One (to put it in hybrid Lacanian-Badiouian locution). Or, in other words borrowed from Žižek's German idealist inspirers, the primal *Urgrund* of reality is the groundlessness of an *Ungrund*, an abyssal vortex of out-of-synch entities and forces saturated with antagonisms, conflicts, gaps, negativities, and so on. From a Žižekian standpoint, any portrayal of existence as ultimately governed by a cosmic order, whether above or below, responsible for a harmonious coordination and integration of the entirety of existent objects and occurrences is tantamount to positing the One-All of a big Other (for example, a God-like Nature-with-a-capital-N as a Whole-sustaining homogeneous substance or bundle of eternal universal laws). Although his ontology forbids such a posit, Žižek is at risk of violating this very prohibition through the ways in which he mobilizes quantum physics. This danger of self-contradiction will become increasingly clear and evident shortly.

In his reply (2011), Žižek soon proceeds to spell out some of what is required of a scientifically informed materialism. He declares:

> In its effort to grasp reality 'independently of me,' mathematized science erases me out of reality, i.e., it ignores (not the transcendental way I constitute reality, but) the way I am PART OF this reality. The true question is

therefore: how do I (as the site where reality appears to itself) emerge in 'objective reality' (or, more pointedly, how can the universe of meaning arise in the meaningless Real). As materialists, we should take into account two criteria that an adequate answer should meet:

(1) the answer should be really materialist, with no spiritualist cheating;
(2) one should accept that the ordinary mechanistic-materialist notion of 'objective reality' will not do the job.

I endorse almost everything said in these remarks, including the two stipulated criteria. But, looking at this passage in its surrounding context, I want to resist and call into question the move of tethering a materialist philosophical account of the genesis of subjectivity to an interpretation of quantum physics. To state the problem bluntly, Žižek, in flirting with the making of this move, teeters on the brink of falling into either reductive or analogical modes of thinking, both equally incompatible with the true systematic core of his interwoven ontology and theory of the subject.

The twin pitfalls of the reductive and the analogical, to be delineated further momentarily, are both opened up by Žižek's rather un-Žižekian apparent elevation of quantum physics to the status of an ontological master-matrix covering a massive range of being's scales (and not just this specific science's proper disciplinary domain limited to the tiny universes of the extremely small). In his response to me, Žižek makes ground-zero quantum materialization *ex nihilo*, creation arising from the nothingness of a vacuum or void, epitomize everything from the Being of Heidegger's fundamental ontology to drives as per Freudian-Lacanian psychoanalysis (the death drive first and foremost) and the delicate art of fierce socio-political struggle. With reference to the energetics of quantum systems, he asserts, "This is why 'there is something and not nothing': because, energetically, something is cheaper than nothing" (2011). Having formulated this abstract ontological principle of economy on the basis of quantum physics, he then leaps into the psychical realm of analytic meta-psychology, maintaining apropos the *Todestrieb* that, "The paradox of the death drive is thus strictly homologous to that of the Higgs field: from the standpoint of libidinal economy, it is 'cheaper' for the system to repeatedly traverse the circle of drive than to stay at absolute rest" (2011). I am of the opinion that Žižek's repeated exercises, here and elsewhere, in employing models taken from theoretical physics so as to elucidate aspects of Lacan's teachings are pedagogically brilliant and amazingly illuminating for anyone interested in grasping key Lacanian concepts

(1996: 189–236; 2006: 165–73; Johnston 2008b: 195–203). But, however productively suggestive these cross-disciplinary comparisons might be, using "homologies" resting on broad, vague notions of "cheapness" and "energy" to facilitate effortless movement between the "economies" of the ontological, the natural, the libidinal, and the political seems as though it leads right back to the old onto-theological vision of being as an organic Whole of smoothly enmeshed microcosms and macrocosms, a seamless, enchained continuum of recurring patterns embedded within each other in a fractal-like fashion. Succinctly stated, Žižek's sweeping generalization of the "natural economy" of quantum physics courts the peril of a regressive return to the One-All of a big Other supposedly dismantled and banned by Žižekian ontology. Moreover, it brings him into the dubious intellectual company of the Roger Penrose who proposes a quantum-physicalist theory of mind (Johnston 2011c).

The potential for Žižek inadvertently falling into reductivism already should be obvious by now. His selection of quantum physics in particular as the singularly privileged scientific terrain for renewed materialist speculation heightens the chances of stumbling into this theoretical dead-end. Many philosophical materialisms that see themselves as rooted in the "hard" sciences embrace monistic ontologies. Such monisms dictate that, when all is said and done, each and every level and layer of entities and events is expressive of nothing more than whatever the present-best physics of the smallest constituents of material reality hypothesizes regarding the purportedly ultimate building blocks of incarnate being. Everything boils down to matter at its most minimal.[3] A pre-Kantian, pre-Hegelian, and Spinozistic-style subject-squashing determinism, anathema to a Žižek-inspired proponent of subjects' irreducible autonomy, is only a step or two away, if that. The choice of quantum physics as providing all-purpose cognitive maps for even the biggest and broadest tiers of existence carries with it this sort of unwanted baggage. Additionally, apart from the philosophical fact that reductivism's monism is fundamentally incompatible with Žižekian ontology despite Žižek's evidently unrestricted, free-wheeling extensions of explanatory constructs peculiar to the quantum kingdom of the very small, empirical and experimental constraints (particularly temporal and computational limitations) thwart any efforts whatsoever to carry out an exhaustively thorough reduction of the mid-sized structures and dynamics of human-scale reality to the unimaginably minuscule teeming multitudes of quantum objects and processes. A quantum-based reductivism is in practice impossible to substantiate, condemned to remain a topic of empty speculation straining in the direction of an intangible mirage of a profoundly harmonious universal arrangement of being and beings as a "Great Chain."

As for the status of the analogies Žižek proposes between quantum and other phenomena, these probably aren't grounded on anything resembling the monistic reductivism remarked upon immediately above. Although I perceive Žižek's reliance on physics as luring him into the shady neighborhood of these types of scientistic ontologies, I am confident that, self-consciously faced with the looming prospect of this proximity, he would promptly flee from such neighbors by adamantly reaffirming his investment in a One-less ontology of not-Whole being devoid of overarching or undergirding big Others of whatever kind. However, this would be for Žižek to appeal to the same ontology I consider him as compromising his allegiance to through his analogical deployments of bits and pieces borrowed from quantum physics. As I have argued in other texts, the elaboration of a science-shaped materialist ontology of an Other-lacking barred Real is better served by something along the lines of philosopher of science Nancy Cartwright's theoretical landscape of a "dappled world," with Cartwright quite effectively casting a number of weighty doubts, both philosophical and scientific, on the presumed pride-of-place enjoyed in the eyes of many philosophers (Žižek clearly included) and scientists by the quantum-level physics of the microcosmic (Johnston 2011c; 2014).

But, if Žižek's quantum analogies are meant to be taken as rather looser homologies – this looseness is entailed by them not resting upon presupposed material continuities licensing, at least in principle, strict explanatory reductions of the larger to the smaller – then several significant questions must be asked and answered: Ontologically speaking, what, if any, hypothesized material forces and factors license comparisons connecting things sub-atomic to realities well above the threshold of the atomic? Epistemologically speaking, how can one know whether discerned resemblances prompting the drawing of analogies are really more than arbitrarily selected or created abstract patterns imaginatively superimposed upon the designated referents thus compared? Methodologically speaking, what principles and restrictions guide constructing certain analogies and not others? Žižek leaves queries of this sort unanswered. Unless and until he furnishes ontological, epistemological, and methodological justifications in support of his philosophical appropriations of quantum physics, they will remain somewhat suspect.

Given Žižek's Hegelianism in all its distinctiveness, a Hegelian problematization of his recourse to physics indeed would count as a far-from-insignificant immanent critique.[4] A door is opened for a Hegelian reply on my part when Žižek (2011) muses:

> . . . what if we transpose ontological difference (the difference between entities and the 'nothingness' of the ontological horizon of their disclosure) into the Thing-in-itself, and (re)conceive it as the ontological incompleteness of reality (as quantum physics implicates)? What if we posit that 'things in themselves' emerge against the background of the Void or Nothingness, the way this Void is conceived in quantum physics, as the Void which is not just a negative void, but the void portent of all possible reality? This is the only truly consequent 'transcendental materialism' which is possible after the Kantian transcendental idealism. For a true dialectician, the ultimate mystery is not 'Why is there something instead of nothing?,' but 'Why is there nothing instead of something?': how is it that, the more we analyze reality, the more we found a void?

Žižek's speculative extrapolation from quantum physics to fundamental ontology might qualify, on a certain construal, as one "truly consequent 'transcendental materialism'" – and, with this phrase, he signals that my own position is in the crosshairs at this moment – but I disagree that it's the "only" version of this materialist stance. In addition to me arguing on separate occasions that Žižek is driven into formulating his specific ontological framework starting first from a particular theory of the subject articulated at the intersection of German idealist philosophy and Lacanian analytic metapsychology (2012a; 2012b), the sub-title of Žižek's *Ontology* is *A Transcendental Materialist Theory of Subjectivity*. What I'm getting at is that the genesis of the "something" of material being from the "nothing" of the immaterial void (and the persisting subsistence of the latter within the former) is one thing; the surfacing of subjects out of this thus-generated existent reality is another thing entirely. If Žižek intends for his abstract formal generalizations of quantum-physical phenomena to cover the issue of subjectivity (among a swarm of other issues), then he must supply sound materialist arguments, which I strongly believe cannot be supplied, to the effect that sub-atomic processes can and do resurface directly at scales of materiality (i.e., those at which it's appropriate to speak of minded agents) well above the threshold of the atomic. In other words, he would have to explain how and why quantum-level dynamics are not thoroughly diluted, transmuted, and/or effectively screened-out at larger-sized levels of material reality. To echo the famous assessment of phrenology in Hegel's *Phenomenology* (196–210), the short circuit of an infinite judgment along the lines of "Spirit is a quark" would require supplementation by significant interpretive contortions and counter-intuitive acrobatics so as to amount to more than the inelegant category mistake of an indefensible reduction or analogy.[5] Furthermore, the addition of such supplements would carry one far beyond the circumscribed confines of the proper epistemological and ontological jurisdictions of quantum physics itself.

Žižek refers countless times to Hegel's insistence, in the awe-inspiring preface to the *Phenomenology*, on the (post-Spinoza, anti-Schelling) necessity of "grasping and expressing the True, not only as *Substance*, but equally as *Subject*" (*das Wahre nicht als* Substanz, *sondern ebensosehr als* Subjekt *aufzufassen und auszudrücken*) (Hegel 1970: 23; Hegel 1977: 10; Johnston 2008b: 163–77; Johnston 2012c). Transcendental materialism, at least as I conceive it, strives to formulate a rigorously materialist and scientifically responsible delineation of the emergence of, in Hegelese, spiritual subjectivity from natural substance.[6] At other times, Žižek refers to biology and its branches in his independent and distinct efforts, from which I have benefitted enormously and drawn much inspiration, to outline a narrative recounting those explosive events in which autonomous subjects spring into being out of heteronomous matter(s) (Johnston 2007; Johnston 2008b: 203–9). In sympathy with Catherine Malabou's Hegel-catalyzed and biologically oriented endeavors – her superb book *The Future of Hegel* is understandably one of Žižek's favorite pieces of Hegelian scholarship (along with Béatrice Longuenesse's *Hegel's Critique of Metaphysics* and Gérard Lebrun's *La patience du Concept*) (Žižek 2010b: 68) – he sometimes devotes himself to a project dear to Malabou and me as well: assembling what could be characterized fairly as a modified, updated reconstruction of the real-philosophical transition, within the systematic parameters of Hegel's *Encyclopedia*, from the "Organics" of the *Philosophy of Nature* to the "Anthropology" of the *Philosophy of Mind*.

Given this shared Hegelian project, I feel compelled to propose a twist different from a reversal Žižek proposes when he says, "For a true dialectician, the ultimate mystery is not 'Why is there something instead of nothing?,' but 'Why is there nothing instead of something?'" The twist is this: For a Hegel-indebted transcendental materialist, insofar as a theory of subjectivity is essential to transcendental materialism, the really crucial enigma is "How does the nothing(ness) of the *Cogito*-like subject-as-$ emerge from the something of material substance(s)?" This is my favored question and, from time to time, Žižek's likewise. Moreover, it is the key Hegelian query for any materialist ontology aiming to think the subject as immanently transcending its substantial base *qua* both originary ground and enduring milieu of being.

Before circumnavigating back to Žižek's first sustained engagement with quantum physics, I should add a few final clarifications with respect to his most recent reply to me. My manners of responding to him by no means are meant to announce an uncompromising resistance on my part to his appropriations of quantum physics, with their sparkling, promising nuances. Admittedly, I lack the expertise in physics and mathematics to assess with complete confidence the accuracy and validity of select aspects of Žižek's quantum musings. Nonetheless, as hinted earlier, I am wholeheartedly in favor of his inclination partially to ground materialism on natural-scientific bases.[7] From a dizzying high-altitude vantage point surveying such basic, ground-zero categories and concepts as Being and Nothing, Žižek is one-hundred-percent correct that any philosophical materialism genuinely worthy of the title cannot rightly avoid a sober intellectual reckoning with quantum physics.[8] But, if such a materialism is both to be authentically dialectical as well as to include a non-reductive account of a more-than-material subject emergent from nothing more than material substance, then a detailed speculative engagement with biology over-and-above physics alone is absolutely requisite. Furthermore, in fidelity to a Žižekian ontology of an Other-less, barred Real of non-All/not-One material being, I will continue to stick to an emergentist orientation (coupled with a Cartwrightian "nomological pluralism" [Johnston 2012c; 2014]), an orientation according to which, simply put, the structures and dynamics of biological realities are ontologically as well as epistemologically irreducible to those of physics (especially the physics of the extremely small). A materialist fundamental ontology of the genesis of being by itself might be able to rest content with quantum physics as the sole chosen source of scientific resources for its thinking. But, a viable transcendental materialist theory of subjectivity needs much more than can be extracted and extrapolated from this lone source, particularly if it eschews dependence on the shaky scaffoldings afforded by the big Other of a natural economy.

Keeping all of the above in mind, Žižek's prior reflections on quantum physics in *The Indivisible Remainder* reveal some noteworthy facets, especially with the benefit of present hindsight. Schelling's 1809 *Freiheitschrift* in particular – this text is animated by a desire philosophically to synthesize the apparent opposites of a Spinoza-style system of deterministic natural necessity with a post-Kantian conception of the irreducible spiritual autonomy of free, self-determining subjectivity (Schelling 1936: 3, 7, 9–11) – is a key source of inspiration for Žižek in his 1996 book and elsewhere (Johnston 2008b 19, 69–122). Avowedly inspired by Schelling, Žižek intends to repeat this later-Schellingian synthesizing gesture through a theoretical reinterpretation of quantum-physical experiments and phenomena.

To be more precise, Žižek utilizes quantum physics so as to destabilize and undermine, on a scientific basis, images of nature typically taken for granted and assumed to be valid in various versions of the distinction between, on the one hand, the natural, and, on the other hand (and in the parlance of German idealism), the spiritual (i.e., the more-than-natural *qua* autonomous, cultural, historical, social, etc.). He explains (1996: 220):

> Quantum physics . . . calls into question . . . not the specificity of man, his exceptional position with regard to nature, but, rather, the very notion of nature implied by the standard philosophical formulation of the gap between nature and man, as well as by the New Age assertion of a deeper harmony between nature and man: the notion of nature as a 'closed,' balanced universe, regulated by some underlying Law or Rule. True 'anthropomorphism' resides in the notion of nature tacitly assumed by those who oppose man to nature: nature as a circular 'return of the same,' as the determinist kingdom of inexorable 'natural laws,' or (more in accordance with 'New Age' sensitivity) nature as a harmonious, balanced Whole of cosmic forces derailed by man's *hubris*, his pathological arrogance. What is to be 'deconstructed' is this very notion of nature: the features we refer to in order to emphasize man's unique status – the constitutive imbalance, the 'out-of-joint,' on account of which man is an 'unnatural' creature, 'nature sick unto death' – must somehow already be at work in nature itself, although – as Schelling would have put it – in another, lower power (in the mathematical sense of the term).

Readers familiar with the full sweep of Žižek's *oeuvre* will readily recognize in this passage a number of thematic threads and trajectories of speculation (not to mention polemical refrains) regularly recurring in texts after *The Indivisible Remainder* up through his most recent publications; considering my precise aims here, I will bypass in what follows many of these motifs and theses so as to retain sharpness of focus. Žižek, short-circuiting the abyss between the very small and the very large (a yawning chasm that has yet to be closed, or even bridged, within physics itself), proceeds in the rest of "Quantum Physics with Lacan" to lay claim to a quantum-physical license for an ontological narrative according to which the existence of the entire universe testifies to a moment of creation sparked by (as he puts it in this quotation) a "constitutive imbalance," namely, "some global 'pathological' disturbed balance, . . . a broken symmetry" (1996: 227), a "fundamental disturbance or lost balance" (1996: 227). On this basis, he concludes, "*there is no (balanced, self-enclosed) Nature* to be thrown out of joint by man's *hubris*" (1996: 235) (a conclusion with, among other ramifications, obvious ideological-political implications, especially *vis-à-vis* ecology and "biopower"). Althusser's "aleatory materialism of the encounter" is invoked as a notable precursor of this view (1996: 227; Althusser 2006: 174–5, 188–90).

In addition to insisting on the primacy of imbalance/asymmetry over balance/symmetry, Žižek, via quantum physics, also launches a theoretical line of argumentation resurfacing in his writings of the past few years. This line is adopted in pointed opposition to Lenin's 1908 *Materialism and Empirio-Criticism*. Therein, Lenin rails against allegedly "idealist" (i.e., anti-materialist) philosophical employments of then-cutting-edge physics according to which "matter" (*qua* dense, hefty, solid stuff) "has disappeared" (Lenin 1972: 308–18). By contrast, Žižek, in both *The Indivisible Remainder* (229) and, for instance, *Organs without Bodies* (24) and *The Parallax View* (165–6, 168), maintains that the sole legitimate type of materialism today must be one which joyously affirms the "disappearance of matter," the becoming-immaterial of matter itself as per theoretical physics, in which macro-level sensory-perceptual imaginings of tangible material bodies are rendered null and void and replaced by dematerialized, impossible-to-picture waves/particles, vibrating strings, and the like.

The upshot of the preceding is that, for Žižek, the only nature that exists is dramatically different from the vast majority of standard, traditional envisionings of it by scientists and non-scientists alike.[9] Whatever there is of "the natural," it's nothing more than a lone expanse of an Otherless barred Real, an "unbearably light" being – in other words, an ontological immanence in which a countless multitude of fragmentary, ephemeral beings come and go with no overarching or underlying governing order centrally controlling this detotalized expanse. Although, in solidarity with Žižek, I too affirm a version of this, so to speak, materialist and science-shaped denaturalization of nature (*à la* a naturalist dismantling of Nature-with-a-capital-N), I am ill-at-ease with his appeals to quantum physics as the scientific cornerstone for a materialist ontology accommodating within itself a non-reductive model of autonomous subjectivity.

My discomfort arises for two reasons. First, as I maintained earlier in responding to Žižek's reply to me in the current round of our debate, his transubstantiation of quantum physics into a catch-all structural web of constellations and patterns applicable across the entire size-spectrum of existence (up to and including not only human subjects, but even the universe as a [non-]whole) amounts to a performative contradiction. How so? He reintroduces the supposedly banished One-All of a big Other in the formal guise of a natural economy generalized precisely from the discipline he holds up as entailing the scientific debunking of any and every version of (material) nature as a totalized, self-integrated Whole.[10]

My second reason for discomfort is that, as I've argued many times elsewhere on combined Hegelian and biological grounds (for instance: 2008b: 203–9, 269–87; 2010: 86–7, 89–92; 2011c; 2012a; 2012c; 2013; 2014), a reliance upon quantum physics for a thoroughly materialist account of free subjects is neither necessary[11] nor even remotely feasible.[12] Arguably, Žižek's move of going all the way down to the tiny micro-cosms of quantum realms creates more disturbing difficulties than it resolves and puts to rest. Furthermore, in light of the fact that the sci-entific disciplines most directly and pressingly relevant to materialist investigations addressing minded subjective agents (i.e., such biological fields as the neurosciences, genetics, and evolutionary theory) have spon-taneously on their own come to problematize the same renditions of nature Žižek seeks to dissolve with the help of a theoretical physics at a dauntingly massive distance from human-scale reality, this difficulty-fraught Žižekian move perhaps is better left to the side, if only as the set-aside leftover of an Occam's razor.

Quite interestingly, *The Indivisible Remainder* draws to a close with a set of remarks anticipating a number of my above-voiced objections. At the end of "Quantum Physics with Lacan," Žižek spells out some con-sequences of his preceding efforts to highlight a series of striking similari-ties between features of Lacan's conception of the subject *qua parlêtre* (i.e., speaking being, socio-symbolic creature of language) and crucial aspects of quantum entities and events (220–8), albeit in line with a "realist" reading of physics opposed to well-known anti-realist *cum* subjective idealist and/or socio-linguistic constructivist interpretations of quantum-level science (236). He observes (230):

> . . . in the strange phenomena of the quantum universe, the human Spirit as it were encounters itself outside itself, in the guise of its uncanny double. Quantum processes are closer to the human universe of language than any-thing one finds in "nature" (in the standard meaning of the term), yet this very closeness (i.e., the fact that they seem to "imitate" those very features

which, according to the common understanding of the gap that separates nature from man, define the *differentia specifica* of the human universe) makes them incomparably stranger than anything one encounters in "nature."

There can be little doubt that, in this context, Žižek has in mind the specifically Schellingian definition of the uncanny, the one catching Freud's attention and which the latter psychoanalytically paraphrases as "something which ought to have remained hidden but has come to light" (*SE* 17: 241) and associates with the disturbing, unsettling figure of the *Doppelgänger* (*SE* 17: 234–7). In the senseless mathematized realm of quantum beings and happenings, a weird domain superficially seeming utterly alien from the human standpoint of sense (as both perception and meaning), one is taken by surprise; more precisely, one is startled to find oneself face-to-face with an ensemble of altogether-unexpected resemblances (i.e., an "uncanny double"), something "in nature more than nature itself" (to paraphrase the Lacan of the eleventh seminar) *qua* a part of nature eerily mirroring more-than-natural/denaturalized subjectivity.[13]

Having implicitly waved at psychoanalysis through alluding to the Schellingian-Freudian *Unheimliche*, Žižek immediately proceeds to up the analytic ante. He does so with an eye to a type of reticence apropos his manner of mobilizing quantum physics resonating with some of my reservations articulated earlier (1996: 230):

Is not all we have developed hitherto, however, just a set of metaphors and superficial analogies which are simply not binding? To this criticism, which imposes itself with a self-evident persuasiveness, one can provide a precise answer: the irresistible urge to denounce the homologies between the quantum universe and the symbolic order as external analogies with no firm foundation – or, at least, as mere metaphors – is itself an expression and/or effect of the traditional philosophical attitude which compels us to maintain an insurmountable distance between 'nature' and the symbolic universe, prohibiting any 'incestuous' contact between the two domains.

The final paragraph following immediately on the heels of this penultimate paragraph concludes *The Indivisible Remainder* with a forceful reiteration of the claim that quantum physics vindicates Schelling's 1809 thesis according to which human freedom is an irruptive upsurge, an abrupt resurfacing, of the unruly, always-already-past Real of *Grund* within the tamed and domesticated present reality of *Existenz*; this claim rests on a one-to-one correspondence between the Schellingian "ground" and the quantum universe, on the one hand, and Schellingian "existence" and larger-than-sub-atomic realms, on the other (230–1). That said, I want to close this intervention by answering head-on Žižek's diagnosis of critics of his annexations of quantum physics as philosophical neurotics, namely, thinkers hampered by Oedipal incest-issues around "Mother Nature."

To begin with, and without reiterating the multiple criticisms I've already made here that can't be so easily dismissed in this brusque analytic fashion, Žižek's retort might hit other targets, but it definitely misses me. Why? As should be quite evident, I share with Žižek the desire to overcome the resistances to materialist philosophical engagements with the sciences stubbornly raised again and again by the many species of anti-naturalism, with their suspicions of and hostility to all things scientific – not to mention their underlying nature-spirit ontological dualism, however avowed or disavowed. We concur that a materialist account of the subject requires thinking the Hegelian dialectical-style unity-in-difference/difference-in-unity of natural substance and spiritual subjectivity. We differ in our ways and means of going about this intellectual task.

To operate once again as an immanent critic, I am tempted to hijack Žižek's criterion of uncanniness – for him and on the basis of psychoanalytic (rather than philosophical) standards of evidence, the effect of uncanniness aroused by his quantum considerations is a symptom testifying to the truth of these speculations – and turn it into an additional justification for my insistence that biology, rather than physics, is the key scientific territory for the struggles of today's theoretical materialists.[14] If the uncanny is an effect symptomatic of shocking convergences of phenomena apparently opposed to each other as familiarly near/proximate and foreignly far/distant, then the becoming-unfamiliar of the biological portrait of human beings, *à la* the radical, subversive transformation of the long-outdated image of nature commonly associated with life-scientific renditions of "human nature," ought to provoke a sense of uncanniness at least as strong and perturbing as the one Žižek alleges arises from an appreciation of select structural isomorphisms between symbolic-subjective and quantum logics. For example, the dysfunctional, conflict-ridden, and kludge-like configuration of the haphazardly evolved human central nervous system, along with the permeating socio-linguistic mediation of body and brain transpiring via epigenetic and neuroplastic conduits, are biological findings presenting a picture of subjects' material substratums (i.e., their "natural" bodies) clashing markedly with a plethora of ideology-laden scientistic caricatures of humanity prevalent and popular in the contemporary societies of biopolitical late-capitalism.

What could be more unnerving than an "incestuous" confrontation with a nature so close to home (i.e., one's own body as *heimlich*, as the skin in which one feels oneself to be at home), hitherto presumably so recognizable as one's own, that nonetheless suddenly has morphed into something dramatically different and unsuspected? What would it be like, as it were, to wake up one day to the realization that who one took all along to be one's mother (Nature) never was, that this figure was, at best, an imposter living on under the cover of the masquerade of a case of mistaken identity? Even worse, what if one couldn't disown and escape from this always-excessively close *Doppelgänger* "in you more than yourself" – separating oneself from one's own physical body arguably isn't really possible – once the mask was off and the ruse was up? Whether viewed psychoanalytically or otherwise, a new materialist incursion into the life sciences in the spirit (if not the letter) of Engels' "dialectics of nature" (Johnston 2011b; 2014) – political as well as philosophical stakes hang in the balance of this – has a chance to summon forth the powers of *das Unheimliche*, hopefully for the better.

Notes

1 These appropriations are elaborated primarily in the third and final chapter of his 1996 book *The Indivisible Remainder: An Essay on Schelling and Related Matters*, a chapter entitled "Quantum Physics with Lacan."

2 Elsewhere, I cast doubt upon whether Badiou, in light of proclaiming himself to be an ardent materialist, can rely upon a Heideggerian understanding of ontological difference licensing an unqualified, non-dialectical denial of there being any potential ontological implications flowing from the empirical, experimental sciences (2008a; 2011a: 110; 2011b; 2013).

3 Or, pointing back to Robert Boyle's seventeenth-century corpuscular/ mechanical philosophy, one could speak of "Boyling" down.

4 And, to be mentioned as an aside, Hegel's thinking from his Jena period onward suggests that the only criticisms worth advancing are immanent ones (1977: 9).

5 An example of such speculative contortions and acrobatics is Hegel's interpretive dance with the phrenological judgment "Spirit is a bone," a performance greatly appreciated by Žižek and his close colleague Mladen Dolar (Johnston 2008b: 211–34).

6 Incidentally, in the preceding block quotation, Žižek invokes the idea of emergence, and he, like me, knows full well of this notion-word's Archimedean position in the theorizations of various life scientists who exhibit spontaneous dialectical materialist sensibilities. What's more, the life-scientific paradigm of strong emergentism consistent with the dialectics of both Hegelianism and Marxism blocks anything like quantum-physicalist reductivism and/or the *grand Autre* of an ubiquitous natural economy of singular universality.

7 This is by contrast with the tendencies either of a caricatured Hegelian hyper-rationalist panlogicism or Badiou's persisting dependence upon the Heideggerian distinction between the ontological and the ontic. As an aside, I love Žižek's physics-inspired problematizations of Heidegger's ontological difference in his reply to me (2011).

8 A genuine materialism also must reckon with whatever further developments unfurl themselves in this scientific realm of the micro and the miniscule – for example, string theory if and when it satisfactorily consolidates its scientific standing.

9 These envisionings usually represent nature as a harmonious, unified, and exhaustively self-coherent Whole of a One-All, the omnipresent lawful order of an inescapable big Other.

10 Žižek's pointing at Schelling's concept of "powers" (*Potenzen*) likewise is symptomatic of this insofar as the Schellingian philosophies of identity and nature, in which this concept features centrally, are what lead Hegel to quip famously and scathingly about the former's "Absolute" as a "night in which all cows are black" (1977: 9).

11 This is because of such life-scientific resources as emergentism, neuroplasticity, and epigenetics, all of which break with the deterministic and monistic naturalism of mechanistic/non-dialectical materialisms.

12 As observed a while ago here, insurmountable practical limitations having to do with time and number-crunching power thwart in advance attempts at drawing reductive links that would substantiate parallels between quantum worlds and those in which living (and human) beings dwell.

13 Hegel's absolute idealism, with its objective realism, likely lurks around the edges of these musings as a supporting frame (Johnston 2011c; 2014).

14 For the sake of clarity and to head off any potential confusions or misunderstandings at this juncture, my privileging of biology over physics rests on two claims. First, in practice, an empirical-scientific substantiation of hypothesized reductions of the biological to the quantum-physical is impossible due to limits of time and computational power (as I've observed here already). Second, in principle – this holds if one affirms, as I do, the sorts of philosophical principles at the core of the ontology and theory of subjectivity Žižek constructs at the intersection of German idealism and Lacanian psychoanalysis – one shouldn't posit a profound continuity between the

biological and the quantum-physical. Rather, a science-influenced material-ism of an Otherless barred Real and the subjects genetically arising out of this not-One/non-All plane ought to push one into philosophically hypoth-esizing that the epistemological limit of the gap of irreducibility between biology and physics is, in truth, more than a mere impossibility internal to subjects' practical ability to know. Instead, this impossibility is directly revela-tory of a really existing ontological gap, an actual difference-in-kind, between the physical and the biological. Kant and Hegel insist on this in terms of identifying teleological, self-organizing structures and dynamics as the distin-guishing features of organisms over-and-above other material bodies. And, by my lights, a systematic, consistent-with-himself Žižek likewise ultimately would have to abandon his quantum musings so as to stay faithful to his underlying Hegelian-Lacanian fundamental ontology. I also would add that the relevance of biology to reflections on human beings as minded subjects is as solidly established at the empirical-scientific level as reasonably could be demanded, whereas the links (if any there are) between quantum physics and theories of thinking subjectivity, however fascinating and intriguing, have thus far remained a matter of pure (and, as in the case of Penrose, contro-versial and discredited) speculation and nothing more.

References

Althusser, Louis (2006) "The Underground Current of the Materialism of the Encounter." *Philosophy of the Encounter: Later Writings, 1978–1987*, ed. François Matheron and Oliver Corpet, trans. G. M. Goshgarian. London: Verso, pp. 163–207.

Freud, Sigmund (1953–74) *The Standard Edition of the Complete Psychological Works of Sigmund Freud*, 24 vols., ed. and trans. James Strachey, Anna Freud, Alix Strachey, and Alan Tyson. London: Hogarth Press and the Institute of Psycho-Analysis.

— "The Uncanny." *SE* 17: 217–56.

Hegel, G. W. F. (1970) *Phänomenologie des Geistes, Werke in zwanzig Bänden*, 3rd edn., Eva Moldenhauer and Karl Markus Michel. Frankfurt am Main: Suhrkamp.

— (1977) *Phenomenology of Spirit*, trans. A. V. Miller. Oxford: Oxford University Press.

Johnston, Adrian (2007) "Slavoj Žižek's Hegelian Reformation: Giving a Hearing to *The Parallax View*." *Diacritics: A Review of Contemporary Criticism* 37.1: 3–20.

— (2008a) "What Matter(s) in Ontology: Alain Badiou, the Hebb-Event, and Materialism Split from Within." *Angelaki: Journal of the Theoretical Humanities* 13.1: 27–49.

— (2008b) *Žižek's Ontology: A Transcendental Materialist Theory of Subjectivity.*
Evanston: Northwestern University Press.

— (2010) "The Misfeeling of What Happens: Slavoj Žižek, Antonio Damasio,
and a Materialist Account of Affects." *Subjectivity* 3.1: 76–100.

— (2011a) "Hume's Revenge: À Dieu, Meillassoux?" *The Speculative Turn: Continental Materialism and Realism*, eds Levi Bryant, Nick Srnicek, and Graham
Harman, Melbourne: Re.press, pp. 92–113.

— (2011b) "Repeating Engels: Renewing the Cause of the Materialist Wager
for the Twenty-First Century," *Theory @ Buffalo* 15: 141–82.

— (2011c) "Second Natures in Dappled Worlds: John McDowell, Nancy
Cartwright, and Hegelian-Lacanian Materialism." *Umbr(a): A Journal of the
Unconscious.* "The Work," ed. Matthew Rigilano and Kyle Fetter, pp. 71–91.

— (2012a) "'Naturalism or anti-naturalism? No, thanks – both are worse!':
Science, Materialism, and Slavoj Žižek." *La Revue Internationale de Philosophie*
66, no. 261: 321–46.

— (2012b) "Slavoj Žižek." *The Blackwell Companion to Continental Philosophy*,
2nd edn., ed. William Schroeder. Oxford: Blackwell Publishing.

— (2012c) "Think Big: Toward a Grand Neuropolitics – or, Why I am not an
immanent naturalist or vital materialist," *Neuroscience and Political Theory:
Thinking the Body Politic*, ed. Frank Vander Valk. New York: Routledge, pp.
156–77.

— (2013) *The Outcome of Contemporary French Philosophy: Prolegomena to Any
Future Materialism*, vol. 1: *The Outcome of Contemporary French Philosophy.* Evanston: Northwestern University Press.

— (2014) *A Weak Nature Alone: Prolegomena to Any Future Materialism*, vol. 2:
A Weak Nature Alone. Evanston: Northwestern University Press, 2012b.

Lenin, V. I. (1972) *Materialism and Empirio-Criticism.* Peking: Foreign Languages
Press.

Schelling, F. W. J. (1936) *Philosophical Inquiries into the Nature of Human Freedom
and matters connected therewith*, trans. James Gutmann. Chicago: Open Court
Publishing Company.

Žižek, Slavoj (1996) *The Indivisible Remainder: An Essay on Schelling and Related
Matters.* London: Verso.

— (2004) *Organs without Bodies: On Deleuze and Consequences.* New York:
Routledge.

— (2006) *The Parallax View.* Cambridge: MIT Press.

— (2010a) "Some Concluding Notes on Violence, Ideology, and Communist
Culture." *Subjectivity* 3.1: 101–16.

— (2010b) *À travers le réel: Entretiens avec Fabien Tarby.* Paris: Nouvelle Éditions
Lignes.

— (2011) "Reply to Adrian Johnston." *La Revue Internationale de Philosophie.*

6

Slavoj Žižek's Eco-Chic

Verena Andermatt Conley

Agent provocateur par excellence of critical and cultural theory, Slavoj Žižek has touched both directly and obliquely on every type of culture war waged in the arena of capitalism today. It comes as no surprise that he should pronounce himself on issues concerning the environment. Žižek faces squarely what is often perceived as a difficult and somewhat uncertain area that many culture critics are reticent to broach. Ecology resonates in his exchanges with Glyn Daly in the same author's *Conversations with Žižek* (2004); it figures in an address on "The Liberal Utopia" he delivered in Athens (2007); it is at the center in his conversation with Astra Taylor in *Examined Life: Excursions with Eight Contemporary Thinkers* (2008 dvd; 2009). In 2008 he also engaged the environment in both a lecture "Censorship Today: Violence or Ecology as a New Opium for the Masses" and an article, "Nature and its Discontents" (reprinted under the title "Unbehagen in der Natur" in his *In Defense of Lost Causes*). Most recently, ecology is actively present in *Living in the End Times* (2010).

However scattered or circumstantial they may appear, the reflections are of a consistent and forceful voice and of strong and avowedly Euro-centric philosophical tenor. Repeatedly calling into question the effects of global capitalism, they examine what the latter has wrought and were it may lead us. For Žižek the environment concerns all and everyone and, as a rule, it cannot be countenanced outside of capitalism. When pronouncing himself on ecology, the philosopher condemns unsparingly a capitalist system that keeps expanding, reinventing itself and, in a doomsday scenario forever surpassing its own limits. Against common assumptions he declares that capitalism is a universal and ecology a particular (*Living in the End Times*, 334). At our historical moment, we witness everywhere, especially in the media, a tendency to naturalize capitalism – to the point where it is replaced with "economy" and simply goes without saying. In their common struggle against anything that is perceived to be even remotely socialist, liberals and conservatives alike present capitalism in the name of the best of all worlds. Žižek argues that a true ecology cannot be thought without socialism or even without communism. Ecology too calls for a genuine collective experience shared by one and all. In the paragraphs to follow, I will work through Žižek's pronouncements on ecology, especially at the core of "Nature and its Discontents," before examining how they percolate through his other writings and, finally, assessing his theory in terms of ecological dilemmas today.

Ecology and the Emancipatory Subject

Žižek wonders if there exist today any areas of disruption that can be found within global capitalism's own process. The response is affirmative. Within capitalism what he calls four antagonisms or counteractive inter-related areas can be located: (1) ecology *per se*; (2) private property, including intellectual property but also vital resources such as water and raw materials; (3) socio-ethical implications of new techno-scientific development, above all in biogenetics where the profit-motive reigns supreme and covert manipulations of humans abound; (4) around the globe, forms of new apartheid, national borders as well as real or symbolic walls that cities have erected, mainly since the turn of the new century, in order to contain the sprawling slums at their peripheries ("Nature and its Discontents," 38–41). These four antagonisms disrupt the smooth functioning of the capitalist system that continuously gives rise to them. The first three pertain to what Žižek, borrowing an expression from Michael Hardt and Toni Negri, calls "the commons" (44). They include culture, shared infrastructure (roads, mail service) as well as external and internal nature (resources such as water, forest and the biogenetic inheritance). In its emphasis on privatization capitalism threatens these commons to the point of self-annihilation of humanity. It is the reference to these commons, neither private nor public, that justifies for Žižek a return to a new "communism" (44). The fourth term, however, is the privileged one. Žižek distinguishes between the Included and the Excluded. The

Included or a rising symbolic class consists of "managers, journalists and PR [public relations] people, academics, artists, etc."[1] The slum dwellers or the Excluded function both as a symptom and the excess of the capitalist system. Theirs is the new proletarian position of the twenty-first century. Žižek implies that until recently ways of finding emancipation from degrading conditions of life had been the purview of utopian social thinkers, Fourierists and others, who saw what industry had done to the European and American landscapes of the nineteenth century. Intellectuals and workers alike had sought to find avenues of release from inhuman confinement.[2] Their acts and actions aimed at changing the nature of things in view of the ongoing history they felt they were shaping. Now, however, faced with the possibility of an ecological or nuclear catastrophe and genetic mutations, we can rely no longer on the safeguarding role that the limited scope of our acts in the sphere of our lives had assured, nor can we say that whatever we do, history will continue along its course ("Censorhips and Violence," 1,1). Unlike the workers of the nineteenth century, the Excluded do not even constitute a class. They live outside the state in areas that are indicated on official maps as blanks. While ecology concerns all of humanity, for Žižek it must be thought in the context of the emancipation of the Excluded.

Considering ecology in the context of the new emancipatory subject, Žižek holds that *contra* the present ideological mystification of ecology, in effect *contra* the limited lessons of a balanced, harmonious nature that many of its New Age adepts impose with righteous sanctimony – a candid view or an ecology that works *against itself* can come about only when we first think the immense emancipatory potential of the slum dwellers. At this juncture antagonism becomes a crucial piece in Žižek's argument and an indication of the simultaneously practical and utopian direction his writings on ecology are taking. Although, as he stated, the threat of an ecological catastrophe – both man-made and purely contingent – is all-encompassing, the antagonism of the new global slum becomes a true site of resistance. The slum inhabitants of the twenty-first century – contrary to those who fly over their dwellings (if dwellings they are) or would wish to forget them, are in terms of sheer numbers, hardly a "marginal phenomenon" ("Nature," 40). Žižek sees zones of excluded populations being one of the "few authentic 'evental sites' in today's society" from where productive antagonism can be marshaled. Slums inspire terror among the Included; they destabilize their quotidian world. They thus open a space that makes possible an event both as interruption and negativity. For Žižek, an event affects all those who are in the field of its situation, including those who choose to ignore it but whose presence causes them to lose their innocence or blissful ignorance of the slum condition. What is revealed to them is precisely the fact that they ignore the event.

While recognizing that the Excluded make do by virtue of improvised models of social life that in fact inspire vital forces of solidarity and have their own economy, Žižek sees them nonetheless as dwelling in free space, excluded from all substantial ties (41).[3] He concludes: "What we should be looking for are the signs of new forms of social awareness that will emerge from the slum collectives. They will be the germs of the future" (42). Germs, which can read equivocally, is taken here as a double entendre, as a sign of growth and conversely, of viral spread.[4] At this historical moment we are witnessing "destructured" masses, poor and deprived in every way that live in utterly destitute urban conditions. As a result, Žižek concludes (perhaps somewhat hastily) that whoever lives in the slums of Bamako or Shanghai is not essentially different from anyone who lives in the *banlieue* of Paris or the ghettos of Chicago. The important task of emancipatory politics of the twenty-first century is to politicize, in other words, to organize and discipline the slum dwellers. In slums where state intervention is non-existent emancipatory politics must begin from the ground up – but with the help of someone to organize the inhabitants. Action must shape and form, it must confer a signature upon the currently "destructured masses" of slum-dwellers, those whom the adepts of global capitalism regard as "the animals of the globe" ("Nature," 42).

We need (and on this point Žižek is adamant) a proletarian position, that is, in the words of Jacques Rancière, the part of no part. We cannot simply have recourse to an empty signifier like the "people" that would be an avatar of the utopian image of a "rainbow coalition" (43). Žižek finds a qualitative difference in the gap that separates the first three antagonisms (ecology, private property, biogenetic interventions) from that which separates the Excluded from the Included. It is this last antagonism that is the point of reference for the others (45). The very terror inspired by the Excluded creates the conditions that will allow the *event* to stabilize in a new order.

Without this fourth antagonism all others lose their political edge and their subversive potential. The field of study turns the environment toward issues of sustainable development; the idea of "property" toward physical and intellectual inflections of the word (where battles over rules of law bear on the environment); and, no less, biogenetics into a welter of ethical issues.[5] When all is said and done, if we fight for the environment without keeping in view the fourth antagonism between the Included and the Excluded we obtain not true universality, but only private concerns in the Kantian sense of the term (45). Žižek repeatedly invokes the example of liberals who patronize Whole Foods or Starbucks because they sell products that in and of themselves claim to be politically progressive acts. Inert political gestures and consumption merge. Indulging in "green chic," these liberals engage, Žižek asserts, in pseudo-activity rather than in a truly symbolic act.[6] A truly symbolic act that interrupts the system, such as the one that would emancipate the destructured masses, is needed. How this organization of slum dwellers will come about, Žižek does not say. Adapting Winston Churchill's famous dictum to the effect that democracy is a terrible system but it is the best, he concludes that politics are bad but they are the best we have. We need a new breed of politicians ("Ecology," 174).[7] He remains silent as to where and how *they* will come about.

Ecology without Nature

The acting out by the Included thus inspires in them an additional feel-good moralism. It is felt in the way the pressure of the Excluded is experienced within established political spaces. This pressure always carries both fear and terror ("Nature," 46). The true choice, Žižek writes, is between fear and terror. From the fear of the unidentified *other* who destabilizes the navigational charts that guide the Included to their fear of losing the "Big Other" (or symbolic forces of meaning that structure their daily lives and govern their pseudo-activities), the Included – "we" in Žižek's parlance – sense terror when realizing that no meaning can palliate menace or symbolic wall isolate them from the Excluded. Hence we need an ecology *without nature* since it is the latter that gives illusory depth and texture to our life-world (48). We need entirely new coordinates. However, the Included want to avoid risk and thus defer the recognition of their own freedom from symbolic ties. Within capitalism, New Ageism, Žižek argues, replaces terror with fear. The Included want to avoid seeing that structurally their life-world does not exist. In addition, nature as a stable background has now, because of ecological troubles, also become a source of danger. It is within ecology that a line can be drawn that separates emancipatory terror from a politics of fear at

its purest (53). Now that ecology as a socio-political movement has all
but disappeared, a new "ecology of fear," an expression Žižek borrows
from Mike Davis, has every chance of developing into the predominant
ideology of global capitalism – "a new opium of the masses replacing the
declining religion" (53). Žižek concludes that what "we" need first and
foremost is an ecology without nature. Borrowing the formula from the
title of Tim Morton's eponymous book, he argues that nature as we
know it, that is, as a background or a life-world made up of heavy symbolic texture and ties does not exist. There is no such harmonious, balanced nature to which humans can be constantly urged to return. Such
a nature, Žižek vituperates, is pure ideology.

It can be noted that Žižek joins the theoretical debates on nature and
ecology at a late stage. Following Claude Lévi-Strauss' early lead, the
environment in theory was present in post-1968 thinkers, from Gregory
Bateson to Michel Serres, Gilles Deleuze, Félix Guattari and others.
Much of Žižek's argument, while valid, has been discussed by others and,
for the most part, also in the context of a critique of capitalism. Nature
as a background against which humans move about was replaced with
feedback loops, cybernetics and atom theory, complemented by Ilya
Prigogine and Isabelle Stenger's influential book, *La nouvelle alliance* (1979,
translated as *Order out of Chaos, Man's New Dialogue with Nature*, 1984),
the sum of which aimed at bringing the humanities and sciences back
together after a hiatus of several centuries. Humans were not so much
said to be "embedded" – one of the main terms Žižek criticizes – in
nature than part of a nature that had been entirely reassessed. Nature was
no longer seen as "harmonious" but always far from equilibrium. In what
became known as complexity theory, nature was always in movement.
In such a system, any "order" is but temporary, emerging out of chaos.
A new order will always either slowly or abruptly, that is, often randomly,
come about. Stephen J. Gould, a popular scientist known for his dictum
that evolution is a random walk in complexity and not an ordered progression is not far from such hypotheses. Gould, whose statement to
the effect that nature is but a series of contingencies and major catastrophes Žižek likes to quote, is himself part of such complexity thinking
("Censorship" I, 3).

It was also in the post-1968 years under the influence of new scientific
discoveries in an era of emancipatory discourses that many projects of
modernity were being criticized and reformulated. With a reassessment
of nature and its relation with culture, many practices destined to control
nature, from the building of dams to the growing of ill-suited crops

during the Green Revolution or the introduction of non-productive technologies that often resulted in ecological catastrophes, illness and starvation of Third World inhabitants who were forced to become slum dwellers, were being abandoned.[8] Žižek bypasses this kind of thinking to focus on a New Ageism that came about during the Reagan years and that can now be seen as a conservative appropriation of the emancipatory discourses of the sixties. The latter obfuscated a very productive way of thinking in the context of the political rhetoric of the sixties.[9] We cannot not agree with Žižek who criticizes New Ageism to argue that a romanticized nature as life world is pure ideology. The philosopher disparages a mystified relation between humans and nature that in his estimation always goes hand in hand with a fear of change, a position taken by religious leaders and environmentalists alike. While praising science, Žižek nonetheless adds that overly rational scientists too who practice what he calls a "university discourse" based on knowledge and power, hold on to a worldview that is also heavily ideologized. Yet, he is adamant, we have to do away with nature as Big Other that tells humans they are embedded. Nature does not exist, we all live in second nature and in language. Furthermore, technologies and the discovery of the genome did away with concepts of nature and humans altogether.

The discovery, as we have seen, is not entirely new. Žižek elaborates what was well known in his own terms. To what he dismisses as "the embedded human," he opposes the Cartesian subject as the subject of modernity, separated from nature.[10] Without rehearsing what he had developed over the years on the construction of the subject and the Big Other, he repeats, based on his signature readings of Hegel and Lacan, his conclusion that the Cartesian subject tears itself away from nature, animality and instincts. Humans are born into language, hence always into a certain degree of abstraction. They are born into second nature. It is this empty subject that ideology appropriates and manipulates.

Related to ecology, are other issues of the common, that is, mainly those concerning intellectual property laws and biogenetics where fear prevents real progress. Žižek also blames the media for spending time on mindless issues rather than debating what is happening in the area of intellectual property laws that prevent free circulation of information and especially in the area of biogenetics.[11] He warns that while "we in the West" are mired in endless debates on ethical and legal limits of biogenetic experiments and procedures, the Chinese simply press their own agendas ahead. Not only does the state control and steer the biogenetic mass of its citizens, but biogenetics are also engaged in a race for profits

(*Living in the End Times*, 341). At the same time, biogenetics have unlimited possibilities to help humans live in today's world. Their possibilities, when imagined in today's terms, seem to border onto science fiction. Žižek emphasizes that projects, from "micro-organisms that detect and eliminate cancer cells to whole factories that transform solar energy into usable fuel" ("Nature," 55) cannot be realized where a politics of fear reigns supreme. Since we are now capable of manipulating and recreating human and natural life, we should excel in this direction for the betterment of humanity and without being afraid of manipulating "nature" and humans alike in a productive way that benefits ecology.

Fear and Terror

Fear, a product of ideology, must be replaced with the terror of existence. We must – Žižek likes to be prescriptive – realize that there is no Big Other and face the abyss of our existence, something even Heidegger did not dare to do ("Nature," 64). When there is no Big Other, humans are free to invent and reinvent themselves and the world. Introduced via quotations from Aeschylus, Sophocles and Che Guevara – Žižek likes to mix levels – this freedom leads him to conclude by appealing to the four moments of what his friend Badiou called "the eternal Idea" of revolutionary-egalitarian Justice" (69) without which there is no possibility for facing ecology politically:

1. Strict egalitarian justice – all people should pay the same price in renunciation of what promotes ecological degradation.
2. Terror – ruthless punishment of all who violate the imposed protective measures (aimed at curbing environmental destruction).
3. Voluntarism – the only way to confront the threat of ecological catastrophes by large-scale, collective decision that will run counter to the 'spontaneous' immanent logical of capitalist development.
4. Trust in people – a wager that the large majority of the earth's populations will support these severe measures, will see them as their own, and will be ready to participate in their enforcement (and, along the way, will celebrate public heroes who enable these measures).

Such a mix of egalitarian justice, terror and quasi-Stalinist measures, Žižek believes, will help humanity face and resolve its ecological dilemmas.

In his last words, Žižek asks: "Could this chance have arisen without the division that colors the entire terrain of struggle, the separation between the Excluded and the Included? Isn't nature no less than culture impossible without its discontented? (70) Nature suddenly reappears and the Excluded introduce the contingency from which change can take place. Thus, the Excluded are needed to introduce a chance for change. When it is lifted from the original text and transposed into "Unbehagen in der Natur" the controversial statement attesting that the excluded are essential for a productive antagonism and a political ecology is erased! (461)

Apocalypse vs Apocalypticism

By way of the Idea of revolutionary-egalitarian Justice, linking Western philosophy and the French revolution, Žižek searches for a true ecology not recuperated by ideology. Paraphrasing Walter Benjamin, Žižek states that "the task of a revolution is not to help the historical tendency or necessity to realize itself, but to 'stop the train' of history that runs toward the precipice of global catastrophe" ("Nature," 69). This insight, he sustains, takes on new importance today with the prospect of an ecological catastrophe. Never doubting the reality of ecological problems, Žižek nonetheless continues to caution about the uncertainties and the difficulties of interventions ("Ecology," 170). Ecology, he repeats tirelessly, quoting Donald Rumsfeld, contains many "unknown unknowns." The outcome of any intervention is uncertain. To illustrate this point, over and again he repeatedly (and I believe, somewhat unfortunately) provides the example of birds in China such as in his conversation with Astra Taylor (171). In the late nineteen-forties, the Chinese Communists noticed that birds were eating too many seeds in the fields. They decided to kill the birds only to discover that parasites were now eating the seeds. It turned out that the birds ate not only the seeds but also the parasites. The Chinese now had to import birds from the Soviet Union. For Žižek, the episode shows that the birds were not simply trash but had a "function." It can also be said that the birds provided a link in a complex system and that elements in a habitat are interconnected. A missing link can easily lead to a catastrophe that is not always productive. Much of ecology now aims at repairing similar damages, often by reverting to older orders and technologies.

Yet Žižek as a philosopher of the abyss does not recognize such links. Asserting boldly that because of ecological catastrophes, genetic mutations and nuclear perils, we may all disappear, he continues to criticize ideology that mystifies and also mythifies a real that, for him, is not simply unattainable. Faithful to his training in psychoanalysis he updates the discipline in order to adapt to an increasingly abstract world of computers bereft of symbolic ties or their textures and tesselations. When elaborating his thoughts, he works mainly from and with other texts such as Lacan, Hegel, and Alain Badiou – whom he chooses to be a current intercessor. In addition, each of his texts seems to be written in dialogue with someone else's article or book such as Tim Morton in "Nature and its Discontents," or Elisabeth Kübler-Ross in his recent *Living in the End Times*. The Swiss-born psychologist discussing human's reactions when faced with a terminal illness distinguishes five stages of experience, from denial, anger, bargaining, and depression to acceptance (*Living*, xi). Giving his philosophical argument a strong psychoanalytic inflection, Žižek further elaborates on ecology throughout the book but mainly in "Interlude Four: Apocalypse at the Gate," inserted between "Depression" and "Acceptance." He also draws on a study by Catherine Malabou, *Les Nouveaux Blessés*, in which the philosopher makes the case that trauma today comes from the outside and does not refer to any previous sexual trauma as in Freud. Humans today are facing external shocks (from genocide and wars to starvation and ecological catastrophes). They live, Žižek concludes, in apocalyptic times. The four antagonisms from the earlier texts have now become the four horsemen of the apocalypse, i.e. the ecological crisis, imbalances within the system (stemming from privatization and intellectual property to resources and raw materials), the consequences of the biogenetic revolution, and the explosive growth of social divisions and exclusions. Already in "Nature and its Discontents," Žižek had argued that religion more than science might become a site of resistance for ecological issues. In *Living in the End Times*, ecological justice, derived from an egalitarianism introduced by the French Revolution, is now complemented by another inherited from Christianity. As in other instances, ideology mystifies reality: its imaginary dimension clouds the truth everyone knows but does not want to see with three types of apocalypticisms, Christian fundamental, New Age and techno-digital-post-human. As he did with fear and terror, Žižek now opposes apocalypticism to apocalypse. We should not see the end-times arriving with the fanfare of a big bang, after which something entirely unforeseen will take place, but rather as a series of small-scale ecological disturbances

(*Living*, 350). With a signature mix of wit and irony, Žižek declares that capitalism will recuperate everything, from melting ice caps to the greening of Greenland.

Reviewing the stages that the intensification of capitalism had taken since the nineteen-sixties, he argues that a new network-capitalism has replaced a more hierarchical model. [12] A new "'spirit of capitalism' triumphantly recuperated the egalitarian and anti-hierarchical rhetoric of 1968, presenting itself as a successful libertarian revolt against oppressive social organization of corporate capitalism and of 'really existing socialism'" (356). This capitalism, Žižek maintains, is exemplified by a further shift in advertising, that is even more pernicious than the one Jean Baudrillard criticized several decades ago. Over the last decade, Žižek notes an increasing mobilization of socio-ideological motifs such as ecology or social solidarity in advertisement (356). The experience is that while consuming a product, anyone and everyone is part of a larger collective movement helping nature or the poor. The "ethical consumer" is born when the "very act of participating in consumerist activity is simultaneously presented as a participation in the struggle against the evils ultimately caused by capitalist consumerism" (356). The logo, the symbolic coin of capitalism now sustains a whole world of meaning.

Having argued throughout his writings that every catastrophe, including those of ecology, brings with it a new opening, an emergent possibility, to illustrate the point, he appeals to one of his standard examples from the seventh art: in the Los Angeles of Robert Altman's *Short Cuts*, conflating a number of Raymond Carver's short stories, a car crash opens a possibility and brings about an entirely new configuration that bears on a variety of protagonists in their different situations. Žižek develops what he broached in "Nature and its Discontents" with the Eternal Idea of revolutionary-egalitarian Justice in the context of ecology, to open the possibility of a communism that would replace capitalism. "When our natural commons – that include ecology – are threatened, neither market nor state will save us, but only a properly communist mobilization" (334). In these "end times," only the collective experience of a true "communism now" will bring about the required changes. The refrain is familiar. For Žižek there can be no true ecology under capitalism. Culture wars are always waged from within capitalism, that is, among the Included. To be truly political, ecology has to deal with the emancipatory subject. Communism as outlined in the four points under the heading of "revolutionary-egalitarian Justice" would be better suited to ecology. In addition, he introduces a "Christian materialism" that brings together both "the rejection of a divine Otherness and the element of unconditional commitment" (352). Yet, when again asking the question, what is to be done? Žižek refers one more time to art.[13] The first indications of the "cause regained," he concludes, "are given in art" (365).

The examples he provides run from the nineteenth century to our days, from Kafka, Wagner and Melville to Dziga Vertov and the television show, *Public Heroes* and others.[14] Žižek places emphasis on Kafka's last story, "Josephine the Singer," whose topic is a truly collective experience in which no charismatic leader is found. The mouse community in Kafka's story knows that Josephine cannot sing. It treats her as a celebrity but without fetishizing her, that is, without giving her any material privilege (368). Vertov's *Man with a Movie Camera* becomes an "exemplary case of cinematic communism" (378) in its affirmation of life in its multiplicity and its daily activities. What makes it "communist" is the underlying assertion of the "univocity of being" so that the usual hierarchies are all equalized, including the communist opposition between old and new (378).[15] If the first two deal with a collective experience, with a genuine celebration of a communism now, "Bartleby" deals with an unlinking, or an act of refusal and non-participation in the system. Bartleby's famous formula, "I would prefer not to," is a truly symbolic act that distances the passive character from the agitation and pseudo-activity around him.

The refusal of pseudo-activity and embrace of symbolic action that would interrupt the system cannot be done without passionate and unconditional commitment. A truly symbolic act makes possible the collective experience of a "communism now" (*Living*, x). Žižek makes it clear. The question is not: What can we use of communism today, but what does it mean to live the Idea of communism in our times? This question is followed by a commitment based on belief. Reversing the formula of advertisement, Žižek writes that "we must believe it to perceive it" (338), he opts for passion against rational science, that in his opinion is tainted with ideology. As already hinted at in "Nature and its Discontents," he turns religion, or rather, a belief without religion, into a site of resistance. More strongly than before, he criticizes science based on knowledge and power. On the one hand, both belief without religion and passionate commitment are now capable of opening an evental site as they do in Kafka's animal Utopia and in Dziga Vertov. On the other, Bartleby's simple refusal becomes a symbolic act interrupting liberal pseudo-activity of the New Age-Whole-Foods-Starbucks-buy-a-jean-and-save-Haiti variety. Ironically, Žižek reaches this conclusion at the end of a four hundred-page book. Describing elsewhere his own failed analysis, he mentions that he could not be analyzed because he talked all the time to fill the void.[16] Is Žižek's voluminous writing also filling a void? Or is it creating one, thus opening a space from which one can engage in a more just and political ecological thinking?

"What is to be done"?

Stressing the importance of ecological dilemmas, Žižek states that "ecology is the question where the fate of humanity is decided. We may all disappear" ("Nature," 58). In an interview on Al Jazeera with Riz Kahn (November 11, 2010) he remarks that laws will not suffice to solve ecological problems. We need other ways of thinking. Recently, he quotes Saint Paul (*Ephesians* 6:12): "For our struggle is not against the flesh and blood but against leaders, against authorities, against the world rulers of this darkness, against the spiritual wickedness in the heavens" (*Living*, xv). Translating the apostle's rhetoric into today's language, he writes: "Our struggle is not against actual corrupt individuals but against those in power in general, against their authority, against the global order and the ideological mystification which sustains it" (xv).

And Žižek certainly does just that. He praises those like Badiou who take risks and engage in fidelity to a Truth-Event, even if it ends in catastrophe, as well as those who reject the liberal ideology of victimhood that reduces politics to a program avoiding the worst ecological scenarios, to renouncing all positive projects and pursuing the least bad option. He elaborates on his own avowedly political philosophy predicated on the abyss of human existence and on contingencies to the point of suggesting, provocatively, "what if the world as a Whole is not a thing-in-itself but merely a regulative Idea of our mind, something our mind imposes on the raw multitude of sensations in order to be able to experience it as a well-rendered meaningful Whole?" ("Nature," 57). What if our "relationship of faith in Nature, in the primordial harmony between mind and reality, is the most elementary form of idealism, of reliance on the big Other? What if the true materialist position starts (and in a way ends) with the acceptance of the In-itself as a meaningless chaotic manifold?" (58). Žižek tears himself away from any kind of order that would smack of ideology and forces his readers to confront the fact that in the current world meaning is imposed, and it is almost invariably imposed by those in power. A real is always the product of ideology. He now urges his readers to commit themselves passionately to bring an egalitarian order to this chaos that would also be ecological.

Regardless of whether one wants to enter into Žižek's philosophical framework or not, his is a very strong and stark position that serves as a wake up call for many liberals, New Agers and academics whose bad faith he repeatedly admonishes. With his wit and his force, the philosopher is at his best when he antagonizes the liberal position with what he derides as its "feel-good moralism" ("Ecology," 177). It remains nonetheless that the deliberate level of abstraction becomes a problem for ecological practices. Unlike a philosopher like Etienne Balibar who argues that in an accelerated world, theory and practice must merge more than ever, Žižek keeps his philosophizing deliberately at a distance from any specific situation to which it might apply.

The remoteness becomes apparent in his concrete pronouncements on ecology – a term that is never really defined, from the ill-chosen example of the birds eating seeds in China to others he also enumerates in a conversation with Astra Taylor. When Žižek ironizes that true ecologists should not want to have a perfect garden (166), he may be closer to the truth than he thinks. Indeed, perfect gardens obtained with the services of "Chemilawn" and weed killers are the obsession of the non-believers who imitate colorful pictures from magazines. The "true ecologist" will choose native plants adapted to the soil where he or she lives. In the same conversation, Žižek derides ecologists for drinking water and taking a walk in pristine woods (163–4). In rejecting those who drink water out of plastic bottles marketed and sold by the Coca Cola conglomerate, his salutary words merit strong applause. However, pristine forests are more likely the result of management that breeds monocultures, trees genetically modified for faster growth and higher profits. "True" ecological forests, far from pristine, do not welcome eco-tourists. They are full of rotting and decaying trees, thorny bushes and hordes of biting bugs.

Žižek's notion of revolutionary-egalitarian Justice that brings together ecology and the Excluded is fortuitously welcome. Questionable is the high level of abstraction that seems closer to intellectual gesture than commitment or praxis. Ecology, for sure, as Deleuze and Guattari put it in the wake of Paul Virilio, has to be thought from today's conditions. For Deleuze, in our world a chosen voice is no longer to be heard and even art, which often has an ecological edge in its political aesthetic, it too is colored by money (Deleuze, *Negotiations*, 1995). In the early

nineteen-nineties, he sees only the possibility of opening of small inter-
ruptions – vacuoles – from which to think otherwise. As Derrida had
argued for democracy both as an absolute idea and as a series of empirical
practices, so also micro-practices are vital to ecology, from restoring
habitat to bringing water to dealing with drought and famine and protest-
ing forced evacuation. Trivializing micro-practices, perhaps as a consequence of the high logical category of his argumentations, Žižek accuses
ecologists of being liberals obsessed with "green chic." But is he not
himself in danger of being tainted by radical or eco-chic, in other words,
far from biology and chemistry, and even the dynamic processes that
informed ecology requires? For the question of the emancipatory subject,
we can also turn to Etienne Balibar whom Žižek elsewhere praises. We
can refer to Balibar by recalling how persisting is the pressure of the
Excluded on the Included. The demands of the former, he notes, are
always refused, but in the end they remain urgent and compelling. Over
time, openings are created and changes do come about.

Not unlike Deleuze, Žižek himself avowedly thinks by difference and
rectificaton. In the context of ecology he addresses his own repetitions
and, too, his contradictions. When, in the course of their conversation,
Astra Taylor reminds Žižek of his protean shifts of position, within
minutes the philosopher had told her, "one must love this world" only
to say a little later, "one must hate this world." He responds that she
should choose what she wants and whatever works ("Ecology," 170,
181). We ought not be afraid, he tells another interlocutor, to change
our own position (*A travers le réel*, 85). Over time, repetitions enable the
emergence of new possibilities. This is, for Žižek, an eternal idea. Truth
cannot be attained directly. Choices always need to be made. Sometimes
a wrong choice is the condition of possibility for a true choice. However,
for the philosopher, today's choice is between a liberal hierarchical order
or egalitarian terror. Only after the worst choice, something will open
for a new choice. What then is the Idea of communism today? At the
empirical level, writes Žižek, it is always Beckett. He recalls the sentence
of Beckett according to which one always fails, tries again, in a slightly
better manner (85).

Would that be the Idea of ecology? How can we think of ecology
today? We can hypothesize, at the risk of assuming a liberal stance, that
ecologists have to proceed at the "empirical" level in ways similar to
those Žižek proposes. Both global and local, ecology involves many different areas from pollution to changing wrong technologies to assuring
the survival of humans but also of animals and plants and, to quote one

of the philosopher's favorite codas, "etc." Many of these ecologists from all over the world, far from being simply New Agers do have the "belief" that Žižek finds crucial for action. While we cannot agree more with Žižek that we need a new breed of politician, we can say that in the meantime many groups of grassroot ecologists who often assist the "Excluded" proceed by trial and error toward an ever-changing truth. They too are in the situation of the Beckett character whom Žižek likes to quote: Will fail, must go on.

Notes

1 Paul Virilio argues that the "new social pyramid" is comprised of CEOs, media people, bureaucrats at the top and consumers at the bottom. He also sees the majority of people living in a worldwide *banlieue* or slum. However, in this configuration, there is no more space for intellectuals.

2 Jacques Rancière's *The Night of Labor. The Worker's Dream in Nineteenth Century France* (1989).

3 For a provocative and somewhat controversial analysis of the "ecology of slums," see Sam Kwinter (2010). He argues that in addition to having what he calls a "third ecology," slum dwellers are vital to the dominant economy with which they interact as well.

4 It is reminiscent (at least for readers trained in French cultural studies) of what the novelist Emile Zola had articulated in *Germinal*, the novel in the Rougon-Macquart saga in which the promise of a future community among coal mines in northeastern France arises from the depths of a network of sordid tunnels. Unlike Zola's monumental and majestic stuff of social and environmental contradiction that was apace of its own time, Žižek envisages today's slums as nodes in the ganglia of global capitalism.

5 Peter H. Raven, *Nature and Society: The Quest for a Sustainable World*. Washington, DC: National Academy Press, 2000.

6 Žižek is relying on psychoanalysis but also on the lapidary distinction between *gesture* and *action* that Sartre had developed in his political writings of the postwar era. It can be added that gaps open among Žižek's Included as well, that is, between those who frequent these places and the majority who cannot afford to enjoy them.

7 In "Censorship" Žižek observes most astutely how today's predominant model of politics is that of "postpolitical biopolitics." The latter replaces ideological struggles with expert management and administration, while regulating the welfare of human life. He concludes that with a depoliticized, socially objective expert administration and coordination of interests as the

zero level of politics, the only way to introduce passion is through fear (II, 3).

8 Examples of forced displacements include people affected by the building of dams from the Sardar Sarovar Dam on the Narmada river, documented by Arundhati Roy, to those on the Mekong in Cambodia that drained the Tonle Sap, once lyrically sung by Marguerite Duras, to that of the Three Gorges on the Yangtze. Other examples of forced displacements are those due to the vanishing of Lake Chad after that of the Aral Sea. Yet it also includes a return to former better-suited agricultural productions, to older technologies of storing and carrying water in the Middle East as well as in India or even the restoration of wetlands such as along the Rhine river in Europe.

9 For a similar conclusion, see again Sam Kwinter (2010).

10 For a critical reading of such a continuity, see Etienne Balibar's "Citizen-Subjects" in Eduardo Cardono, Jean-Luc Nancy et al. eds, *Who Comes After the Subject?* New York: Routledge, 1992.

11 Žižek's circulation of many of his own texts and lectures on line helps precisely to subvert the idea of intellectual property.

12 Žižke is critical implicitly of the concept of network proposed by many thinkers including Bruno Latour and, explicitly, by that advocated by Hardt and Negri.

13 Žižek has repeatedly recourse to aesthetics to make his point about a new politics. In "Nature and its Discontents," he introduces Egalitarian Justice via Aeschylus and Beckett; in "Ecology," a conversation with Astra Taylor, he calls for an aesthetics of decay, such as that exemplified in Andrei Tarkovsky's *The Stalker*. In an Interview on VPROinternational (2010) based on *Living in the End Times*, he declares that we "live in images."

14 In his four points that would counter the ecological catastrophe, he mentions informers as "public heroes" (69).

15 Žižek rehearses a component of Rancière's studies of Vertov. *The Man with a Movie Camera* realizes immediately "a communism that consists only in the relation among all movements and all intensities . . . [and] the immediate realization of a new world . . . a communism of the universal exchange of movements," in his *Les Écarts du cinéma* (Paris: La Fabrique, 2011) 41.

16 Slavoj Žižek, *A travers le réel. Entretiens avec Fabien Tarby*. Paris: Lignes, 2010.

References

Balibar, Etienne (1998) *Droit de cite*. Editions de l'Aube.
— (1992) "Citizen-Subjects." *Who Comes After the Subject*, eds Eduardo Cardono and Jean-Luc Nancy. New York: Routledge.

Bateson, Gregory (1975) *Steps to an Ecology of Mind*. New York: Ballantine.

Conley, Verena Andermatt (1997) *Ecopolitics. The Environment in Poststructuralist Thought*. New York: Routledge.

— (2012) *Spatial Ecologies*. Liverpool: Liverpool University Press.

Cronon, William (1996) *Uncommon Ground*. New York: Norton.

Davis, Mike (1998) *The Ecology of Fear: Los Angeles and the Imagination of Disaster*. New York: Metropolitian Books.

Deleuze and Guattari (1987) *A Thousand Plateaus*, trans. Brian Massumi. Minneapolis: University of Minnesota Press.

Deleuze, Gilles (1995) *Negotiations*, trans. Martin Joughin. New York: Columbia University Press.

Derrida, Jacques (2005) *Rogues: Two Essays on Reason*, trans. Pascale-Anne Brault and Michael Naas. Palo Alto: Stanford University Press.

Guattari, Felix (2000) *The Three Ecologies*, trans. Ian Pindar and Paul Sutton. New York: Continuum.

Gould, Stephen, Jay (1999) *Rocks of Ages: Between Science and Religion and the Fullness of Life*. New York: Ballantine.

Hardt, Michael and Toni Negri (2000) *Empire*. Cambridge: Harvard University Press.

— (2004) *Multitude: Democracy in the Age of Empire*. New York: Penguin.

Herzogenrath, Bernd, ed. (2009) *An (Un)likely Alliance: Thinking the Environment(s) with Deleuze/Guattari*. New York: Palgrave.

Kwinter, Sam (2010) "Notes on a Third Ecology." In *Ecological Urbanism*, eds Mohsen Mostafavi and Gareth Doherty. Baden: Lars Müller, pp. 84–95.

Malabou, Catherine (2007) *Les nouveaux blesses: de Freud à la neurologie, penser les traumatismes contemporains*. Paris: Bayard.

Malabou Catherine and Xavier Emmanuelli (2009) *La grande exclusion*. Paris: Bayard.

Morton, Tim (2005) *Ecology without Nature*. Cambridge, MA: Harvard University Press.

Parr, Adrian (2009) *Hijacking Sustainability*. Cambridge, MA: MIT Press.

Prigogine, Ilya and Isabelle Stengers (1984) *Order out of Chaos: Man's New Dialogue with Nature*. New York: Bantam Books.

Rancière, Jacques (1989) *The Night of Labor. The Workers' Dream in Nineteenth Century France*, trans. John Drury. Philadelphia: Temple University Press.

— (1991) *The Ignorant Schoolmaster. Five Lessons In Intellectual Emancipation*, trans. Kristin Ross. Palo Alto: Stanford University Press.

— (2011) *Les Écarts du cinéma*. Paris: La Fabrique.

Raven, Peter (2000) Nature and Society: The Quest for a Sustainable World. Washington, DC: National Academic Press.

— (2004) *Environment*. Hoboken, NJ: Wiley.

Roy, Arundhati (1999) *The Cost of Living*. New York: Modern Library.

Serres, Michel (1995) *The Natural Contract*, trans. Elizabeth MacArthur and William Paulson. Ann Arbor: University of Michigan Press.

Shiva, Vandana (2002) *Water Wars: Water Pollution and Profits*. Toronto: Between the Lines.

Žižek, Slavoj (2007) "Liberal Utopia." Address. Athens, Greece. October 4. Web. April 10, 2011.

— (2008a) "Nature and its Discontents." *Substance* 117,37.3: 37–72.

— (2008b) "Unbehagen in der Natur." *In Defense of Lost Causes*. New York: Verso, pp. 420–61.

— (2011) "Censorship Today: Violence or Ecology as a New Opium for the Masses." www.lacan.com/zizecology 1 and 2 htm. April 15.

— with Astra Taylor (2008) "Ecology." *Examined Life: Excursions with Eight Contemporary Thinkers*. New York Zeitgeist Film, DVD.

— (2009) "Ecology," ed. Astra Taylor. *Examined Life: Excursions with Eight Contemporary Thinkers*. Cambridge, MA: New Press, pp. 155–83.

— (2010a) *Living in the End Times*. New York: Verso.

— (2010b) "Living in the End Times." *Interview*. VPROinternational. March 11. Web. April 10, 2011.

— (2010c) "Are We Living in the End Times?" Interview with Riz Kahn. Al Jazeera. November 11, 2010. Youtube.com. April 1.

— with Fabien Tarby (2010d) *A travers le réel*. Entretiens. Paris: Lignes.

7

Žižek and Fanon: On Violence and Related Matters

Erik Vogt

The present chapter engages in a mutual illumination of Slavoj Žižek's and Frantz Fanon's conceptions of violence.[1] Far from suggesting that their respective approaches to the issue of violence could simply be mapped onto each other, it will be argued that these two political analyses, while employing distinct theoretical frameworks, nonetheless converge in a trenchant critique regarding the perceived dissimulation of the systemic, objective violence central to the capitalist (neo)-colonialist system – a dissimulation that is generated in large part by depoliticizing representations of different manifestations of subjective violence. Although Žižek and Fanon concur that forms of subjective violence often have to be treated as versions of a politically impotent *passage à l'acte*, they insist that these can also be grasped as potential sites for a radical re-politicization of certain socio-political impasses; in particular, they seem to agree that the passage, within subjective forms of violence, from violence as mere inherent transgression perpetuating the existing oppressive system to violence as possible opening toward proper politics can take on the guise of self-violence ("self-beating") on the part of the oppressed and exploited subjects. Moreover, this self-violence – a violence directed primarily against those fantasies that keep subjects bound to their own subjection and oppression by promising, for instance, some particular cultural or even national identity supposedly providing alternative avenues of escape from the capitalist (neo)-colonialist system – contains the germs for modes of collective political subjectivization arising out of a space where the excluded masses, militants, and those intellectuals identifying with "the wretched of the earth" (can) meet on strictly egalitarian grounds; however, if this new collective political subjectivization is not to exhaust itself in mere spontaneous voluntarism, specific structures for its political organization must be devised so as to enable and stabilize proper universal politicization. Furthermore, neither Fanon nor Žižek dismiss the relevance of existing cultural, racial, or ethnic differences for the project of a postcolonial universal politics; that is, they maintain that these differences remain important, as long as they are sustained by the collective, transversal, and egalitarian struggle on the part of militant subjects against the repressive and oppressive cores concealed within their own respective cultures and civilizations.

The Ambiguity of Subjective Violence Facing Objective-Systemic Violence

Contemporary post-political societies are marked not only by an allegedly successful overcoming of earlier forms of "totalitarian" universal politics in the name of "peaceful" and pragmatic deliberations and negotiations aiming at consensus, but also by the more or less implicit ideological conviction that violence presents no longer an eminently political problem; that is, violence today appears paradoxically as disavowed violence both in the quasi-naturalist form of the objective-anonymous machine of market forces simply taking its course and in ubiquitous spurious claims as to the final realization of an allegedly multi-cultural and even postcolonial coexistence of different cultures and ethnicities, or, on the other hand, as "excessive" and "irrational" violent eruptions, supposedly unrelated to the current socioeconomic order and the persistence of neo-colonialist structures of subjugation and exclusion, to be dealt with by decreeing different kinds of statist police actions. In other words, one encounters, on the one hand, an anonymous socioeconomic machine that, by "*detotalizing meaning*," deprives "the large majority of people of any cognitive mapping," and, on the other hand, eruptions of subjective violence as utterly "senseless" forms of protest (Žižek 2008: 67–8). Between the objective-anonymous violence of a naturalized socioeconomic neo-colonialist system and the "senseless" modes of subjective violence, there seems to be no (longer any) place for a politics that would not be thwarted in advance by one of these two post-political poles complementing each other.

What is thus completely obfuscated is violence as a *political* phenomenon that continues to be operative in current Western (and non-Western) societies; for this very reason, one of the most important tasks for radical political thought today must consist in a "*dispassionate* conceptual development of the typology of violence" that distances itself from the fascination with immediately visible "subjective" violence *and* reveals the very "objective" and systemic violence hidden behind the supposedly "politically neutral" and nonviolent socioeconomic order of the present (Žižek 2008: 3). However, this kind of analysis requires a perspectival shift in terms of a dialectical analysis of the complex relationship between subjective and objective violence that can demonstrate that subjective violence is (often) counter-violence, that is, a reaction to the prevailing objective violence. What is more, only this dialectical investigation can discern in subjective violence a proper political dimension, for "irrational" and "excessive" violent outbursts should be grasped as complementary modes of the structural violence of the current socioeconomic neo-colonial system whose suffocating closure seems to generate "automatically" and "naturally" an increasing number of "superfluous" individuals and social groups excluded by the current fundamental societal divide. Thus, a dialectical analysis of contemporary violence trying to re-articulate the project of universal politics must identify in those "irrational" violent eruptions the possibility of a "universality-in-becoming." Žižek explains:

> The only way for a universality to come into existence, to 'posit' itself 'as such', is in the guise of its very opposite, of what cannot but appear as an excessive 'irrational' whim. These violent *passages à l'acte* bear witness to some underlying *antagonism* that can no longer be formulated-symbolized in properly political terms. The only way to counteract these excessive 'irrational' outbursts is to approach the question of what none the less remains foreclosed in the very all-inclusionary/tolerant post-political logic, and to actualize this foreclosed dimension in some new mode of political subjectivization. (Žižek 2000: 204)

Žižek's account of the riots in the Parisian suburbs that took place in fall 2005 can illustrate this seminal point: As "senseless" and "irrational" violent protests lacking any direct political and socio-economic demands, these riots appeared to be perfect exemplifications of a "*passage à l'acte*," that is, of "an impulsive movement into action which can't be translated into speech or thought and carries with it an intolerable weight of frustration" (Žižek 2008: 65).[2] These riots did not so much pursue concrete socio-economic goals, but they "were simply a direct effort to gain *visibility*" (Žižek 2008: 65) on the part of the protesters who, excluded from the socioeconomic realm, attempted to challenge the still persisting neo-colonialist wall of inclusion and exclusion by identifying the continuing presence of French neo-colonialism in France as a problem that must not longer be ignored.[3] Their violent revolts were therefore not simply "senseless"; rather, the insistence of the protesters to enforce their visibility as the excluded from within the neo-colonialist French republic can be deciphered as a demand for recognition that also invoked implicitly the need for the political construction of a new universal framework for recognition.

Moreover, the Parisian *passages à l'acte* signaling the continuous socio-economic and neo-colonialist exploitation and oppression in France demonstrate that "irrational" violent outbursts can introduce a certain distance to the violent socioeconomic and neo-colonialist status quo and open up the space to be occupied (in a next step) by a mode of politicization that pushes beyond mere reforms with the existing socio-political system toward the transformation of its fundamental coordinates. It is precisely with regard to this crucial passage to proper politicization that Žižek seems to advocate a return to the anti-colonial "problematic of Frantz Fanon" (Daly/Žižek 2004: 121). For Fanon's anti-colonial politics contains both the crucial insight into the necessity of (political) violence, of the violent traumatic shattering of particular ideological predicaments – often either neglected or strongly criticized by some postmodern and postcolonial thinkers[4] – and, importantly, also the crucial definition of (transformative) political violence "as 'work of the negative', . . . as a violent reformation of the very substance of subject's being" (Daly/Žižek 2004: 121). Wherein consists, however, the ongoing significance of Fanon's theory of (anti-colonial) violence?

(Neo)-Colonial fantasy and political over-identification

In *Black Skin, White Masks*, Fanon strives to provide, primarily from the perspective of the colonized intellectual, the black "colonized" with visibility; that is to say, he endeavors to demonstrate how the black "colonized" who have been violently excluded by the racist-colonialist system can acquire some kind of identity as black subjects against this very racist-colonial system. Since racist colonialism has constituted the black as "the eternal victim of an essence, of an *appearance* for which he is not responsible," he must first "say *no* to those who attempt to build a definition of him" (Fanon 1967: 35; 36). What is more, since the racist colonial apparatus grants social integration to the black subject, only if he "accepts the separation imposed by the European" and assimilates himself to the hierarchical "range of colors," a different solution must consist in the black subject making himself "known" (Fanon 1967: 82–3; 115). This attempt to gain self-recognition against the background of racist colonialism's claim regarding the alleged non-existence of any black culture or history whatsoever initially leads Fanon to considerations that seem to prove "the existence of a black civilization to the white world at all costs" (Fanon 1967: 34). He develops these reflections primarily with regard to the way in which the colonized intellectual relates to the movement of négritude[5] in which he encounters "Negro culture" rehabilitating "the Negro," providing him with the tools of recognition: "At last I had been recognized, I was no longer a zero" (Fanon 1967: 129).

But the assumption of black self-identity provided by négritude is expropriated from Fanon, as soon as he comes across Jean-Paul Sartre's "Black Orpheus"; for in Sartre's text, black self-identity achieved through the subjective violence of négritude, that is, through its anti-racist racism consisting in a positive revalorization of those very negative values attributed to blacks by the white racists-colonialists, becomes quickly a mere "dialectical step" (Fanon 1967: 132). This means not only that Sartre ultimately asserts (and dismisses) the mere relativity of négritude's subjective violence, but also, as Fanon puts it, that this "born Hegelian had forgotten that consciousness has to lose itself in the night of the absolute, the only condition to attain to consciousness of self" (Fanon 1967: 133–4). Sartre's quasi-dialectical rendition and overcoming of black anti-racist racism aims too quickly at an abstract non-racial "postcolonial" synthesis, thereby missing both the crucial dimension of subjective violence espoused in black anti-racist racism and its construction of black self-identity, as well as the recognition that the violent racist-colonial construction of blacks has profoundly determined their very being and social existence.

For this very reason, Fanon insists on the need of "losing myself in négritude" (BS 186); however, the purpose of this immersion in négritude as "irrational" outburst is not to assert or retrieve some (lost) stable racial-cultural self-identity, but rather to take the first steps toward a radical political challenge of racist-colonial oppression. That is to say, after re-visiting the site of this oppression and exploitation in order to create some distance to the existing racist-colonial system, the colonized intellectual engaged in the process of decolonization must no longer misrecognize négritude as an oppositional cultural force to racist colonialism, but rather has to re-stage or – to use one of Žižek's terms – over-identify[6] with négritude's own specific libidinous attachments to the socio-symbolic order of racist colonialism finding expression precisely in négritude's evocation of the unfathomable substance of those practices and attributes supposedly making up "black" and/or "African" (self-) identity. By bringing to light in a literal manner the unspoken assumptions and rules tacitly organizing négritude as (fantasized) past (and future) collective identity, over-identification can take full subversive effect by disclosing the ways in which négritude as racial-cultural fantasy remains complicit with colonialism. Moreover, over-identification with the fantasy of négritude is necessary for the colonized intellectual, if he wants to discern in it "the fires, the segregations, the repressions, the rapes, the discriminations, the boycotts" (Fanon 1967: 186–7). Thus, he has to "*come down*" and "see what is happening at the very depths" of négritude, and only then can he "go up" (Fanon 1967: 195).

This over-identification with the libidinous components characterizing the fantasy of négritude makes it possible for the colonized intellectual to realize that the desire for cultural and racial recognition on the basis of appeals to a "re-discovered African culture" is not only grounded in the fetishism of cultural-racial identity, but also in the fixation of the black and/or African subject as sublime object of an anti-colonial or even "postcolonial" ideology that is nothing but a kind of inherent transgression with regard to the colonial system. For this reason, Fanon increasingly intensifies his critique of those colonized intellectuals who remain passionately attached to the cause of négritude even in the context of decolonization. He remarks that "the colonized intellectual, steeped in Western culture and set on proving the existence of his own culture, [. . .] does so in the name of [. . .] African culture" (Fanon 2004: 150); again, the effort by the colonized intellectuals to "escape the sting of colonialism" by means of an invocation of the ideology of négritude based on race and on the assumption of rigorously identical cultures even "obeys the same rules" of the colonial logic (Fanon 2004: 150). This becomes particularly clear when these intellectuals employ négritude as a particular organization of enjoyment for the purpose of creating out of the splintered and disoriented decolonized society a "postcolonial" community held together by what Žižek, following Lacan, designates "the nation as Thing."[7] When Fanon states that the "cultured class of colonized intellectuals" is concerned primarily with "the recognition of a national culture and its right to exist represents their favorite stamping ground" (Fanon 2004: 147), he rejects not only their attempt to forge certain national or "African" myths by means of particularist aesthetic-ideological practices[8] entertaining a relation to the "nation" or to "Africa" as Thing;[9] like Žižek after him, he also draws attention to the dangerous implications of this kind of nationalism. That is to say, the deployment of négritude as cultural-aesthetic instrument for the (re-)establishment of a racially and culturally differentiated community relies not only on the assumption that individuals and collectives are ultimately nothing but bearers of one single homogeneous culture, but also on anthropological universals such as the ideas of cultural tradition and cultural rootedness. Additionally, négritude potentially betrays an affinity to other (both earlier and later European) deeply problematic versions of constructing the nation as Thing in that its cultural raci(ali)sm operates as well a kind of fantasmatic loop in form of a regressive and infinite search for some lost fantasmatic point in the (glorious cultural) past that is to be retrieved.[10]

Négritude as cultural fantasy of postcolonial nationalism is thus not only a political impasse that, as reverse image of colonialism, betrays political "irresponsibility" (Fanon 2004: 150–1) with regard to need for true anti-colonial politics, but it is also "very often nothing but an inventory of particularisms" (Fanon 2004: 160). Ultimately, négritude as (cultural, racial, and nationalist) identity politics perpetuates a (long history of a) "politics" of recognition lacking the central feature of any genuine political and, thus, violent struggle for freedom:[11] namely the concomitant acceptance of "convulsions of death, invincible dissolution" on the part of the colonized subjects. In short, since its cultural policies remain separated from militant anti-colonial struggle and continue to affirm inversely (Western) colonialism's bourgeois-individualist and elitist residues, négritude as such cannot be a sufficient condition for the liberation from colonial subjugation.[12] This explains why the (liberal-bourgeois) representative proponents of négritude cannot but fail to grasp "the possibility of the impossible" characterizing radical anti-colonial politics (Fanon 1967: 218).

Self-Violence as Passage to Proper Political Subjectivization

Fanon elaborates a genuine anti-colonial politics as the "possibility of the impossible" precisely in the context of decolonization that "is always a

violent event" because decolonization must be grasped as the struggle
between two antagonistic forces within colonialism's utterly divided
world, incapable of any synthesis or reconciliation (Fanon 2004: 1, 2).

Again, colonialism produces in the colonized intellectuals fantasies that
allow them to participate in and profit from the surplus-enjoyment of
the colonial system even after decolonization, thereby supporting and
perpetuating their own oppression; what is more, colonized intellectuals
often adopt in the process of decolonization "the abstract, universal values
of the colonizer" and are "prepared to fight so that colonist and colonized
can live in peace in a new world" (Fanon 2004: 9). But this abstract-
universal discourse disavowing the colonial antagonisms ultimately testifies
only to the distance of those colonized intellectuals to those real others
who do not have any proper place in the (neo)-colonial system: "the
fellah, the unemployed and the starving"; they *are*, however, precisely
"the truth in their very being" (Fanon 2004: 13). For this very reason,
this abstract-universal discourse with its traditional invocations of the
liberal-humanist heritage will simply not suffice to break open the closure
of colonized subjectivity; rather, "self-beating" has to occur as a kind of
intermediate stage in the passage from oppressed (and oppressive) colonized subjectivity to a type of subjectivity forged in the heat of anti-
colonial struggles. As Žižek explains perspicaciously:

> The abstraction, the foreclosure of others, the blindness to the other's suffering
> and pain, has first to be broken in a gesture of taking the risk and reaching
> directly out to the suffering other – a gesture which, since it shatters the very
> kernel of our identity, cannot fail to appear extremely violent: However, there
> is another dimension at work in *self*-beating: the subject's scatological (excre-
> mental) identification, which is equivalent to adopting the position of the
> proletarian who has nothing to lose. (Žižek 2002: 252).

Moreover, "self-beating"[13] not only brings to light the fact that one's
oppression is sustained by libidinous attachments generating surplus-
enjoyment for the oppressed but also, since oppression cannot be thought
apart from material practices, the recognition that one's liberation has to
occur via "some kind of bodily performance" (Žižek 2002: 253). Žižek
stresses also not only the traumatic physical (and socio-symbolic) dimensions of objective violence, but refers also to the significance of the bodily
aspects of subjective (counter)-violence, the more so as the body cannot
be separated from the socio-symbolic realm. Fanon too holds that the
subjective violence of the colonized subject that is condemned to

immobility within the violent Manichean colonial system manifests itself
first as "muscular dreams, dreams of action, dreams of aggressive vitality"
(Fanon 2004: 15) Like Žižek, who remarks that the violence of the
protesters in the Parisian suburbs "was almost exclusively directed against
their own" (Žižek 2008: 64), Fanon claims as well that the "colonized
subject will first train this aggressiveness . . . against his own people," as
can be seen in the very violence periodically erupting "into bloody fighting between tribes, clans, and individuals" (Fanon 2004: 15, 17). In
addition to this kind of suicidal *passage à l'acte*, Fanon mentions as other
collective "'head-in-the-sand' behaviors" to be rejected fatalistic recourses
to "religion," "myth," "magic," "ecstasy of dance," and "rituals of possession" (Fanon 2004: 19–20).

Are these collective *Ersatzhandlungen* not exemplary cases of inherent
transgression, that is, measures that only help to stabilize the colonial
system? Do they not simply stage the obscene underside of colonialism
and its subjects? Or is their severity rather "a proof *a contrario* of the possibility of the authentic [. . .] revolution: its excessive energy can be read
only as a reaction to the ('unconscious') awareness of the missed revolutionary opportunity" (Žižek 2002: 256)? For a transformative approach
to these collective *Ersatzhandlungen* is initiated when the colonized subject
– "with his back to the wall, the knife at his throat, or to be more exact
the electrode on his genitals" – realizes that he "is bound to stop telling
stories" (Fanon 2004: 20). That is to say: "After years of unreality . . . the
colonized subject . . . finally confronts the only force which challenges
his very being: colonialism" (Fanon 2004: 20); he discovers the violent
reality of colonialism and "transforms it through his praxis, his deployment and his agenda for liberation" (Fanon 2004: 21). This discovered
colonial reality reveals itself as contradictory and ultimately impotent
precisely in its increasing practices of oppression and violence directed at
those militant subjects and groups that are engaged in anti-colonial struggle. What is more, oppression changes sides. While the "atmospheric"
violence of the colonized, before its transformation into "praxis," was
characterized by the impasse of a *passage à l'acte*, after its transformation,
the colonial system itself and its impotent excessive violence manifests
features of a *passage à l'acte* and can barely conceal any longer that colonialism "does not (no longer) exist."

The passage from "atmospheric" to "active" violence occurs when the
colonized grasps violence as absolute praxis, that is, when violence "transforms the spectator crushed to a nonessential state into a privileged actor,"
into "a worker" (Fanon 2004: 2, 44). But this praxis of violence can

truly liberate the colonized subject, only if violence is simultaneously grasped as self-violence accompanied by the assumption and the consequent traversal of the colonized subject's fantasies, which entails risking his own imaginary and symbolic identity. For the colonized subject engaged in anti-colonial struggle, the passage from spontaneous-reactive to active violence occurring within subjective violence enables not only access to a realm no longer marked by mere survival and fear of death, but, within that realm, also the re-politicization of surplus-enjoyment as (failed) revolutionary possibility. Fanon concludes: "We have seen that this violence throughout the colonial period, although constantly on edge, runs on empty. We have seen it channeled through the emotional release of dance or possession. We have seen it exhaust itself in fratricidal struggles. The challenge now is to seize this violence as it realigns itself. Whereas it once reveled in myths and contrived ways to commit collective suicide, a fresh set of circumstances will now enable it to change directions" (Fanon 2004: 21).

Violence and the Question of Political Organization

Clearly, this "fresh set of circumstances" raises the question as to how revolutionary violence can acquire permanence; this problem cannot be separated from the question of political organization, for if it is not adequately addressed, the anti-colonial struggle remains subject to "blind voluntarism with the terribly reactionary risks this implies" (Fanon 2004: 21). Fanon identifies those forces that can organize the violence of the colonized in terms of an alliance between the (rural) masses, the *lumpenprotelariat*, and urban revolutionaries and intellectuals forced into illegality; this alliance has to overcome by means of political organization the initial "spectacular" voluntarism since this voluntarism "which was to lead the colonized people in a single move to absolute sovereignty" has "proved in the light of experience to be a very great weakness" (Fanon 2004: 88). As Fanon remarks, the initial leaders of the revolt must control and direct these spontaneous revolts by providing them with the organizational framework of the party (Fanon 2004: 126–7); it is then from within the political structure of the party that a mobilization of the people can occur by the formation of a "national consciousness" that, however, must reject any kind of identitarian nationalism à la négritude by actively opening itself up toward anti-capitalist international-universal socialism.[14] Fanon thus insists that the structural organization of postcolonial politics has to arise out of a space where the masses, the militants, and the intellectuals (who have identified themselves with the previously excluded masses as their political reference point) meet on egalitarian grounds; while he endorses the significance of the party as centralizing political form during the early stages of the revolution, he stresses at the same time the need for a decentralized and democratizing political organization of the party itself in the postcolonial period.[15]

It is precisely at this point that Fanonian politics once more converges with Žižekian politics. Žižek maintains as well that the excluded and "de-structured masses" of the slums, "poor and deprived of everything, [. . .] constitute one of the principal horizons of the politics to come," if these masses can be politically organized together with a mixture of different agents so that their revolutionary force can be transformed into a new socio-political order (Žižek 2008a: 426).[16] True, Žižek's elaboration of new forms of political organization takes recourse to the notion of the "dictatorship of the proletariat." While this appeal to a centralized party-state seems to indicate a marked difference to Fanon's political project, this impression is nonetheless deceptive, for "dictatorship of the proletariat" means precisely a radical transformation of the state itself in terms of new popular (and democratic) forms of participation. As Žižek explains with regard to the government of Morales in Bolivia, the Maoist government in Nepal, and the government of Chávez in Venezuela, these different governments have succeeded in exercising power in a non-statal manner: that is, by means of a direct mobilization of their supporters, by bypassing the liberal-democratic representative party network (Žižek 2009: 155).[17] The example of Hugo Chávez, his successful politicization of the slum dwellers, can illustrate this point. Referring to Chávez's "risky choice" to found his own political party, Žižek remarks: "However, one should fully endorse this risky choice: the task is to make this party function not like the usual (populist or liberal-parliamentary) party, but as a focus for the political mobilization of new forms of politics" (Žižek 2008a: 427). Although the central role of the party for the possibility of political universalization continues to be emphasized, the party has no longer, as Jodi Dean points out, the function of the "master" but that of a "catalyst" formally providing the position of truth from which the existing ideological coordinates are suspended in order to invent a space for a new form of political organization. In short, the party is no longer conceived of as the embodiment of some objective historical necessity, but as the "relation between truth and the singular symptom or point of disruption. The form of the social from the perspective of the truth of the Party is the excluded element" (Dean 2006: 201). Furthermore, insofar as the "dictatorship of the proletariat" as projected replacement of the State-form of liberal democracy is not in external opposition to "democracy" which, in its purely formal determination, is itself a form of dictatorship,[18] and insofar as it does not designate a State-form in which the "proletariat" would simply be the new ruling class, it *"is another name for the democratic explosion itself"* (Žižek 2008a: 416). In other words, "dictatorship of the proletariat" names that moment in which the existing political-representative structures are suspended by the *demos*, that is, by those that, precisely as excluded from the social totality, present themselves as true universality and intervene into and restructure the field of the political. Consequently, Žižek draws a conclusion echoing Fanon's own refashioning of postcolonial political organization: "We effectively have the 'dictatorship of the proletariat' only when the State itself is radically transformed, relying on new forms of popular participation" (Žižek 2010: 220).

For a Postcolonial Universal Politics

Fanon's revolutionary postcolonial politics does *not* fall into the trap of a mere "culturalization of politics" (Žižek 2008: 119). Political antagonisms are *not* translated into mere nationalist and/or cultural differences; rather, the revolutionary anti-colonial struggle inaugurating a new postcolonial order challenges allegedly fixed racial, cultural, and nationalist identities inherited from colonialism's Manicheanism by giving "a quasi-universal dimension to the most local disputes" (Fanon 2004: 95, 35). One has to abandon fantasies of a particular ("black" or "white," "African" or "European") culture, especially of a particular (nationalist) culture that, desperately attempting "to defend its identity, has to repress the universal dimension which is active at its very heart, that is the gap between the particular (its identity) and the universal which destabilizes it from within" (Žižek 2008: 133). In a truly postcolonial world, there would thus neither be a "black world that laid down my course of conduct," nor would there be "a white world, [. . .] white ethic [. . .] white intelligence" (Fanon 1967: 228, 229). Since neither the "Negro nor the White" *is*, there "are in every part of the world men who search" (Fanon 1967: 231, 229) – that is, men concerned "that the enslavement of man by man cease forever" (Fanon 1967: 231).

Both Fanon's and Žižek's politics are sustained by the gesture of an identification with the standpoint of the "most excluded ones," making those "most excluded ones" into representatives for a claim to egalitarian universality. True political universalization comes about by means of an identification of one's own commitment with the commitment of those who have been excluded from the existing social order, and who become, in the words of Alain Badiou, "vectors of humanity as a whole" (Badiou 2003: 20). Crucially, neither Fanon nor Žižek imply that political universalization could simply disregard existing cultural, racial, or ethnic differences. The struggle for a truly postcolonial order continues to encounter racial and racist differences (Fanon 2004: 95); what they suggest, however, is that these differences have to be traversed in order for universality to be constructed and invented; this traversal is, perhaps, best illustrated by Badiou's proposal: "Differences can be transcended only if benevolence with regard to customs and opinions presents itself as *an indifference to difference*" (Badiou 2003: 99). In other words, cultural differences or particularities play a certain role in the construction of postcolonial universal humanity; it is not simply a matter of abolishing those particularities and differences, but rather of "animating them internally" in such a manner that they can be subjectivized in terms of the universal. In turn, the postcolonial universal has "to expose itself to all differences and show, through the ordeal of their division, that they are capable of welcoming the truth that traverses them" (Badiou 2003: 106). Against the multiculturalist *doxa*, according to which victimized identities are *per se* politically "emancipatory" once rights will have been conferred upon them (thereby not only ignoring that this demand for rights may simply leave intact the status quo, but also that this conferral of rights is often policed by particularist and differentialist logics),[19] Fanon and Žižek insist that they be politicized in such a manner so as to become heterogeneous to any post-political demand for integration, to any valorization of one's particularity in the existing state of things. This politicization subtracts colonized, oppressed subjects from the homogeneous and homogenizing space of the oppressive (neo)-colonial system in such a way that they can combine, by means of an affirmation of their own non-identity, into a postcolonial egalitarian collective that is founded upon an unconditional universalism traversing a line of separation (neo)-colonial society and suspending its existing cultural and racial differences.

Finally, the postcolonial society envisioned by Fanon and Žižek is not based on a simple affirmation of either "Europe" or of the "Third World." Both insist that this new type of postcolonial humanity both must go beyond Manicheanism and must not be severed from revolutionary anti-colonial struggle; furthermore, it must take as its point of departure the crucial recognition – acquired precisely through the praxis of anti-colonial struggles – that cultural identities are fragile and never identical with themselves; that the gap in their self-identity is precisely the universal separating them from themselves – the space in which new concepts of humanity have to be worked out, must be "innovated" (Fanon 2004: 239). It is for this reason that Fanon's appeal to humanity cannot be reduced to a version of liberal humanism, but constitutes rather a form of "generic" humanism.[20] As Badiou remarks with regard to Sartre's radical humanism (that certainly overlaps with Fanon's projected generic humanism), it is to be grasped as "the occupation of an empty place" (Badiou 2007: 169). This project to make man "arise at the place of the absolute" aims at "generic humanity" to be established in the context of and by means of historical-political struggles. Moreover, this radical "generic" humanism exhibits, in certain circumstances, an affinity to the kind of radical anti-humanism espoused by Žižek.[21] Badiou accounts for this affinity in the following manner:[22] "Radical humanism and radical anti-humanism agree on the theme of Godless man as opening, possibility, programme of thought. That is why the two orientations will intersect in a number of situations, in particular in all the revolutionary episodes. In a certain sense the politics of the century or revolutionary politics more generally, creates situations that are subjectively undecidable between radical humanism and radical anti-humanism" (Badiou 2007: 171–2).

While both Fanon and Žižek clearly reject the temptation to define the "Third World" in culturalist, that is, identitarian terms, they *also* reject any identitarian conception of "Europe" (to be emulated by the "Third World"); that is, neither Fanon nor Žižek subscribe to some kind of mimetological program concerning "Europe." However, this does not amount to a dismissal *tout court* of "European thought." As Fanon readily concedes: "All the elements for a solution to the major problems of humanity existed at one time or another in European thought" (Fanon 2004: 237) For this reason, both Fanon and Žižek urge a reading of "European thought" against the grain, an expropriation of "Europe" which, "by appropriating key elements of the 'white' egalitarian-emancipatory tradition, *redefines that very tradition*, transforming it not so

much in terms of what it says as in what it *does not say* – that is, obliterating the implicit qualifications which have *de facto* excluded Blacks
from the egalitarian space" (Žižek 2009: 120). In other words, neither
Fanon nor Žižek consider it sufficient "to find new terms with which
to define oneself outside of the dominant white tradition – one should
go a step further and deprive the whites of the monopoly on defining
their own tradition" (Žižek 2009: 120). Reading "Europe" against the
grain implies for Fanon and Žižek to both remain faithful to "lost" revolutionary causes and to invent a new political space for revolutionary
solidarity. Put succinctly "For Europe, for ourselves and for humanity,
comrades, we must make a new start, develop a new way of thinking,
and endeavor to create a new man" (Fanon 2004: 239); consequently,
both Fanon and Žižek are committed to an unconditional affirmation of
solidarity among and across revolutionary collectives both from "Europe"
and the "Third World," equally sustained by egalitarian universalism;[23]
finally, these collectives do not represent "a pact of civilizations, but a
pact of struggles which cut across civilizations, a pact between what, in
each civilization, undermines its identity from within, fights against its
oppressive kernel" (Žižek 2008: 133). True anti-colonial politics striving
for the establishment of a proper postcolonial society consists therefore
not in a tolerant dialogue between civilizations or cultural identities, but
rather in the common incessant and "intolerant" struggle of "the repressed,
the exploited and suffering [. . .] of every culture" (Žižek 2008: 134).

Notes

1 I am very grateful to both editors of this volume for providing me with
   numerous comments and valuable suggestions that have allowed me to re-
   think and clarify the argument of my chapter.
2 However, as Bjerre and Laustsen point out, these riots were accompanied
   by attempts to translate them into speech and thought (Bjerre/Laustsen 2010:
   113).
3 After all, is it not the case that many of the Parisian suburbs are occupied
   by "citizens" from former French colonies?
4 Examples for the postcolonial and postmodern distance to or even rejection
   of Fanonian violence can be found in (Bhaba 1999: 179–96) and (Butler
   2008: 211–231).
5 Although the significance of négritude in Fanon's thought has been a truism
   in the secondary literature on Fanon, only James Penney grasps négritude as

fantasy – I follow here closely his convincing arguments (Penney 2004: 49–67).

6 Žižek repeatedly asserts the ideological-critical potential of over-identification; for one of its earliest accounts see (Žižek 1994: 72).

7 See (Žižek 1993: 202).

8 While the approach of negritude has reached "unusual heights in the sphere of poetry," its central notions and ideas nonetheless (must) remain intransitive with regard to the revolts at the center of anti-colonial politics (Fanon 2004: 157).

9 Fanon is equally critical of attempts to revive "the legacy" of an Arab "past" (Fanon 2004: 151–152).

10 In addition to German National Socialism and its attempt to re-build the Aryan nation (also) by aesthetic means, one could mention the different eruptions of nationalism in the wake of the dissolution of former Yugoslavia; Žižek has not only developed his notion of the nation as Thing precisely in that specific socio-political context; what is more, he has also pointed the crucial role of art (especially literature and poetry) for the construction of a national aestheticism in Serbia, Croatia, and Slovenia. See also (Vogt 2003: 83–101) for an account of the ways in which the (aesthetic) nation as Thing continues to be at the center of contemporary far-right politics in Europe (and, particularly, in Austria).

11 On Fanon and his account of Hegel's dialectic of master and slave, see (Ato Sekyi-Out 1996: 28–31; 58–64); see also (Gibson 2003: 29–41).

12 However, négritude must not be seen as an entirely homogeneous movement since there exist clear and decisive political differences among some of its representatives; that is, Fanon certainly rejects Senghor's conception of négritude, while he endorses its militant version in Césaire; by the way, the recognition of these political differences between these two can already be found in Sartre's "Black Orpheus."

13 Fabio Vighi and Heiko Feldner have brilliantly elaborated the necessarily "masochistic" dimension of liberation; although I follow closely their account of the notion of "self-beating," I attempt to re-contextualize their arguments (restricted to the movie *Fight Club*) in reference to the more properly politico-revolutionary situation of anti-colonial struggle; see (Vighi/Feldner 2007: 109–120).

14 Briefly, Fanon's notion of the "people" does not succumb to populism because the revolutionary anti-colonial struggle also implies the re-structuring of the "people" so that the "people" after the revolution should no longer be grasped in terms of the populist opposition between a "unified," homogeneous "people" and its "external enemy." The "people" simply does not exist for Fanon; for this reason, Fanon's political-hegemonic strategy of appealing to "national consciousness" does not abet an ontological identity politics, as has been claimed by Udo Wolter (Wolter 2001: 204).

15 See (Gibson 2003: 201).

16 I emphasize here the centrality of the question of the political organization of revolutionary violence in Žižek; this also means that I put, perhaps erroneously, less emphasis on Žižek's invocation of Walter Benjamin's "divine violence." Although Žižek insists that "we should fearlessly identify divine violence with positively existing historical phenomena, thus avoiding any obscurantist mystification" (Žižek 2008: 167), the concrete examples that he provides are, as Reinhard Heil states, not always convincing (Heil 2010: 116). For this reason, I prefer to pursue the question of revolutionary violence and its transformation into structures of political organization along Leninist lines.

17 See also (Žižek 2011: 56 –7).

18 Here, Žižek is of course indebted to Lenin.

19 See (Vogt 2011: 155–208).

20 This is the claim put forth by Homi K. Bhaba – see (Bhaba 1999: 191); see also (Gibson 2003: 188–205) for a very different account of Fanon's humanism.

21 For Žižek's reflection on anti-humanism and the in-human see (Žižek 2006: 337–42).

22 Of course, Badiou cites Michel Foucault as representative of radical anti-humanist thought, pairing Sartre and Foucault.

23 Although Žižek has been repeatedly accused of promoting a kind of "Eurocentrism," and although he himself has at times subscribed to a "progressive Eurocentrism"(Žižek 2000: 205–12), things are not that simple; after all, is it not the case that many of his more recent publications re-examine again and again political events outside "Europe" in terms of their repetition, that is, their appropriation/expropriation, of "European" theory? And is it not also the case that he has increasingly paid attention to the ways in which "European" theory and politics have been over-determined by "non-European" thought and practice so that, for instance, Hegel's conception of revolution cannot be fully recognized without "*the significance of the Haitian Revolution for Europe*" (Žižek 2009: 121)? In this regard, Žižek states unequivocally, thereby affirming Buck-Morss' central claim (Buck-Morss 2009): "It is not only that one cannot understand Haiti without Europe – one cannot understand either the scope or the limitations of the European emancipation process without Haiti" (Žižek 2009: 121).

References

Badiou, Alain (2002) *Ethics: An Essay on the Understanding of Evil*, trans. Peter Hallward. London and New York: Verso.

— (2003) *Saint Paul: The Foundation of Universalism*, trans. Ray Brassier. Stanford: Stanford University Press.

— (2007) *The Century*, trans., with a commentary and notes, by Alberto Toscano. Cambridge UK: Polity.

Bhaba, Homi K. (1999) "Remembering Fanon: Self, Psyche, and the Colonial Condition," in *Rethinking Fanon: The Continuing Dialogue*, Gibson, Nigel (ed.) Amherst and New York: Humanity Books, pp. 179–96.

Bjerre, Henrik Joker and Laustsen, Cartsen Bagge (2010) *The Subject of Politics: Slavoj Žižek's Political Philosophy*. Penrith, CA: Humanities-Ebooks.

Buck-Morss, Susan (2009) *Hegel, Haiti, and Universal History*. Pittsburgh: University of Pittsburgh Press.

Butler, Judith (2008) "Violence, Nonviolence: Sartre and Fanon," in *Race After Sartre: Antiracism, Africana Existentialism, Postcolonialism*, Jonathan Judaken (ed.) Albany: SUNY Press, pp. 211–31.

Dean, Jodi (2006) *Žižek's Politics*. New York and London: Routledge.

Fanon, Frantz (1967) *Black Skin, White Masks*, trans. from the French by Charles Lam Markman. New York: Grove Press.

— (2004) *The Wretched of the Earth*, trans. from the French by Richard Philcox, with commentary by Jean-Paul Sartre and Homi K. Bhaba. New York: Grove Press.

Gibson, Nigel (2003) *Fanon: The Postcolonial Imagination*. Cambridge, UK: Polity.

Heil, Reinhard (2010) *Zur Aktualität von Slavoj Žižek*. Wiesbaden: VS Verlag.

Penney, James (2004) "Passing into the Universal: Fanon, Sartre, and the Colonial Dialectic," in *Paragraph*, vol. 27, no. 3: 49–67.

Sekyo-Otu, Aro (1996) *Fanon's Dialectic of Experience*. Cambridge, MA and London: Harvard University Press.

Vighi, Fabio and Feldner, Heiko (2007) *Žižek: Beyond Foucault*. Hampshire and New York: Palgrave MacMillan.

Vogt, Erik (2003) *Zugaenge zur politischen Aesthetik*. Vienna: Turia + Kant.

— (2011) *Slavoj Žižek und die Gegenwartsphilosophie*, foreword by S. Žižek. Vienna: Turia + Kant.

Wolter, Udo (2001) *Das obskure Subjekt der Begierde. Frantz Fanon und die Fallstricke des Subjekts der Befreiung*. Muenster: Unrast-Verlag.

Žižek, Slavoj (1993) *Tarrying with the Negative*. Durham, NC: Duke University Press.

— (1994) *Metastases of Enjoyment*. London: Verso.

— (2000) *The Ticklish Subject*. London and New York: Verso.

— (2002) "Afterword: Lenin's Choice," in *Revolution At the Gates: Žižek On Lenin, The 1917 Writings*, ed. with an Introduction and Afterword by S. Žižek. London and New York: Verso, pp. 165–336.

— and Daly, Glyn (2004) *Conversations With Žižek*. Cambridge, UK: Polity.

— (2006) *The Parallax View*. Cambridge, MA and London: MIT Press..

— (2008a) *On Violence*. London: Profile Books.

— (2008b) *In Defense of Lost Causes*. London and New York: Verso.

— (2009) *First as Tragedy, Then as Farce*. London and New York: Verso.

— (2010) "How to Begin from the Beginning," in *The Idea of Communism*, Douzinas, Costas and Žižek, Slavoj (eds) London and New York: Verso, pp. 209–26.

— (2011) "Welcome to Interesting Times!" Unpublished manuscript.

8

Žižek's Infidelity: Lenin, the National Question, and the Postcolonial Legacy of Revolutionary Internationalism

Jamil Khader

Arguing against all unwritten discursive taboos (the *Denkverbot*) that waste no time invoking the specter of totalitarianism, its history of the gulag and Third World catastrophes, Slavoj Žižek makes the case for the need to reactualize the Leninist act of the October Revolution today (Žižek 2002: 168). Elsewhere, he calls this critical confrontation with the Leninist legacy as "retrieval-through-repetition" (*Wieder-Holung*) (Žižek 2007: 95). While Žižek is more than ready to recognize the monstrous failure of the solutions that Lenin's legacy embodies (the one-party system and the dictatorship of the proletariat), he still believes that there is "a utopian spark in [Lenin's legacy] worth saving."[1] For Žižek, the Lenin to be reloaded is the "Lenin-in-becoming," the one that has not yet become a part of the Soviet institution; this is the Lenin who is "thrown into an *open* situation" (emphasis in original; Žižek 2002: 6). As such, the Lenin to be recovered is the Lenin full of potentialities, whose language of possibilities can be located in "what he *failed to do*, his missed opportunities" which can never be predicted or foreclosed (emphasis in original; Žižek 2002: 310). To repeat Lenin is to recuperate, as Žižek memorably says, what was "in Lenin more than Lenin himself" (Žižek 2002: 310). Above all, this excess in Lenin represents for Žižek the freedom to think outside the common discursive prohibitions of the neo-colonial, global capitalist regime. This Lenin, he writes, "stands for the compelling freedom to suspend the stale existing (post) ideological coordinates, the debilitating *Denkverbot* in which we live – it simply means that we are allowed to think again" (Žižek 2002: 11). As Adrian Johnston succinctly puts it, repeating Lenin "broadly signifies a disruptive break that makes it possible to imagine, once again, viable alternatives to liberal democratic capitalism by removing the various obstacles to thinking seriously about options forcefully foreclosed by today's reigning ideologies" (Johnston 2009: 115).

For Žižek, however, Lenin signifies more than just this freedom to think outside the box of the neo-colonial, global capitalist regime. For all his talk about "passive aggressivity" (Žižek 2006b: 209–26), Žižek's invocation of Lenin's name ultimately lies in his historic act, the event of the October Revolution, precisely in his call for immediate revolution.[2] He thus notes Lenin's anti-evolutionary conviction that there can be no waiting for the "right moment" of the revolution to mature on its own and explode, but that under certain conditions, it is legitimate, even advisable, to catalyze and force the revolution to come into existence (Žižek 2002: 8). Although he perceived the situation to be desperate, Lenin realized that it could be "creatively exploited for new political choice" (Žižek 2008: 360). In Lacanese, therefore, Lenin's revolutionary act was "not covered by the big Other" – that is, for Žižek, Lenin was neither afraid of a premature seizure of power nor did he demand full guarantees for the revolution to succeed in order for him to embark on the road to revolutionary change (Žižek 2002: 8). In short, because Lenin was capable of looking into the "abyss of the act" in the eye that he insisted that there is no right time for the revolution.

For Žižek, therefore, these completely hopeless times clear a space for enacting Lenin's freedom of experimentation and rejection of determinism, for "there is *always* a space to be made for an act" (emphasis in original; Žižek 2008: 361). In his implicit response to Žižek's claim, Fredric Jameson asserts that Lenin's significance can be located neither in politics nor in economics, but rather in the fusion of both together "in that Event-as-process and process-as-Event we call revolution" (Jameson 2007: 68). Jameson thus states: "The true meaning of Lenin is the perpetual injunction to keep the revolution alive, to keep it alive as a possibility even before it has happened, to keep it alive as a process at all those moments when it is threatened by defeat or worse yet, by routinization, compromise, or forgetfulness" (Jameson 2007: 68). As such, Žižek reappropriates Lenin to foreground the need for reenacting another revolution, although not necessarily a communist one since Marx's Communist society, in his opinion, is an "inherent capitalist fantasy" (Žižek 2000: 19), but a revolution in the abstract whose content still requires remapping and specification. In this sense, Žižek's rejection of a Communist Utopia is indeed an example of, in Johnston's words, a "Marxism deprived of its Marxism" (Johnston 2009: 112). Nonetheless, it is precisely this weak form of "positive Marxism," embodied in his insistence on keeping the revolution alive, that constitutes the highest expression of fidelity to Marx and to the Lenin who identifies "what is decisive in Marxism" as "its revolutionary dialectics" (Lenin 1923: 476–7).

Although this exhortation to repeat Lenin has radical implications for the "gesture of reinventing the revolutionary project in the conditions of imperialism and colonialism, more precisely" (Žižek 2002: 11), Žižek's turn to Lenin is an example of the kind of repetition to salvage alternative history that Žižek claims as a critical gesture for maintaining a revolutionary stance. Yet, strangely enough, Žižek himself misses one of Lenin's most useful linkages for promoting the revolution on a global scale – the revolutionary potential of the postcolonial subject. After the 1914 crisis and his disenchantment with the Second International, I will show, Lenin's writings increasingly reinscribe the subject of the national liberation movements in the colonies, not the Western working class, as one of the fundamental articulations of the "real" revolutionary subject. It is not that Lenin disavowed the proletariat and their world-historic mission altogether or that he assigned an a priori ontological value to the postcolonial subject as the ultimate locus of revolutionary subjectivity, and Žižek is fully aware, of course, that there *"never was"* a "predestined revolutionary subject," not even the working class (Žižek 2008: 289; emphasis in original). Rather, it must be recognized that in the years leading to the Third International and until his death, Lenin's faith in the "awakening of hundreds of millions" in the colonies became more pronounced.

If Lenin is to be repeated today, I argue, postcoloniality should (retroactively) be considered one of those causal nodes around which a Leninist act is formed. Repeating Lenin, that is, will not transform the coordinates of the political, unless one recuperates and accounts for Lenin's mediation of the national question and his increasing faith in the capacity of the subjects of colonial difference to serve as the vanguard of revolutionary internationalism. In Žižek's own radical Marxist understanding of the contingency of the past and the freedom we have to "(over) determine the past which will determine us" (Žižek 2008: 314), Lenin's revolutionary politics can thus be seen as being over-determined in a retroactive endorsement of the postcolonial link that will determine the future of revolutionary internationalism. Nonetheless, Žižek has been reluctant to locate the world-historic mission of socialist internationalism in the field of possibilities and potentialities that characterizes the history

of postcoloniality, repudiating thus the capacity of the postcolonial subject
to subjectivize the position of the proletariat and the revolutionary class
that was envisioned by Lenin.[3] In part, he represents the postcolonial as
both an ideological supplement to global capitalism, specifically in the
case of Tibet and Buddhism, and its excremental remainder especially,
the favelas and slums of the Third World. Consequently, Žižek does not
only obliterate the history of the national liberation movements in the
postcolonial world, but also forecloses the possibility of the construction
of the postcolonial as the subject-for-itself, or more specifically, the
subject of history and revolutionary internationalism. Žižek's infidelity to
this other/wise Lenin notwithstanding, a genealogy of the position of
postcoloniality in Lenin's work can retroactively foreground the exclusion
in Žižek's revolutionary politics, clearing a space for its politicization.

Žižek and the Postcolonial: Between a Supplement and an Excremental Remainder

The postcolonial subject of difference assumes an ambivalent position in
Žižek's work, a position that evolves within the contradictions between
his culturalist and political understanding of the postcolonial. On the one
hand, there is a culturalist representation of the postcolonial (mostly
Tibetan Buddhism) as a fetish, a fantasmatic object upon which the
Western melancholic subject projects his own anxieties, embodying the
lie that allows this subject to endure the unbearable truth that the source
of his secret of enjoyment is to be found within, not somewhere else
outside. On the other, there is a political representation that considers
the postcolonial (mostly the favelas in Latin America and the slums in
South East Asia) as a symptom of the logic of global capitalism, modernization, and developmentalism, which functions as the point of the return
of the repressed truth of class antagonism within, in his words, the "field
of global capitalist lies" (Žižek 2008: 424). In both cases, however, Žižek
fails to reimagine the subject of postcolonial difference as a genuine locus
of the revolutionary act, a subject-for-itself, opting instead for envisioning
a true revolution emerging only from a Europe-centered "Second World,"
where it becomes possible to put up a resistance front to the global
hegemony of the United States.

Within the current economy of exchange between Europe and Asia,
Žižek postulates, the Western melancholy subject identifies Tibet and its

religious (Buddhist) traditions as its lost object-cause of desire. This idealization of Tibet, however, all too easily turns into its opposite, a through-going defilement and devaluation as an "excremental object" (Žižek 2001: 59). Indeed, Žižek points out that these contradictory Western representations of Tibet coincide all the time, noting that the natives and their capital city, Lhasa, including its central palace (Potala) always appear to Westerners as both the epitome of spirituality and the sublime AND the embodiment of filth and corruption (Žižek 2001: 64). In its fantasmatic status as both a jewel and an excremental object, Tibet constitutes a "'reflexive determination' of the split attitude of the West itself, combining violent penetration and respectful sacralization." Elsewhere, Žižek describes the fetishistic function of Tibet for Westerners as a "screen for the projection of Western ideological fantasies," a "screen concealing the liminal experience of their own impotence" (Žižek 1997: 103). Ultimately, the East is defined by its empty and illusory reality, its "positive void," impassivity, and indifference to the world through the renunciation of desire, but this East still possesses that lost object of desire that the Western subject is after and which this subject tries to claim through an arduous journey, struggle, and violent encounters.

Žižek's description of the Western subject's quest for wisdom in the East, however, is in itself a depoliticized form of Eurocentrism. For him, Eurocentrism is all about decenterment, the ex-centricity of Europeans – that is, instead of searching for the lost object in Europe itself, Europeans look for that object in the midst of the Other, outside Europe. This quest, however, took many forms of not only erotic and aesthetic investment in the Other, but most importantly economic exploitation and violent extermination from cannibalization to genocidal colonization. Strangely enough, Žižek contends that colonization was never about imposing Western values or even about economic exploitation, but about cultural envy and a false respect for the Other. His warning about obfuscating economic sources of neo-colonial capitalism notwithstanding, Žižek's seems to abandon, rather too quickly, his earlier insight into the economic exploitation of the Tibetans in the global capitalist economy that renders the Tibetan condition homologous to that of the Native Americans. Consequently, his discussion of Tibet smacks of a culturalist rhetoric that invokes the same pseudo-psychoanalytic vocabulary for which he criticizes the postmodernist trend in postcolonial theory. At stake here is Žižek's reduction of the East to some essence (Buddhism/ Emptiness) which allows, as Ananda Abeysekara claims, to produce a religio-cultural difference that can serve not only as a foil to an alleged Christian core or legacy that one must fight for over and over again, but also as the projection screen of Europeans' worst nightmare, namely the Holocaust and its anti-Semitic subtext (Abeysekara 2008: 73–4).[4]

Žižek's reduction of the postcolonial East to a space of both emptiness and excrementality whence no true subjectivity can ensue underwrites his representation of the favelas and slums around the Third World. With the growth of the "destructured" population in the slums and shanty towns of the Third World, he contends, these forms of alternative communities, or "supernumerary" collectives, are excluded from the benefits of citizenship, existing "outside the structured social field" in extra-juridical spaces and beyond state control where the system itself is suspended (Žižek 2008: 425). In fact, according to Žižek, the state has withdrawn its power to control the slums and their dwellers, leaving them to "vegetate in the twilight zone," even though they are still subject to integration within the global capitalist economy as its "systematically generated 'living dead'" (Žižek 2008: 425). Grounded in the possibility of "self-transparent organization," nonetheless, these marginalized and dispossessed dwelling spaces have led to the construction of an emergent form of agency and social awareness. Hence, Žižek dubs these spaces "liberated territories," where the "horizon of the politics to come" is actualized (Žižek 2008: 426). To this extent, the subject of postcolonial difference in the favelas and slums subjectivizes the position of Marx's proletariat. Although the slum dwellers are defined in socio-political not economic terms like the working class, he argues that they embody, even exceed, the definition of the "free" proletarian revolutionary subject. He writes that they are "'freed' from all substantial ties; dwelling in a free space, beyond the police regulations of the state; they are a large collective, forcibly thrown together, 'thrown' into a situation where they have to invent some mode of being-together, and simultaneously deprived of any support in traditional ways of life, in inherited religious or ethnic life-forms" (Žižek 2008: 425).

Unlike other leftists who altogether dismiss the favelas, where the valorization of both religious fundamentalism and survival strategies over political mobilization they find to be utterly objectionable, Žižek celebrates the vitality and energy of the slums and favelas, finding more in the favelas than the favelas.[5] Nevertheless, he inevitably renounces the capacity of these Other utopian spaces to affect a subversion of the whole edifice of the system. In Žižek's analysis, these alternative spaces are typified by a limited, indeed extra-revolutionary, potentiality that may at best allow for escaping the system, providing a temporary respite from its constraints, but they miserably fail to become truly authentic "evental sites" from which to mount the next revolutionary act against neo-liberal global capitalism and affect a total transformation of the system. The problem here is three-fold: First, Žižek is inconsistent in his representation of the precise location of these communities and spaces within the system, for he shuttles back and forth between identifying their location as existing in a space completely exterior to the system and their position "in conditions *half* outside the law" in a terrain where the state has "*partially at least*" withdrawn from the favelas and slums (Žižek 2008: 224–5). Second, Žižek seems to believe that the "improvised modes of social life" that proliferate in the slums, namely religious fundamentalist ideologies, criminal gangs, the black economy, and diverse forms of socialist solidarity and social programs, are capable of facilitating the "political mobilization of new forms of politics."[6] It remains unclear, however, how such forms of agency and resistance, if indeed that is what they are, can produce direct forms of democratic governance that would reinvent the function of the party and "preclude political alienation" (Žižek 2006: 51–3). He even admits that these spaces are "in terrible need of minimal forms of self-organization" (Žižek 2008: 424).

And third, Žižek seems to think that these spaces can only be embedded in negative and inhuman forms of vitality and energy, what he refers to as "divine violence." Like the biblical locusts, Žižek surmises, the slum dwellers strike "blindly" out of nowhere, "demanding *and* enacting immediate justice/vengeance," an act or a decision not "covered by the big Other," and as such, without any external guarantees invoking the passion of risk of a contingent decision and requiring the suspension of the ethical (Žižek 2008: 162). Although the content of the violence of the slum dwellers (it exists outside the law within the realm of excessive inhuman terror and it disrupts the socio-symbolic field) may sound identical to that of the Jacobins or Lenin in his analysis, the form of that violence (subhuman/zoological; inhumanly blind and vengeful) dramatically and drastically varies among them. In his analysis, the violence in the favelas is exclusively directed internally, against each other, problematically invoking colonial representations of Third World barbaric thugs and hooligans who are not capable of mounting an effective act of resistance to the system itself. For Žižek, it seems, the postcolonial subject does not, even will not, have the ability to rearticulate acts of resistance in a different register beyond itself altogether, failing thus to turn these practices of resistance into an authentic revolutionary act.

"Beyond the Pale of History": Lenin, the National Question, and the Postcolonial Legacy of Revolutionary Internationalism

By reducing postcoloniality to Tibet and the favelas, the cultural imaginary and the excremental exclusion of global capitalism, Žižek overlooks other postcolonial sites and acts, especially the national liberation movements as possible sources of revolutionary transformation. Such an approach subverts his attempt at reclaiming Lenin, because Lenin's mediation of anti-colonialism and the national question constitutes another possible outcome that still "haunt[s] us as specters of what might have been" (Žižek 2010: 86). Accounting for Lenin's faith in the power of the national liberation movements to lead the world revolution to come, nonetheless, has radical implications for retroactively redeeming postcoloniality, especially the constitution of the postcolonial subject as one of the main loci of the production of a revolutionary internationalist subjectivity and its world-historic mission. Lenin did not simply provide a new language and broader theoretical vocabulary for articulating the concerns of the national liberation movements in the colonies, as the standard postcolonial critiques of Lenin have it. Rather, he located the language of hope and messianism that characterizes socialist internationalism in the postcolonial field of possibilities. Although Lenin did not simply abandon the potential of the proletariat for revolution, he seems to consider the subjects of the national liberation movements in the colonies more than just "one of the ferments, one of the bacilli, which help the real anti-imperialist force, the socialist proletariat, to make an appearance on the scene."[7] By embracing the subject of the national liberation movements, as Kevin Anderson writes, Lenin widened "the orthodox Marxist notion of the revolutionary subject" (Anderson 2007: 143). Lenin's position on the potential of the subject of colonial difference to assume the leadership of the revolutionary movement, I maintain, developed in dialogue and debates with many Third World Marxist activists and intellectuals most importantly, the Indian M. N. Roy and the Muslim Mir Said Sultan-Galiev.[8]

It is important first to note that Lenin's uncompromising socialist internationalist position on the problematic of the subject of colonial difference was first articulated at the 1907 Stuttgart Congress of the Second International (1889) especially, at the 1899 Brunn Congress. At Brunn, the solidarity of the oppressed, the Western proletariat and the subjects of colonial difference, took center stage over the preoccupation with intra-European colonialism that characterized the First International and the early congresses of the Second (Young 2001: 116). Lenin firmly rejected the pervasive conviction in the Congress that colonialism was an integral part of the socialist movement, criticizing its underlying racist bourgeois policies for "introducing virtual slavery into the colonies and subjecting the native populations to untold indignities and violence" (Young 2001: 116–17).

Lenin's understanding of this common bond of oppression between colonials and proletariat and the importance of class struggle for forging a link between them was rearticulated three years later (1910) at a world conference of colonized peoples and at the 1916 Lausanne conference. In a 1916 essay, he asserted that the struggle for national self-determination in the colonies was a leading force in the opposition to imperialist capitalism (Young 2001: 125; Anderson 2007: 129). As Kevin Anderson notes, Lenin was "the first major theorist, Marxist or non-Marxist, to grasp the importance that anti-nationalist movements would have for global politics in the twentieth century" (Anderson 2007: 128). Indeed, his references and examples in *Imperialism* (1916) and *The State and Revolution* (1917) were mostly drawn not from Russia but from anti-imperialist national liberation movements in India, Ireland, China, Turkey, and Iran. In his debates about the Irish Easter Rebellion of 1916, in particular, with leading Marxists especially, Radek and Trotsky, Lenin dissented from their Bukharinian renunciation of all forms of nationalism as obsolete, distinguishing between the chauvinist nationalism of colonial powers and the revolutionary nationalism of the national liberation movements which he described as "the dialectical opposite of global imperialism" (Anderson 2001: 131). In the years leading to the October Revolution, moreover, Lenin reconciled the claims of nationalism and national self-determination with the need for the proletariat to "fight in conjunction with it against colonial oppression," by anticipating the dissolution and renunciation of bourgeois nationalism in favor of the establishment of proletarian internationalism (Young 2001: 121–2).

As he began considering himself a leader of international Marxism, nonetheless, Lenin viewed the production of anti-imperialist subjectivity, one constituted through the dialectics of national struggle in the colonies, as central to his vision of world revolution and communist internationalism. Indeed, in his critique of Rosa Luxemburg's Eurocentric proletarian messianism, that only the "workers of the advanced capitalist countries . . . can lead the army of the exploited and enslaved of the five continents," Lenin forcefully argues that "the national liberation politics of the colonies will *inevitably* be continued by national wars of the colonies *against* imperialism" (emphasis in original; Lenin 1972, 22: 307). While the First Congress of the Third International, the Communist International, or the Comintern (1919), mainly reiterated Luxemburg's faith in the messianic powers of the Western urban proletariat to overthrow the European colonial states, so that "the workers and peasants not only of Annam, Algiers, and Bengal, but also of Persia and Armenia [may] gain their independence," by the time of the Second Congress Lenin was becoming very skeptical about the ability of the Western proletariat to affect an immediate revolution in Europe (Young 2001: 128). With the encouragement of Sultan-Galiev, Lenin began increasingly to "identify the countries of the east as being of more potential revolutionary significance" (Young 2001: 129). In *The National Liberation-Movement in the East*, therefore, Lenin writes: "And it should be perfectly clear that in the coming decisive battles of the world revolution, this movement of the majority of the world's population, originally aimed at national liberation, will turn against capitalism and imperialism and will, perhaps, play a more revolutionary role than we have been led to expect" (Lenin 1969: 289–90).

At and after the Second Congress, moreover, Lenin identified his critique of imperialism with that of the Indian Marxist M.N. Roy, putting thus "colonial revolution at the forefront of the priorities of the new communist government, regarding it as a central factor in the Soviet fight against capitalism" (Young 2001: 125). Indeed, Roy was instrumental in Lenin's recognition of the subject of colonial difference as one of the main loci of revolutionary subjectivity. Drawing on and revising Marx's analysis of Ireland in his debate with Lenin on the importance of Asia in developing world revolutions, Roy argued that "because of the economic dependency of imperialist powers on their colonial structures, 'the fate of the revolutionary movement in Europe depends *entirely* on the course of the revolution in the East. Without the victory of the revolution in the eastern countries, the communist movement in the West would come to nothing" (emphasis added; qtd in Young 2001: 131–2). While Lenin thought that Roy's use of the word "entirely" was hyperbolic, Lenin in his address to the Second Congress, nonetheless, announced: "World imperialism shall fall when the revolutionary onslaught of the exploited and oppressed workers in each country . . . merge with the revolutionary onslaught of hundreds of millions of people who have hitherto stood beyond the pale of history and have been regarded merely as the objects of history" (Lenin 1972, 31: 207–8). The power of the subjects of colonial difference is thus embedded in their rejection of that status as "objects of history" and their ability to reclaim the potential for embodying the idea of revolution. Indeed, Lenin stated that "the awakening to life and struggle of the new classes in the East (Japan, India, China) . . . serves as a fresh confirmation of Marxism" (Lenin 1972, 33: 234).

Lenin's radical idea from the Second Congress until his death, then, was his ability to recodify the subjects of colonial difference into the vanguard subjects of socialist internationalism, an idea that he had presciently anticipated in a 1913 article entitled, "Backward Europe and Advanced Asia" (Lenin 1972, 19: 99–101). This idea took full form in The First Congress of the Peoples of the East, or the Baku Congress of 1920, which convened at his own instigation to underscore the revolutionary potential of the subjects of colonial difference. Lenin's understanding of the primacy of anti-colonial struggle of the national liberation movements in the march toward socialist internationalism does not thus simply mean that he bracketed the potential of the proletariat to lead the revolution, but rather the opposite, that above all Lenin was increasingly convinced that the national liberation movements in the colonies provided a new language of anti-imperial struggle and liberation with which to inject the stale legacy of socialist internationalism. Even in the last article he wrote, Lenin reiterated his faith in the future role of the subject of colonial difference in the coming world revolution, stating that the mobilization of the national liberation movements in the colonies will ensure socialist victory (Lenin 1972, 45: 416–17). Such a position would not be far from Lenin's dialectical "concrete analysis of concrete situations" which, as Etienne Balibar maintains, "assumed incorporating into the concept of revolutionary process the *plurality of forms* of proletarian political struggle ("peaceful" and "violent"), and the *transition* from one form to another (hence the question of the specific duration and successive contradictions of the revolutionary transition" (emphasis in original; Balibar 2007: 211). This is not only to acknowledge that the socialist revolution is inconceivable without a diverse and international insurgency, as Kevin Anderson argues (Anderson 1995: 135–41), but that the idea of the revolution itself will inevitably be, and will have been, "exported" to the world from without Europe. To invert Stalin's statement on "The International Significance of the October Revolution," it could be said in regards to Lenin's position on the revolutionary potential of postcolonial subjectivity that the struggle of national liberation movements in the colonies created a "new line of revolution against world imperialism," extending from the oppressed nations of the East, through the Russian revolution, and to the "proletarians of the West" (qtd in Young 2001: 126).

The Postcolonial Hypothesis: Two Words for Žižek

Reconfiguring this postcolonial trajectory of Lenin's revolutionary pedagogy is in line with Žižek's view that "while the pure past is the transcendental condition for our acts, our acts not only create an actual new reality, but also retroactively change this very condition" (Žižek 2008: 315). As such, Lenin's October Revolution should be perceived only as "being one possible, and often even not the most probable, outcome of an 'open' situation" (Žižek 2010: 86), and that the postcolonial impetus of Lenin's revolutionary politics is the specter that will continue to haunt the future of the radical left and the Western revolutionary theories and politics. This perception of an alternate postcolonial history of revolutionary internationalism does not simply amount to disavowing the October Revolution the way conservative, revisionist what-if historians do, but constitutes the site where the "felt *urgency* of the revolutionary act" unfolds in actuality (Žižek 2010: 86).

Shifting the focus from the October Revolution to the history of postcolonial revolutionary experimentation can therefore be more productive for thinking through not only the practical difficulties of constructing a revolution, but also the ultimate end of the revolution. Despite the disparity in the success of postcolonial revolutionary practices, one cannot simply overlook the record of postcolonial revolutions that were thickly invested in reimagining extra-capitalist social totalities. As one of the major repressed points of exclusion under the hegemony of global capitalism today, postcolonial spaces indeed constitute the most important locus for exacerbating the antagonisms inherent to the capitalist system, turning them into a collective evental site that even in, or precisely because of, its failures can offer a radical challenge to the totality of the liberal-capitalist socio-symbolic order and actualize the "revolutionary explosion."

My wager then is that, especially at this juncture in the rise of mezzanine regimes that refuse to do the bidding of US imperial power, Žižek's call for the "political mobilization of new forms of politics" must not only be predicated upon a "practical alliance" with the "new prole-tarians from Africa and elsewhere," as Alain Badiou states (Badiou 2010: 99).[9] Rather, they must be organized from the beginning at the level of the real by those same new postcolonial proletarians who recognize themselves in the socialist revolutionary Event. Indeed, under the current hegemony of neo-colonialist global capitalism, it is the subjects of post-colonial difference that have assumed the position of and been able to "subjectivize" Marx's "vanishing" proletariat. As Badiou correctly points out in regards to the Cultural Revolution, and by implication other postcolonial revolutionary acts, Žižek fails to understand not only the long series of postcolonial revolutionary acts that constitute the ultimate embodiment of the "principles of the Paris Commune," but also the "element of universality in [their] terrible failure" (Badiou 2010: 274, 273). As Žižek himself recently noted, the subject's fidelity to a cause like the revolutionary Event can be only regulated through "incessant betrayals" (Žižek 2010: xiv).

Despite the disparity in the history and practice of revolutionary ideol-ogy in the postcolonies, the postcolonial subject seems to be the one best suited these days to reinvent and stabilize a radically egalitarian politics as well as alternative forms of political organization "in the immediate" (Žižek 2008: 427). Chavez's call for a Fifth International and the recent current revolutionary developments in Tunisia, Egypt, Bahrain, and Libya, and the increasing signs of social upheaval and unrest that are sweeping Yemen, Jordan, and Syria, are the ultimate proof of the explo-sive, utopian potential of postcolonial emancipatory politics.[10] In Tahrir square, that is, Žižek needs to see that we were "allowed to act as if the utopian future is . . . already at hand, there to be seized" (Žižek 2002: 260). Indeed, it is this revolutionary postcolonial moment that proves beyond the shadow of doubt that "the 'right choice' is only possible the second time, after the wrong one; that is, it is only the first wrong choice which literally creates the conditions for the right choice" (Žižek 2010: 88).

Notes

1 When Ernesto Laclau faults Žižek's call to repeat Lenin, he is wary that such a call risks re-implementing the one-party political system and the dictator-ship of the proletariat (Laclau 2000). But, as I will argue below, Žižek's weak

form of "positive Marxism" makes it almost impossible to tell a priori the precise substance of such a repetition. Hence, the emphasis on the Badiouian event in Žižek's formulation of the act. For Žižek's response to Laclau, see his "A Leninist Gesture" and *In Defense of Lost Causes*.

2 For a history of the October Revolution and Lenin's surprise call for immediate revolution in October, see Rabinowitch (1976).

3 Žižek calls for rehabilitating Marx's distinction between the working class, as an "objective" social category, and the proletariat, as a certain subjective position or, in Kantian terms, the class "for itself" (Žižek 2002: 336). In response to his question as to "who occupies, who is able to subjectivize, today [the working class's] position as proletarian," my unequivocal answer is: the subject of postcolonial difference.

4 Abeysekara is clearly offended by the way in which Žižek obsessively lays the blame of the Nazi industrial genocide on the doctrine of noninvolvement in the Bhagavad Gita; for Žižek, this principle of disinterested action "provided the justification for the burning of the Jews in the gas chambers" (qtd in Abeysekara 2008: 81).

5 For a more pessimistic analysis of the revolutionary potential of the slums, see Davis who views religion in the favelas as the major reactionary political force and believes the dwellers care more about survival rather than protest. As he succinctly puts it, "making do is more conservative than revolutionary" (Davis 2006: 18, 35).

6 One must here contrast Žižek's endorsement of religious fundamentalism in the favelas with his critique of Islamic fundamentalist movements such as Hezbollah which is bound, in Badiou's words, to their "religious particularity." While in the former he locates a capacity for mediating direct democratic governance, in the latter he can only find the blurring of the "distinctions between capitalist neo-imperialism and secular progressive emancipation: within the Hezbollah ideological space, women's emancipation, gay rights, etc., are nothing but the "decadent" moral aspect of Western imperialism" (Žižek, "The Palestinian"). Ironically, Hizbollah is widely recognized as a trailblazer in the emergence of "mezzanine regimes" which seem to offer precisely that for which Žižek is condemning them.

7 V. I. Lenin, *Collected Works* (Moscow: Progress Publishers, 1972), vol. 22, p. 357. All subsequent references to Lenin from this edition will be cited by volume and page numbers in the text.

8 This reconstructive reading of Lenin's position on the true subject of revolutionary internationalism draws on the work of John Riddell's history and documentation of the Baku Conference and the Second Congress of the Third International. See also Young (2001: 115–39), and Kevin Anderson (1995; 2003) whose important work on Lenin's position on the national question which was grounded in Hegelian dialectics has refocused attention on this neglected issue in the criticism of Lenin's work.

9 For more on these mezzanine regimes, see Crawford and Miscik 2010.

10 Although Žižek praises the populist regimes of Hugo Chávez and Juan Evo Morales, his assessment of their regimes are framed within his debate on populism with Laclau. Given that sovereign power is always already cut through by a "totalitarian excess" (based on the recognition of the law's "obscene unconditional self-assertion" as the obverse side of its legitimate authority), Žižek maintains, the Chávez and Morales regimes successfully tilted that totalitarian excess of power towards the dispossessed "part of no-part," actualizing thus what he considers to be the "contemporary form of the dictatorship of the proletariat" (Žižek 2008: 379). Nonetheless, and this was the substance of his debate with Laclau, this populist commitment to the poor and the suspension of the big Other, in the guise of democratic electoral process, are invariably effective only as a "short-term pragmatic compromise." For him, such a populism then cannot bring a radical change in the system, because not only that the big Other is still present in the form of the "People as the substantial agent legitimizing power," but most importantly because populism can only normalize the "violent intrusion of the egalitarian logic" through democratic regulated procedures. In other words, populism fails to institutionalize itself as "revolutionary democratic terror" (Žižek 2008: 265, 266). More recently, Žižek has even condemned Chávez's anti-American populism which like Mugabe's failed economic policies exploit "racial divisions in order to obfuscate the class division," by playing the race card and "place the blame on the old white colonialists" (Žižek 2010: 385n36).

References

Abeysekara, Ananda (2008) *The Politics of Postsecular Religion: Mourning Secular Futures*. NY: Columbia University Press.

Anderson, Kevin B. (1995) *Lenin, Hegel, and Western Marxism: A Critical Study*. Champaign, IL: University of Illinois Press.

— (2007) "The Rediscovery and Persistence of the Dialectic in Philosophy and in World Politics." In *Lenin Reloaded: Towards a Politics of Truth*, eds Sebastian Budgen, Stathis Kouvelakis, and Slavoj Žižek. Durham and London: Duke University Press, pp. 120–47.

Badiou, Alain (2010) *The Communist Hypothesis*. London: Verso.

Balibar, Etienne (2007) "The Philosophical Moment in Politics Determined by War: Lenin 1914–1916." In *Lenin Reloaded: Towards a Politics of Truth*, eds Sebastian Budgen, Stathis Kouvelakis, and Slavoj Žižek. Durham and London: Duke University Press, pp. 207–21.

Crawford, Michael, and Jami Miscik (2010) "The Rise of the Mezzanine Rulers." *Foreign Affairs*, 89.6 (Nov./Dec.): 123–32.

Davis, Mike (2006) *Planet of Slums*. London: Verso.

Jameson, Frederick (2007) "Lenin and Revisionism." Budgen, Kouvelakis, and Žižek 59–73.

Johnston, Adrian (2009) *Badiou, Žižek, and Political Transformations: The Cadence of Change*. Evanston, IL: Northwestern University Press.

Laclau, Ernesto (2000) "Structure, History, and the Political." In *Contingency, Hegemony, Universality: Contemporary Debates on the Left* by Judith Butler, Ernesto Laclau, and Salvoj Žižek. NY and London: Verso, pp. 182–212.

Lenin, V. I. (1972) *Collected Works*. 45 vols. Moscow: Progress Publishers.

— (1969) *National-Liberation Movement in the East*. Moscow: Progress Publishers.

Rabinowitch, A. (1976) *The Bolsheviks Come to Power*. NY: Norton.

Riddell, John, ed. (1993) *To See the Dawn: Baku, 1920 – First Congress of the Peoples of the East*. NY: Pathfinder Press.

— ed. (1991) *Workers of the World and Oppressed Peoples Unite! Proceedings and Documents of the Second Congress, 1920*. 2 Volumes. NY: Pathfinder Press.

Young, Robert J. (2001) *Postcolonialism: An Historical Introduction*. Malden, MA: Blackwell.

Žižek, Slavoj (1997a) "The Palestinian Question." Lacan.com. Web.

— (1997b) *The Plague of Fantasies*. London and NY: Verso.

— (1999) *The Ticklish Subject*. London and NY: Verso.

— (2000) *The Fragile Absolute, or Why the Christian Legacy is Worth Fighting For?* London: Verso.

— (2001) *On Belief*. NY: Routledge.

— ed. (2002) *Revolution at the Gate: Selected Writings of Lenin from 1917* by V. I. Lenin. London: Verso.

— (2006) *The Universal Exception: Selected Writings*, vol. 2, eds Rex Butler and Scott Stephens. NY and London: Continuum.

— (2007) "A Leninist Gesture Today: Against the Populist Temptation." In *Lenin Reloaded: Towards a Politics of Truth*, eds Sebastian Budgen, Stathis Kouvelakis, and Slavoj Žižek. Durham and London: Duke University Press, pp. 74–98.

— (2008) *In Defense of Lost Causes*. NY and London: Verso.

— (2010) *Living in the End Times*. NY: Verso.

Part Four

9

King, Rabble, Sex, and War in Hegel

Slavoj Žižek

The most famous passage in Jack London's *Martin Eden* is the final paragraph, describing the hero's suicide by drowning:

> He seemed floating languidly in a sea of dreamy vision. Colors and radiances
> surrounded him and bathed him and pervaded him. What was that? It seemed
> a lighthouse; but it was inside his brain – a flashing, bright white light. It
> flashed swifter and swifter. There was a long rumble of sound, and it seemed
> to him that he was falling down a vast and interminable stairway. And some-
> where at the bottom he fell into darkness. That much he knew. He had fallen
> into darkness. And at the instant he knew, he ceased to know.

How did Martin arrive at this point? What pushed him to suicide was
his very success – the novel presents the crisis of investiture in its simple
but most radical form: after long years of struggle and hard work, Martin
finally succeeds and becomes a famous writer; however, while he is float-
ing in wealth and fame, one thing puzzles him,

> a little thing that would have puzzled the world had it known. But the world
> would have puzzled over his bepuzzlement rather than over the little thing
> that to him loomed gigantic. Judge Blount invited him to dinner. That was
> the little thing, or the beginning of the little thing, that was soon to become
> the big thing. He had insulted Judge Blount, treated him abominably, and
> Judge Blount, meeting him on the street, invited him to dinner. Martin
> bethought himself of the numerous occasions on which he had met Judge
> Blount at the Morses' and when Judge Blount had not invited him to dinner.

Why had he not invited him to dinner then? he asked himself. He had not changed. He was the same Martin Eden. What made the difference? The fact that the stuff he had written had appeared inside the covers of books? But it was work performed. It was not something he had done since. It was achievement accomplished at the very time Judge Blount was sharing this general view and sneering at his Spencer and his intellect. Therefore it was not for any real value, but for a purely fictitious value that Judge Blount invited him to dinner.[1]

This little puzzling thing grows larger and larger, turning into the central obsession of his life:

His thoughts went ever around and around in a circle. The centre of that circle was "work performed"; it ate at his brain like a deathless maggot. He awoke to it in the morning. It tormented his dreams at night. Every affair of life around him that penetrated through his senses immediately related itself to "work performed." He drove along the path of relentless logic to the conclusion that he was nobody, nothing. Mart Eden, the hoodlum, and Mart Eden, the sailor, had been real, had been he; but Martin Eden! the famous writer, did not exist. Martin Eden, the famous writer, was a vapor that had arisen in the mob-mind and by the mob-mind had been thrust into the corporeal being of Mart Eden, the hoodlum and sailor.

Even his beloved Lizzy who didn't want to marry him, is now desperately throwing herself at him, proclaiming that she loves him totally; when she proclaims that she is ready to die for him, Martin tauntingly replies:

Why didn't you dare it before? When I hadn't a job? When I was starving? When I was just as I am now, as a man, as an artist, the same Martin Eden? That's the question I've been propounding to myself for many a day – not concerning you merely, but concerning everybody. You see I have not changed, though my sudden apparent appreciation in value compels me constantly to reassure myself on that point. I've got the same flesh on my bones, the same ten fingers and toes. I am the same. I have not developed any new strength nor virtue. My brain is the same old brain. I haven't made even one new generalization on literature or philosophy. I am personally of the same value that I was when nobody wanted me. And what is puzzling me is why they want me now. Surely they don't want me for myself, for myself is the same old self they did not want. Then they must want me for something else, for something that is outside of me, for something that is not I! Shall I tell you what that something is? It is for the recognition I have received. That recognition is not I. It resides in the minds of others.

What Martin cannot accept is the radical gap that forever separates his "real" qualities from his symbolic status (in the eyes of the others): all of a sudden, he is no longer a nobody avoided by respectable public but a famous author invited by the pillars of society, with even the beloved woman now throwing herself at his feet – but he is fully aware that nothing changed in him in reality, he is now the same person as he was, and even all his works were already written when he was ignored and despised. What Martin cannot accept is this radical de-centering of the very core of his personality which "resides in the minds of others": he is nothing in himself, just a concentrated projection of others' dreams. This perception that his *agalma*, what now makes him desired by others, is something that is outside of him, not only ruins his narcissism, but also kills his desire: "Something has gone out of me. I have always been unafraid of life, but I never dreamed of being sated with life. Life has so filled me that I am empty of any desire for anything." It is this "conclusion that he was nobody, nothing," which drove him to suicide.

Insofar as symbolic castration is also one of the names of the gap between my immediate stupid being and my symbolic title (recall the proverbial disappointment of an adolescent: is that miserable coward really my *father*?), and since a symbolic authority can only function insofar as, in a kind of illegitimate short-circuit, this gap is obfuscated and my symbolic authority appears as an immediate property or quality of me as a person, each authority has to protect itself from situations in which this gap becomes palpable. For example, political leaders know very well how to avoid situations in which their impotence would have been revealed; a father knows how to hide from the gaze of his son his humiliating moments (when his boss shouts at him, etc.). What is protected by such strategies of "saving one's face" is *appearance*: although I know very well my father is ultimately impotent, I refuse to believe it, which is why the effect of witnessing the open display of his impotence can be so shattering. Such humiliating moments fully deserve to be called "castrating experiences," not because father is shown castrated-impotent, but because the gap between his miserable reality and his symbolic authority is rendered palpable and can no longer *be* ignored by way of the fetishist disavowal.

For Hegel, the definition of a king is a subject who accepts this radical decenterment, i.e., to quote Marx, the fact that he is a King because others treat him as a King, not the other way round – otherwise, if he thinks that he is a King "in himself," he is a madman (recall Lacan's claim that a madman is not only a beggar who thinks he is a King but also a

King who thinks he is a King). According to a legend, during the decisive battle between the Prussian and the Austrian army in the 1866 war, the Prussian king, formally the supreme commander of the Prussian army, who was observing the fight from a nearby hill, looked worried at (what appeared to him) the confusion in front of his eyes, where some of the Prussian troops even seemed to be retreating. General von Moltke, the great Prussian strategist who planned the battle deployment, turned to the King in the middle of this apparent confusion and told him: "May I be the first to congratulate your majesty for a brilliant victory?" This is the gap between S_1 and S_2 at its purest: the King was the Master, the formal commander totally ignorant of the meaning of what went on in the battlefield, while von Moltke embodied strategic knowledge – although, at the level of actual decisions, the victory was Moltke's, he was correct in congratulating the King on behalf of whom he was acting. The stupidity of the Master is palpable in this gap between the confusion of the master-figure and the objective-symbolic fact that he already won a brilliant victory. We all know the old joke referring to the enigma of who really wrote Shakespeare's plays: "Not William Shakespeare, but someone else with the same name." This is what Lacan means by the "decentered subject," this is how a subject relates to the name which fixes its symbolic identity: John Smith is (always, by definition, in its very notion) not John Smith, but someone else with the same name. As already Shakespeare's Juliet knew, I am never "that name" – the John Smith who really thinks he is John Smith is a psychotic. This key point was missed by the young Marx in his critique of Hegel's *Philosophy of Right*; after quoting the beginning of Par 281:

> Both moments in their undivided unity – (a) the will's ultimate ungrounded self, and (b) therefore its similarly ungrounded objective existence (existence being the category which is at home in nature) – constitute the Idea of something against which caprice is powerless, the 'majesty' of the monarch. In this unity lies the actual unity of the state, and it is only through this, its inward and outward immediacy, that the unity of the state is saved from the risk of being drawn down into the sphere of particularity and its caprices, ends and opinions, and saved too from the war of factions round the throne and from the enfeeblement and overthrow of the power of the state.[2]

Marx adds his comment full of (all too commonsensical) irony:

> The two moments are [a] the contingency of the will, caprice, and [b] the contingency of nature, birth; thus, His Majesty: Contingency. Contingency

is thus the actual unity of the state. The way in which, according to Hegel, an inward and outward immediacy [of the state] is to be saved from collision, [due to caprice, factions,] etc., is incredible, since collision is precisely what it makes possible. /. . ./ The prince's hereditary character results from his concept. He is to be the person who is specified from the entire race of men, who is distinguished from all other persons. But then what is the ultimate fixed difference of one person from all others? The body. And the highest function of the body is sexual activity. Hence the highest constitutional act of the king is his sexual activity, because through this he makes a king and carries on his body.[3]

Marx concludes with the sarcastic note that the Hegelian monarch is nothing more than an appendix to his penis – to which we should say: yes, but that's precisely Hegel's point, i.e., such an utter alienation, such a reversal by means of which a person becomes an appendix of its biological organ of procreation, is the price to be paid for acting like the state's sovereignty embodied. (Note also the irony of the situation: insofar as the gap between my immediate bodily being and my symbolic identity is the gap of castration, being reduced to one's penis is the very formula of castration.) One can clearly see, from the quoted Par 281, how the institution of hereditary monarchy is for Hegel the solution to the problem of caprices and war of factions, in short, of the contingency of social life of power. One overcomes this contingency not with a deeper necessity (say, in the sense of Plato's philosophers-kings, rulers whose knowledge legitimizes their power), but with an even more radical contingency: one posits at the top a subject reduced to an appendix of his penis, a subject who did not make himself what he is (through the labor of mediation), but is immediately born into it. Of course, Hegel is fully aware that there is no deeper necessity secretly pulling the strings and guaranteeing that the monarch will be a wise, just and courageous person – on the contrary, in the figure of the monarch, contingency (of his properties and qualifications) is brought to an extreme, all that matters is his birth. (Also in inherent philosophical terms, we can see here how radical Hegel is in his assertion of contingency: the only way to overcome contingency is through its redoubling.) In socio-political life, stability can only be regained when all subjects accept the result of this contingent process, since the contingency of birth is exempted from social struggles.

An obvious counter-argument arises here: does Hegel not remain caught in an illusion of purity – namely of the purity of expert-knowledge of state bureaucracy which only works rationally for the common good? True, he concedes an irreducible impurity (being caught in the contingent play of partial interests and factional struggles) of political life, but is not his illusory wager that, if one isolates this moment of impurity (subjective caprice) in the figure of the monarch, this exception will make the rest, the body of state bureaucracy, rational, exempted from the play of conflictual partial interests? Is thus, with this notion of state bureaucracy as the "universal class," the state not depoliticized, exempted from the properly political *differend*? However, while Hegel is well aware that political life consists of the contingent "war of factions round the throne," his idea is not that the monarch takes upon himself this contingency and thus magically turns state bureaucracy into a neutral machine, but that, on account of his being-determined by the contingency of biological descendance, *the King himself* is in a formal sense elevated above political struggles.

In Lacanese, the passage from inherent notional self-development which mediates all content to the act/decision which freely releases this content is, of course, the passage from S_2 (knowledge, the chain of signifiers) to S_1 (the performative Master-Signifier). (In a strictly homologous sense, the Hegelian Absolute Knowing is a knowledge which is "absolved" from its positive content.) Schelling was thus wrong in his critique of Hegel: the intervention of the act of decision is purely immanent, it is the moment of the "quilting point," of the reversal of constative into performative. Does the same not go for the King in the case of State, according to Hegel's defense of monarchy? The bureaucratic chain of knowledge is followed by the King's decision which, as the "completely concrete objectivity of the will," "reabsorbs all particularity into its single self, cuts short the weighing of pros and cons between which it lets itself oscillate perpetually now this way and now that, and by saying 'I will' makes its decision and so inaugurates all activity and actuality." Hegel emphasizes this apartness of the monarch already when he states that the "ultimate self-determination" can "fall within the sphere of human freedom only in so far as it has the position of a pinnacle, explicitly distinct from, and raised above, all that is particular and conditional, for only so is it actual in a way adequate to its concept."(Ibid.) This is why "the conception of the monarch" is

> of all conceptions the hardest for ratiocination, i.e., for the method of reflection employed by the Understanding. This method refuses to move beyond isolated categories and hence here again knows only *raisonnement*, finite points of view, and deductive argumentation. Consequently it exhibits the dignity

of the monarch as something deduced, not only in its form, but in its essence. The truth is, however, that to be something not deduced but purely self-originating is precisely the conception of monarchy.

In the next paragraph (280) Hegel further elaborates this speculative necessity of the monarch:

> This ultimate self in which the will of the state is concentrated is, when thus taken in abstraction, a single self and therefore is immediate individuality. Hence its 'natural' character is implied in its very conception. The monarch, therefore, is essentially characterized as this individual, in abstraction from all his other characteristics, and this individual is raised to the dignity of monarchy in an immediate, natural, fashion, i.e., through his birth in the course of nature.
>
> *Remark*: This transition of the concept of pure self-determination into the immediacy of being and so into the realm of nature is of a purely speculative character, and the apprehension of it therefore belongs to logic. Moreover, this transition is on the whole the same as that familiar to us in the nature of willing, and there the process is to translate something from subjectivity (i.e., some purpose held before the mind) into existence. But the proper form of the Idea and of the transition here under consideration is the immediate conversion of the pure self-determination of the will (i.e., of the simple concept itself) into a single and natural existent without the mediation of a particular content (like a purpose in the case of action).
>
> In the so-called 'ontological' proof of the existence of God, we have the same conversion of the absolute concept into existence. /. . ./
>
> *Addition*: It is often alleged against monarchy that it makes the welfare of the state dependent on chance, for, it is urged, the monarch may be ill-educated, he may perhaps be unworthy of the highest position in the state, and it is senseless that such a state of affairs should exist because it is supposed to be rational. But all this rests on a presupposition which is nugatory, namely that everything depends on the monarch's particular character. In a completely organized state, it is only a question of the culminating point of formal decision (and a natural bulwark against passion. It is wrong therefore to demand objective qualities in a monarch); he has only to say 'yes' and dot the 'i', because the throne should be such that the significant thing in its holder is not his particular make-up. /. . ./ In a well-organized monarchy, the objective aspect belongs to law alone, and the monarch's part is merely to set to the law the subjective 'I will'.

The speculative moment that Understanding cannot grasp is "the transition of the concept of pure self-determination into the immediacy of being and so into the realm of nature." In other words, while Understanding can well grasp the universal mediation of a living totality, what it cannot grasp is that this totality, in order to actualize itself, has to acquire actual existence in the guise of an immediate "natural" singularity. (The Marxists who mocked Hegel here paid the price for this negligence: in the regimes which legitimized themselves as Marxist, a Leader emerged who, again, not only directly embodied the rational totality, but embodied it fully, as a figure of full Knowledge and not merely the idiotic point of dotting the i's. In other words, a Stalinist Leader is NOT a monarch, which makes him much worse . . .) One can also say that Understanding misses the *christological* moment: the necessity of a singular individual to embody the universal Spirit. – The term "nature" should be given its full weight here: in the same way that, at the end of Logic, the Idea's completed self-mediation releases from itself Nature, collapses into the external immediacy of Nature, the State's rational self-mediation has to acquire actual existence in a will which is determined as directly natural, unmediated, *stricto sensu* "irrational."

Recall here Chesterton's appraisal of the guillotine (which was used precisely to behead a king):

> The guillotine has many sins, but to do it justice there is nothing evolutionary about it. The favourite evolutionary argument finds its best answer in the axe. The Evolutionist says, 'Where do you draw the line?' the Revolutionist answers, 'I draw it *here*: exactly between your head and body.' There must at any given moment be an abstract right or wrong if any blow is to be struck; there must be something eternal if there is to be anything sudden.[4]

It is from here that one can understand why Badiou, THE theorist of the Act, has to refer to Eternity: act is only conceivable as the intervention of Eternity into time. Historicist evolutionism leads up to endless procrastination, the situation is always too complex, there are always some more aspects to be accounted for, our pondering of pros and cons is never over . . . against this stance, the passage to act involves a gesture of radical and violent simplification, a cut like that of the proverbial Gordian knot: the magical moment when the infinite pondering crystallizes itself into a simple "yes" or "no."

A propos school exams, Lacan pointed out a strange fact: there must be a minimal gap, delay, between the procedure of measuring my qualifications and the act of announcing the result (grades). In other words, even if I know that I provided perfect answers to the exam questions, there remains a minimum element of insecurity, of chance, till the results are announced − this gap is the gap between *constatif* and *performatif*, between *measuring* the results and *taking note* of them (registering them) in the full sense of the symbolic act. The whole mystique of bureaucracy in its most sublime hinges on this gap: you know the facts, but you can never be quite sure of how these facts will be registered by bureaucracy. And, as Jean-Pierre Dupuy points out, the same holds for elections: in the electoral process also, the moment of contingency, of hazard, of a "draw," is crucial.[5] Fully "rational" elections would not be elections at all, but a transparent objectivized process. Traditional (pre-modern) societies resolved this problem by invoking a transcendent source which "verified" the result, conferring authority on it (God, King . . .). Therein resides the problem of modernity: modern societies perceive themselves as autonomous, self-regulated, i.e., they can no longer rely on an external (transcendent) source of authority. But, nonetheless, the moment of hazard has to remain operative in the electoral process, which is why commentators like to dwell on the "irrationality" of votes (one never knows where votes will swing in the last days before elections . . .). In other words, democracy would not work if it were to be reduced to permanent opinion polling − fully mechanized-quantified, deprived of its "performative" character; as Lefort pointed out, voting has to remain a (sacrificial) ritual, a ritualistic self-destruction and rebirth of society.[6] The reason is that this hazard itself should not be transparent, it should be minimally externalized/reified: "people's will" is our equivalent of what the Ancients perceived as the imponderable God's will or the hands of Fate. What people cannot accept as their direct arbitrary choice, the result of a pure hazard, they can accept if it refers to a minimum of the "real" − Hegel knew this long ago, this is the entire point of his defense of monarchy. And, last but not least, the same goes for love: there should be an element of the "answer of the Real" in it ("we were forever meant for each other"), I cannot really accept that my falling in love hinges on a pure contingency.[7]

Even such a superb reader of Hegel as Gerard Lebrun falls short here in inscribing Hegel into the Platonic tradition of "philosophers-kings": every exercise of power has to be justified by good reasons, the bearer of power has to be properly qualified for it by his knowledge and abilities, plus power should be exercised for the good of the entire community − this notion of power sustains Hegel's concept of state bureaucracy as the "universal class" educated to protect state interests against the particular interests of members and groups of the civil society. According to

Lebrun, Nietzsche counters this received notion by questioning its underlying premise: what kind of power (or authority) is it which needs to
justify itself by evoking the interests of those over whom it rules, i.e.,
which accepts the need to provide reasons for its exercise? Does such a
notion of power not undermine itself? How can I be your master when
I accept the need to justify my authority in your eyes? Does this not
imply that my authority depends on your approval, so that, acting as your
master, I effectively serve you (recall Frederick the Great's famous notion
of the King as the highest servant of his people)? Is it not that authority
proper needs no reasons, since it is simply accepted on its own? As
Kierkegaard put it, for a child to say that he obeys his father because the
latter is wise, honest and good, is a blasphemy, a total disavowal of the
true paternal authority. In Lacanian terms, this passage from "natural"
authority to authority justified by reasons is, of course, the passage from
the master's discourse to the university discourse. This universe of justified exercise of power is also eminently anti-political and, in this sense,
"technocratic": my exercise of power should be grounded in reasons
accessible to and approved by all rational human beings, i.e., the underlying premise is that, as an agent of power, I am totally replaceable, I act
in exactly the same way everyone else would have acted at my place –
politics as the domain of competitive struggle, as the articulation of
irreducible social antagonisms, should be replaced by rational administration which directly enacts the universal interest.

Is, however, Lebrun right in imputing to Hegel such a notion of justified authority? Was Hegel not fully aware that true authority always
contains an element of the tautological self-assertion? "It is so because I
say it is so!" The exercise of authority is an "irrational" act of contingent
decision which cuts short the endless chain of enumerating reasons *pro et
contra*. Is this not the very rationale of Hegel's defence of monarchy? The
State as a rational totality needs at its head a figure of "irrational" authority, an authority not justified by its qualifications: while all other public
servants have to prove their capacity to exert power, the king is justified
by the very fact that he is a king. To put it in more contemporary terms,
the performative aspect of state acts is reserved for the king: the state
bureaucracy prepared the content of state acts, but it is the signature of
the king which enacts them, enforcing them upon society. Hegel was
well aware that it is only this distance between the "knowledge" embodied in state bureaucracy and the authority of the Master embodied in the
king which protects the social body against the "totalitarian" temptation:
what we call "totalitarian regime" is not a regime in which the Master

imposes its unconstrained authority and ignores the suggestions of rational knowledge, but the regime in which Knowledge (the rationally justified authority) immediately assumes "performative" power – Stalin was not (presenting himself as) a Master, he was the highest servant of the people legitimized by his knowledge and abilities.

Hegel's insight points toward his unique position between the Master's discourse (of the traditional authority) and the university discourse (of the modern power justified by reasons or the democratic consent of its subjects): Hegel knew that the charisma of the Master's authority is a fake, that Master is an impostor – it is only the fact that he occupies the position of a Master (that his subjects treat him as a Master) which makes him a Master. However, he was also well aware that, if one tries to get rid of this excess and impose a self-transparent authority fully justified by expert knowledge, the result is even worse: instead of being contained to the symbolic head of State (King), "irrationality" spreads over the entire body of social power. Kafka's bureaucracy is such a regime of expert knowledge deprived of the figure of the Master – Brecht was right when, as Benjamin reports in his diaries, during a conversation on Kafka, he claimed that Kafka is "the *only genuine Bolshevik* writer."[8]

Is, then, Hegel's position cynical? Does he tells us to act as if a monarch is qualified by his properties, celebrate his glory, etc., although we know well that he is nobody in himself? A gap nonetheless separates Hegel's position from cynicism: the Hegelian (utopian?) wager is that one can admire a monarch not for his supposed real qualities, but on behalf of his very mediocrity, as a representative of human frailty. Here, however, things get complicated: is the excess at the top of the social edifice (king, leader) not to be supplemented by the excess at its bottom, by the "part of no part" of the social body, those with no proper place within it, what Hegel called *Poebel* (rabble)? Hegel fails to take note how the rabble, in its very status of the destructive excess of social totality, its "part of no-part," is the "reflexive determination" of the totality as such, the immediate embodiment of its universality, the particular element in the guise of which the social totality encounter itself among its elements, and, as such, the key constituent of its identity.[9] (Note the dialectical finesse of this last feature: what "sutures" the identity of a social totality as such is the very "free-floating" element which dissolves all fixed identity of any intra-social element.)[10] This is why Frank Ruda is fully justified in reading Hegel's short passages on rabble (*Poebel*) in his *Philosophy of Right* as a symptomatic point of his entire philosophy of right, if not of his entire system.[11] If Hegel were to see the universal dimension of the rabble, he would have invented the symptom (as Marx – who saw in the proletariat the embodiment of the deadlocks of the existing society, the universal class – did).[12] That is to say, what makes the notion of rabble symptomatic is that it describes a necessarily produced "irrational" excess of modern rational state, a group of people for which there is no place within the organized totality of the modern state, although they formally belong to it – as such, they perfectly exemplify the category of singular universality (a singular which directly gives body to a universality, by-passing the mediation through the particular), of what Rancière called the "part of no-part" of the social body:

> § 244 When the standard of living of a large mass of people falls below a certain subsistence level – a level regulated automatically as the one necessary for a member of the society – and when there is a consequent loss of the sense of right and wrong, of honesty and the self-respect which makes a man insist on maintaining himself by his own work and effort, the result is the creation of a rabble of paupers. At the same time this brings with it, at the other end of the social scale, conditions which greatly facilitate the concentration of disproportionate wealth in a few hands.

We can easily perceive here the link between the eminently political topic of the status of the rabble and Hegel's basic ontological topic of the relationship between universality and particularity, i.e., the problem of how to understand the Hegelian "concrete universality." If we understand "concrete universality" in the usual sense of the organic subdivision of the universal into its particular moments, so that universality is not an abstract feature in which individuals directly participate, and the participation of the individual in the universal is always mediated through the particular network of determinations, then the corresponding notion of society is a corporate one: society as an organic Whole in which each individual has to find its particular place, i.e., in which I participate in the State by fulfilling my particular duty or obligation. There are no citizens as such, one has to be a member of a particular estate (a farmer, a state official, mother in a family, teacher, artisan . . .) in order to contribute to the harmony of the Whole. This is the Bradleyian proto-Fascist Hegel who opposes atomistic liberalism (in which society is a mechanic unity of abstract individuals) on behalf of the State as a living organism in which each part has its function, and within this space, rabble has to appear as the irrational excess, as the threat to social order and stability, as outcasts excluded and excluding themselves from the "rational" social totality.

But is this truly what Hegel aims at with his "concrete universality"? Is the core of the dialectical negativity not the short-circuit between the genus and (one of) its species, so that genus appears as one of its own species opposed to others, entering a negative relationship with them? Recall Ambedkar's rejoinder to Gandhi: "There will be outcasts as long as there are castes." As long as there are castes, there will always be an excessive excremental zero-value element which, while formally part of the system, has no proper place within it, and as such stands for the (repressed) universality of this system. In this sense, concrete universality is precisely a universality which includes itself among its species, in the guise of a singular moment lacking particular content – in short, it is precisely those who are without their proper place within the social Whole (like the rabble) that stand for the universal dimension of the society which generates them. This is why the rabble cannot be abolished without radically transforming the entire social edifice – and Hegel is fully aware of this; he is consistent enough to confess that a solution of this "disturbing problem" is impossible not for external contingent reasons, but for strictly immanent conceptual reasons. While he enumerates a series of measures to resolve the problem (police control and repression, charity, export of rabble to colonies . . .), he himself admits that these are only secondary palliatives which cannot really resolve the problem – not because the problem is too hard (i.e., because there is not enough wealth in society to take care of the poor), but because there is too much excessive wealth – the more society is wealthy, the more poverty it produces:

§ 245 When the masses begin to decline into poverty, (a) the burden of maintaining them at their ordinary standard of living might be directly laid on the wealthier classes, or they might receive the means of livelihood directly from other public sources of wealth (e.g., from the endowments of rich hospitals, monasteries, and other foundations). In either case, however, the needy would receive subsistence directly, not by means of their work, and this would violate the principle of civil society and the feeling of individual independence and self-respect in its individual members. (b) As an alternative, they might be given subsistence indirectly through being given work, i.e., the opportunity to work. In this event the volume of production would be increased, but the evil consists precisely in an excess of production and in the lack of a proportionate number of consumers who are themselves also producers, and thus it is simply intensified by both of the methods (a) and (b) by which it is sought to alleviate it. It hence becomes apparent that despite an excess of wealth civil society is not rich enough, i.e., its own resources are insufficient to check excessive poverty and the creation of a penurious rabble.

Note the finesse of Hegel's analysis: he points out that poverty is not only a material condition, but also the subjective position of being deprived of social recognition, which is why it is not enough to provide for the poor through public or private charity – in this way, the poor are still deprived of the satisfaction of autonomously taking care of their own lives. Furthermore, when Hegel emphasizes how society – the existing social order – is the ultimate space in which the subject finds his/her substantial content and recognition, i.e., how subjective freedom can actualize itself only in the rationality of the universal ethical order, the implied (although not explicitly stated) obverse is that those who do NOT find this recognition have also the right to rebel: if a class of people is systematically deprived of their rights, of their very dignity as persons, they are *eo ipso* also released from their duties toward the social order, because this order is no longer their ethical substance. The dismissive tone of Hegel's statements about the "rabble" should not blind us to the basic fact that he considered their rebellion rationally fully justified: the "rabble" is a class of people to whom systematically, not just in a contingent way, recognition by the ethical substance is denied, so they also do not owe anything to society, are dispensed of any duties toward it.

The negativity – the non-recognized element of the existing order – is thus necessarily produced, inherent to it, but with no place within the order. Here, however, Hegel commits a failure (measured by his own standards): he doesn't venture the obvious thesis that, as such, rabble should immediately stand for the universality of society. As excluded, lacking recognition for its particular position, the rabble is the universal as such. At this point, at least, Marx was right in his critique of Hegel, since he was here more Hegelian than Hegel himself – as is well known, this is the starting point of the Marxian analysis: the "proletariat" designates such an "irrational" element of the "rational" social totality, its unaccountable "part of no part," the element systematically generated by it and, simultaneously, denied the basic rights that define this totality, as such, the proletariat stands for the universality dimension, i.e., its emancipation is only possible in/through the universal emancipation. In a way, EVERY act is proletarian: "There is only one social symptom: every individual is effectively proletarian, that is to say, he does not dispose of a discourse by means of which he could establish a social link."[13] It is only from such a "proletarian" position of being deprived of a discourse (of occupying the place of the "part of no part" within the existing social link) than an act can emerge.

How, then, do the two excesses (the excess at the top and the excess at the bottom) relate to each other? Does the link between the two not provide the formula of a populist authoritarian regime? In his *18ᵗʰ brumaire*, the analysis of the first populist-authoritarian regime (the reign of Napoleon III), Marx pointed out that, while Napoleon III played one class against the other, stealing from one in order to satisfy another, the only true class base of his rule was the lumpenproletarian rabble. In a homologous way, the paradox of fascism is that it advocates hierarchic order in which "everybody at his/her proper place," while its only true social base is rabble (SA thugs, etc.) – in it, the only direct class link of the Leader is the one which connects him to rabble, it is only among the rabble that Hitler was truly "at home."

Hegel is of course aware that objective poverty is not enough to generate rabble: this objective poverty must be subjectivized, changed into a "disposition of mind," experienced as radical injustice on account of which the subject feels no duty and obligation toward society. Hegel leaves no doubt that this injustice is a real one: society has a duty to guarantee the conditions for a dignified free autonomous life to all its members – this is their right, and if it is denied, they also have no duties toward society:

> Addition: The lowest subsistence level, that of a rabble of paupers, is fixed automatically, but the minimum varies considerably in different countries. In England, even the very poorest believe that they have rights; this is different from what satisfies the poor in other countries. Poverty in itself does not make men into a rabble; a rabble is created only when there is joined to poverty a disposition of mind, an inner indignation against the rich, against society, against the government, &c. A further consequence of this attitude is that through their dependence on chance men become frivolous and idle, like the Neapolitan lazzaroni for example. In this way there is born in the rabble the evil of lacking self-respect enough to secure subsistence by its own labor and yet at the same time of claiming to receive subsistence as its right. Against nature man can claim no right, but once society is established, poverty immediately takes the form of a wrong done to one class by another. The important question of how poverty is to be abolished is one of the most disturbing problems which agitate modern society.[14]

It is easy to discern the ambiguity and oscillation in Hegel's line of argumentation here. He first seems to blame the poor themselves for subjectivizing their position as that of rabble, i.e., for abandoning the principle of autonomy which obliges subjects to secure their subsistence by their own labor, and for claiming as their right to receive means for survival from society. Then he subtly changes the tone, emphasizing that, in contrast to nature, man can claim rights against society, which is why poverty is not just a fact but a wrong done to one class by another. Furthermore, there is a subtle *non sequitur* in his argumentation: he passes directly from indignation against the rich/society/government to the lack of self-respect (implied by the demand to receive from society subsistence without working for it) – rabble is irrational because they demand decent life without working for it, thus denying the basic modern axiom that freedom and autonomy are based on the work of self-mediation. Consequently, the right to subsist without labor

> can only appear as irrational because /Hegel/ links the notion of right to the notion of the free will that can only be free if it becomes an object for itself through objective activity. To claim a right to subsist without activity and to claim this right at the same time only for oneself, according to Hegel, therefore means to claim a right that has neither the universality nor the objectivity of a right. The right that the rabble claims for Hegel is therefore a *right without right* and /. . ./ he consequently defines the rabble as the particularity that unbinds itself also from the essential interrelation of right and duty.[15]

But indignation is not the same as the lack of self-respect: it does not automatically generate the demand to be provided for without working. Indignation can also be a direct expression of self-respect: since rabble is produced necessarily, as part of the social process of the (re)production of wealth, it is society itself which denies them the right to participate in the social universe of freedoms and rights – they are denied the right to have rights, i.e., their "right without right" is effectively a meta-right or reflexive right, a universal right to have rights, to be in a position to act as a free autonomous subject. The demand to be provided for life without working is thus a (possibly superficial) form of appearance of the more basic and in no way "irrational" demand to be given a chance to act as an autonomous free subject, to be included in the universe of freedoms and obligations. In other words, since members of the rabble were excluded from the universal sphere of free autonomous life, their demand is itself universal – their

> claimed *right without right* contains a latent universal dimension and is itself not at all a mere particular right. As a particularly articulated right it is a right that latently affects anyone and offers the insight into a demand for equality beyond the existing objective statist circumstances.[16]

There is a further key distinction to be introduced here, a distinction only latent in Hegel (in the guise of the opposition between the two excesses of poverty and wealth) elaborated by Ruda: members of the rabble (i.e., those excluded from the sphere of rights and freedoms) "can be structurally differentiated into two types: there are the poor and there are the gamblers. Anyone can non-arbitrarily become poor, but only the one that arbitrarily decides not to satisfy his egoist needs and desires by working can become a gambler. He relies fully on the contingent movement of bourgeois economy and hopes to secure his own subsistence in an equally contingent manner – for example by contingently gaining money on the stock-market." The excessively wealthy are thus also a species of rabble in the sense that they violate the rules of (or exclude themselves from) the sphere of duties and freedoms: they not only demand from society to provide for their subsistence without work, they are *de facto* provided for such a life. Consequently, while Hegel criticizes the position of the rabble as being the position of an irrational particularity that egoistically opposes its mere particular interests against the existing and rationally organized universality, this differentiation between the two distinct rabbles demonstrates that only the rich rabble falls under Hegel's verdict: "While the rich rabble is, as Hegel judges correctly, a mere particular rabble, the poor rabble contains, against Hegel's judgment, a latent universal dimension that is not even inferior to the universality of the Hegelian conception of ethics."

One can thus demonstrate that, in the case of the rabble, Hegel was inconsistent with regard to his own matrix of the dialectical process, *de facto* regressing from the properly dialectical notion of totality to a corporate model of the social Whole. Is this inconsequence a simple empirical and accidental failure of Hegel, so that we can correct this (and other) similar points and thereby establish the "true" Hegelian system? The point is, of course, that, here also, one should apply the fundamental dialectical guideline: such local failures to deploy properly the mechanism of the dialectical process are its immanent symptomal points, they indicate a more fundamental structural flaw of the basic mechanism itself. In short, if Hegel were to articulate the universal character of rabble, his entire model of the rational State would have to be abandoned. However, does this mean that all we have to do here is to enact the passage from Hegel to Marx? Is the inconsistency resolved when we replace rabble with proletariat as the "universal class"? Here is how Rebecca Comay summarizes the socio-political limitation of Hegel:

Hegel is not Marx. The rabble is not the proletariat, communism is not on the horizon, and revolution is not a solution. /. . ./ Hegel is not prepared to see in the contradiction of civil society the death knell of class society, to identify capitalism itself as its own gravedigger, or to see in the disenfranchised masses anything more than a surge of blind, formless reaction, 'elemental, irrational, barbarous, and terrifying'/. . ./, a swarm whose integration remains unrealized and unrealizable, an 'ought'. /. . . / But the aporia, untypical for Hegel, points to something unfinished or already crumbling within the edifice whose construction Hegel declares to be completed, a failure of both actuality and rationality that undermines the solidity of the state he elsewhere cele-brates, in Hobbesian language, as an earthly divinity.[17]

Is then Hegel simply constrained by his historical context, did he come too early to see the emancipatory potential of the "part of no-part," so that all he could have done was to honestly register the unresolved and unresolvable aporia of his rational state? But does the historical experience of the XXth century not render problematic also Marx's vision of the revolution? Are we today, in the post-Fukuyama world, not exactly in late Hegel's situation? We see "something unfinished or already crumbling within the edifice" of the liberal-democratic Welfare state which, in the utopian Fukuyama moment of the 1990s, may have appeared as the "end of history," the finally found best possible politico-economic form. Perhaps, then, we encounter here yet another case of non-synchronicity: in a way, Hegel was more right than Marx, the XXth century attempts to enact the *Aufhebung* of the rage of the disenfranchised masses into the will of the proletarian agent to resolve social antagonisms ultimately failed, the "anachronistic" Hegel is more our contemporary than Marx.

We can also see how wrong was Althusser when, in his crude opposi-tion between overdetermined structure and the Hegelian totality, he reduced the latter to a simple synchronicity that he called "expressive totality": for (Althusser's) Hegel, every historical epoch is dominated by one spiritual principle which expresses itself in all social spheres. However, as the example of the temporal discord between France and Germany demonstrated, non-contemporaneity is for Hegel a principle: Germany was politically in delay with regard to France (where the revolution took place), which is why it could only prolong it in the domain of thought; however, revolution itself emerged in France only because France itself was in delay with regard to Germany, i.e., because France missed Ref-ormation which asserts inner freedom and thus reconciles secular and spiritual domains. So far from being an exception or an accidental com-plication, anachronism is the "signature" of consciousness:

experience is continually outbidding itself, perpetually making demands that it (i.e., the world) is unequipped to realize and unprepared to recognize, and comprehension inevitably comes too late to make a difference, if only because the stakes have already changed. (6)

This anachronistic untimeliness holds especially for revolutions: "The 'French' Revolution that provides the measure of 'German' untimeliness is itself untimely. /. . ./ There is no right time or 'ripe time' for revolution (or there would be no need of one). The Revolution always arrives too soon (conditions are never ready) and too late (it lags forever behind its own initiative)" (7). We can see now the stupidity of those "critical Marxists" who propagate the mantra that Stalinism emerged because the first proletarian revolution occurred at the wrong place (the half-developed "Asiatic" – despotic Russia instead of Western Europe – revolutions ALWAYS, by definition, occur at the wrong time and place, they are always "out of place." And was the French Revolution not conditioned by the fact that, because of its absolutism, France was lagging behind in capitalist modernization?

But is this non-contemporaneity irreducible? Is the Absolute Knowing, the concluding moment of the Hegelian system, not the moment when, finally, history catches up with itself, when notion and reality overlaps in full contemporaneity? Comay rejects this easy reading:

> Absolute knowing is the exposition of this delay. Its mandate is to make explicit the structural dissonance of experience. If philosophy makes any claim to universality, this is not because it synchronizes the calendars or provides intellectual compensation for its own tardiness. Its contribution is rather to formalize the necessity of the delay, together with the inventive strategies with which such a delay itself is invariably disguised, ignored, glamorized, or rationalized. (6)

This delay – ultimately not only the delay between the elements of the same historical totality, but the delay of the totality with regard to itself, the structural necessity for a totality to contain anachronistic elements which only make it possible for it to establish itself as a totality – is the temporal aspect of a gap which propels the dialectical process, and far from filling in this gap, "absolute knowing" makes it visible as such, in its structural necessity:

> Absolute knowing is neither compensation, as in the redemption of a debt, nor fulfilment: the void is constitutive (which does not mean that it is not

historically overdetermined). Rather than trying to plug the gap through the accumulation of conceptual surplus value, Hegel sets out to demystify the phantasms we find to fill it. (125)

Therein resides the difference between Hegel and historicist evolutionism: the latter conceives historical progress as the succession of forms, each of which grows, reaches its peak, and then becomes oudated and disintegrates, while for Hegel, disintegration is the very sign of "maturity," i.e., there is no moment of pure synchronicity when form and content overlap without delay.

So, back to Europe, perhaps we should conceive the very European trinity as a Borromean knot of anachronisms: the model-like excellence of each nation (British economy, French politics, German thought) is grounded in an anachronistic delay in other domains (the excellence of German thought is the paradoxical result of their politico-economic backwardness; the French Revolution was grounded in the delay of capitalism due to French state absolutism; etc.In this sense, the European trinity worked like a Borromean knot: each two nations are linked only through the intermediary of the third (in politics, France links England and Germany, etc.).

We should risk here a step further and demystify the very notion of a world-historical nation, a nation destined to embody the level the world history has reached at a certain point. It is often claimed that, in China, if you really hate someone, the curse you address at him is: "May you live in interesting times!" As Hegel was fully aware, in our history, "interesting times" are effectively the times of unrest, war and power struggle with millions of innocent by-standers suffering the consequences: "The history of the world is not the theatre of happiness. Periods of happiness are blank pages; for they are periods of harmony, periods of the missing opposition."[18] Should we then not conceive the succession of great "historical" nations which pass one to another the torch of embodying for a period progress (Iran, Greece, Rome, Germany . . .) not as a blessing of being temporarily elevated into a world-historical range but, rather, as a transmitting of a king of contagious spiritual disease of which one (a nation) can get rid only by passing it over to another nation, a disease which brings only suffering and destruction to the people contaminated by it. Jews were a normal nation living in a happy "blank page" of history until, for reasons unknown, god selected them as a chosen nation, which brought them only pain and dispersion – Hegel's solution is that this burden can be passed on and one can return to the happy "blank page." Or, to put it in Althusserian terms, while people live like individuals, from time to time some of them have the misfortune of being interpellated into subjects of the big Other.

So, back to rabble, one can argue that the position of "universal rabble" perfectly renders the plight of today's new proletarians. In the classical Marxist dispositif of class exploitation, capitalist and worker meet as formally free individuals on the market, equal subjects of the same legal order, citizens of the same state, with the same civil and political rights. Today, this legal frame of equality, this shared participation in the same civil and political spaces, is gradually dissolving with the rise of the new forms of social and political exclusion: illegal immigrants, slum-dwellers, refugees, etc. It is as if, in parallel to the regression from profit to rent, in order to continue to function, the existing system has to resuscitate pre-modern forms of direct exclusion – it can no longer afford exploitation and domination in the form of legal and civil authority. In other words, while the classic working class is exploited through their very participation in the sphere of rights and freedoms, i.e., while their *de facto* enslavement is realized through the very form of their autonomy and freedom, through working in order to provide for their subsistence, today's rabble is denied even the right to be exploited through work, its status oscillating between that of a victim provided for by charitable humanitarian help and that of a terrorist to be contained or crushed; and, exactly as described by Hegel, they sometimes formulate their demand as the demand for subsistence without work (like the Somalia pirates).

One should bring together here Hegel's two failures (by his own standards), rabble and sex, as aspects of the same limitation. Far from providing the natural foundation of human lives, sexuality is the very terrain where humans detach themselves from nature: the idea of sexual perversion or of a deadly sexual passion is totally foreign to the animal universe. Here, Hegel himself commits a failure with regard to his own standards: he only deploys how, in the process of culture, the natural substance of sexuality is cultivated, sublated, mediated – we, humans, no longer just make love for procreation, we get involved in a complex process of seduction and marriage by means of which sexuality becomes an expression of the spiritual bond between a man and a woman, etc. However, what Hegel misses is how, once we are within the human condition, sexuality is not only transformed/civilized, but, much more radically, *changed in its very substance*: it is no longer the instinctual drive to reproduce, but a drive that gets thwarted as to its natural goal (repro-duction) and thereby explodes into an infinite, properly metaphysical, passion. The becoming-cultural of sexuality is thus not the becoming-cultural of nature, but the attempt to domesticate a properly un-natural excess of the metaphysical sexual passion. This excess of negativity discernible in sex and apropos rabble is the very dimension of "unruliness" identified by Kant as the violent freedom on account of which man, in contrast to animals, needs a master. So it is not just that sexuality is the animal substance which is then "sublated" into civilized modes and rituals, gentrified, disciplined, etc. – the excess itself of sexuality which threatens to explode the "civilized" constraints, sexuality as unconditional Passion, is the result of Culture. In the terms of Wagner's *Tristan*: civilization is not only the universe of the Day, rituals and honors that bind us, but the Night itself, the infinite passion in which the two lovers want to dissolve their ordinary daily existence – animals know no such passion. In this way, the civilization/Culture retroactively posits/transforms its own natural presupposition: culture retroactively "denaturalizes" nature itself, this is what Freud called the Id, libido. This is how, here also, in fighting its natural obstacle, opposed natural substance, the Spirit fights itself, its own essence.

Elisabeth Lloyd suggests that female orgasm has no positive evolutionary function: it is not a biological adaptation with evolutionary advantages, but an "appendix" like male nipples.[19] Male and female both have the same anatomical structure for the first two months in the embryo stage of the growth, before the differences set in – the female gets the orgasm because the male will later need it, just like the male gets nipples because the female will later need them. All the standard explanations (like the "uterine upsuck" thesis – orgasm causes contractions that "upsuck" sperm and thus aid conception) are false: while sexual pleasures and even clitoris ARE adaptive, orgasm is not. The fact that this thesis provoked a furor among feminists is in itself a proof of the decline of our intellectual standards: as if the very superfluity of the feminine orgasm does not make it all the more "spiritual" – let us not forget that, according to some evolutionists, language itself is a by-product with no clear evolutionary function. One should be attentive not to miss the properly dialectical reversal of substance at work here: the moment when the immediate substantial ("natural") starting point is not only acted-upon, transformed, mediated/cultivated, but changed in its very substance. We not only work upon and thus transform nature – in a gesture of retroactive reversal, nature itself radically changes its "nature." (In a homologous way, once we enter the domain of legal civil society, the previous tribal order of honor and revenge is deprived of its nobility and all of a sudden appears as common criminality.) This is why the Catholics who insist that only sex for procreation is human, while coupling for lust is animal, totally miss the point, and end up celebrating the animality of men.

Why is Christianity opposed to sexuality, accepting it as a necessary evil only if it serves its natural purpose of procreation? Not because in sexuality our lower nature explodes, but precisely because sexuality competes with pure spirituality as the primordial metaphysical activity. The Freudian hypothesis is that the passage from animal instincts (of mating) to sexuality proper (to drives) is the primordial step from physical realm of biological (animal) life to metaphysics, to eternity and immortality, to a level which is heterogeneous with regard to the biological cycle of generation and corruption. (This is why the Catholic argument that sex without procreation, whose aim is not procreation, is animal, is wrong: the exact opposite is true, sex spiritualizes itself only when it abstracts from its natural end and becomes an end-in-itself.) Plato was already aware of this when he wrote about Eros, erotic attachment to a beautiful body, as the first step on the way toward the supreme Good; perspicuous Christians (like Simone Weil) discerned in sexual longing a striving for the Absolute. Human sexuality is characterized by the impossibility to reach its goal, and this constitutive impossibility eternalizes it, as is the case in the myths about great lovers whose love insists beyond life and death. Christianity conceives this properly metaphysical excess of sexuality as a disturbance to be erased, so it is paradoxically Christianity itself (especially Catholicism) which wants to get rid of its competitor by way of reducing sexuality to its animal function of procreation: Christianity wants to "normalize" sexuality, spiritualizing it from without (imposing on it the external envelope of spirituality (sex must be done with love and respect for the partner, in a cultivated way, etc.), and thereby obliterating its immanent spiritual dimension, the dimension of unconditional passion. Even Hegel succumbs to this mistake when he sees the properly human-spiritual dimension of sexuality only in its cultivated/mediated form, ignoring how this mediation retroactively transubstantiates/ eternalizes the very object of its mediation. In all these cases, the aim is to get rid of the uncanny double of spirituality, of a spirituality in its obscene libidinal form, of the excess which absolutizes the very instinct into the eternal drive.

It is easy to see the parallel between rabble and sex here: Hegel doesn't recognize in rabble (more than in state bureaucracy) the "universal class"; he doesn't recognize in sexual passion the excess which is neither culture nor nature. Although the logic is different in each case (apropos rabble,

Hegel overlooks the universal dimension of the excessive/discordant element; apropos sex, he overlooks the excess as such, the undermining of the opposition nature/culture), the two failures are linked, since excess is the site of universality, the way universality as such inscribes itself into the order of its particular content.

The underlying true problem is the following one: the standard "Hegelian" scheme of death (negativity) as the subordinate/mediating moment of Life can only be sustained if we remain within the category of Life whose dialectic is that of the self-mediating Substance returning to itself from its otherness. The moment we effectively pass from Substance to Subject, from Life(-principle) to Death(-principle), there is no encompassing "synthesis," death in its "abstract negativity" forever remains as a threat, an excess which cannot be economized. In social life, this means that Kant's universal peace is a vain hope, that *war* forever remains a threat of total disruption of organized state Life; in individual subjective life, that *madness* always lurks as a possibility.

Does this mean that we are back at the standard *topos* of the excess of negativity which cannot be "sublated" in any reconciling "synthesis," or even at the naive Engelsian view of the alleged contradiction between the openness of Hegel's "method" and the enforced closure of his "system"? There are indications which point in this direction: as it was noted by many perspicuous commentators, Hegel's "conservative" political writings of his last years (like his critique of the English Reform Bill) betray a fear of any further development which will assert the "abstract" freedom of the civil society at the expense of the State's organic unity, and open up a way to new revolutionary violence.[20] Why did Hegel shrink back here, why did he not dare to follow his basic dialectical rule, courageously embracing "abstract" negativity as the only path to a higher stage of freedom?

Hegel may appear to celebrate the *prosaic* character of life in a well-organized modern state where the heroic disturbances are overcome in the tranquillity of private rights and the security of the satisfaction of needs: private property is guaranteed, sexuality is restricted to marriage, future is safe . . . In this organic order, universality and particular interests appear reconciled: the "infinite right" of subjective singularity is given its due, individuals no longer experience the objective state order as a foreign power intruding onto their rights, for they recognize in it the substance and frame of their very freedom. Lebrun asks here the fateful question: "Can the sentiment of the Universal be dissociated from this appeasement?"(214) Against Lebrun, our answer should be: yes, and this is why war is necessary – in war, universality reasserts its right against and over the concrete-organic appeasement in the prosaic social life. Is thus the necessity of war not the ultimate proof that, for Hegel, every social reconciliation is doomed to fail, that no organic social order can effectively contain the force of abstract-universal negativity? This is why social life is condemned to the "spurious infinity" of the eternal oscillation between stable civic life and wartime perturbations – the notion of "tarrying with the negative" acquires here a more radical meaning: not just to "pass through" the negative but to persist in it.

This necessity of war should be linked to its opposite, the necessity of a rebellion which shatters the power edifice from its complacency and makes it aware of its dependence on the popular support and of its *a priori* tendency to "alienate" itself from its roots, or, as Jefferson famously wrote, "a little rebellion now and then is a good thing": "It is a medicine necessary for the sound health of government. God forbid that we should ever be twenty years without such a rebellion. The tree of liberty must be refreshed from time to time with the blood of patriots and tyrants. It is its natural manure."[21] Both times, a "terrorist" potential is unleashed: the first time, it is the state which unleashes absolute negativity that shatters individual subjects out of their particular complacency; the second time, it is the people themselves who remind the state power of the terrorist dimension of democracy by way of shattering all particular state structures. The beauty of the Jacobins is that, in their terror, they brought together these two opposed dimensions: their terror was simultaneously the terror of the state against individuals and the terror of the people against particular state institutions or functionaries who got too identified by their institutional places (the reproach to Danton was simply that he wanted to raise himself above others . . .). Needless to add that, in a properly Hegelian way, the two opposed dimensions are to be identified, i.e., that the negativity of the state power against individuals sooner or later inexorably turns against (the individuals who exercise) the state power itself.

Apropos war, Hegel is thus again not fully consequent with regard to his own theoretical premises: if he were to be consequent, he would have to accomplish the Jeffersonian move, i.e., obvious dialectical passage from external war (between states) to "internal" war (revolution, i.e., rebellion against one's own state power) as a sporadic explosion of negativity which rejuvenates the edifice of power. This is why, in reading the infamous Paragraphs 322–4 of Hegel's *Philosophy of Right*, where Hegel justifies the ethical necessity of war, one should be very careful to perceive the link between his argumentation here and his basic propositions on the self-relating negativity that constitutes the very core of a free autonomous individual – Hegel here simply applies this basic self-relating negativity constitutive of free subjectivity to relations between states:

§ 322 Individuality is awareness of one's existence as a unit in sharp distinction from others. It manifests itself here in the state as a relation to other states, each of which is autonomous vis-a-vis the others. This autonomy embodies mind's actual awareness of itself as a unit and hence it is the most fundamental freedom which a people possesses as well as its highest dignity.

§ 323 This negative relation of the state to itself is embodied in the world as the relation of one state to another and as if the negative were something external. In the world of existence, therefore, this negative relation has the shape of a happening and an entanglement with chance events coming from without. But in fact this negative relation is that moment in the state which is most supremely its own, the state's actual infinity as the ideality of everything finite within it. It is the moment wherein the substance of the state – i.e., its absolute power against everything individual and particular, against life, property, and their rights, even against societies and associations – makes the nullity of these finite things an accomplished fact and brings it home to consciousness.

/. . ./ An entirely distorted account of the demand for this sacrifice results from regarding the state as a mere civil society and from regarding its final end as only the security of individual life and property. This security cannot possibly be obtained by the sacrifice of what is to be secured – on the contrary.

/. . ./ War is not to be regarded as an absolute evil and as a purely external accident, which itself therefore has some accidental cause, be it injustices, the passions of nations or the holders of power, &c., or in short, something or other which ought not to be. It is to what is by nature accidental that accidents happen, and the fate whereby they happen is thus a necessity. Here as elsewhere, the point of view from which things seem pure accidents vanishes if we look at them in the light of the concept and philosophy, because philosophy knows accident for a show and sees in it its essence, necessity. It is necessary that the finite – property and life – should be definitely established as accidental, because accidentality is the concept of the finite. From one point of view this necessity appears in the form of the power of nature, and everything is mortal and transient. But in the ethical substance, the state, nature is robbed of this power, and the necessity is exalted to be the work of freedom, to be something ethical. The transience of the finite becomes a willed passing away, and the negativity lying at the roots of the finite becomes the substantive individuality proper to the ethical substance.

/. . ./ In peace civil life continually expands; all its departments wall themselves in, and in the long run men stagnate. Their idiosyncrasies become
continually more fixed and ossified. But for health the unity of the body is
required, and if its parts harden themselves into exclusiveness, that is death.
Perpetual peace is often advocated as an ideal towards which humanity should
strive. With that end in view, Kant proposed a league of monarchs to adjust
differences between states, and the Holy Alliance was meant to be a league
of much the same kind. But the state is an individual, and individuality essentially implies negation. Hence even if a number of states make themselves
into a family, this group as an individual must engender an opposite and create
an enemy. As a result of war, nations are strengthened, but peoples involved
in civil strife also acquire peace at home through making wars abroad. To be
sure, war produces insecurity of property, but this insecurity of things is
nothing but their transience – which is inevitable. We hear plenty of sermons
from the pulpit about the insecurity, vanity, and instability of temporal things,
but everyone thinks, however much he is moved by what he hears, that he
at least will be able to retain his own. But if this insecurity now comes on
the scene in the form of hussars with shining sabres and they actualize in real
earnest what the preachers have said, then the moving and edifying discourses
which foretold all these events turn into curses against the invader.

The function of what Hegel conceptualizes as the necessity of war is
precisely the repeated untying of the organic social links. When, in his
Group Psychology, Freud outlined the "negativity" of untying social ties
(*Thanatos* as opposed to *Eros*, the force of social link), he (in his liberal
limitation) all too easily dismissed the manifestations of this untying as
the fanaticism of the "spontaneous" crowd (as opposed to artificial crowds:
Church and Army). Against Freud, we should retain the ambiguity of
this movement of untying: it is a zero level that renders open the space
for political intervention. That is to say, this untying is the pre-political
condition of politics, and, with regard to it, every political intervention
proper already goes "one step too far," committing itself to a new project
(Master-Signifier). (Badiou also jumps all too directly from mere "animal
life" to the political Event, ignoring the negativity of the death-drive
which intervenes between the two.) Today, this apparently abstract topic
is actual again: the "untying" energy is largely monopolized by the New
Right (Tea Party movement in the US, where the Republican Party is
more and more split between Order and its Untying). However, here
also, every Fascism is a sign of failed revolution, and the only way to
combat this Rightist untying will be for the Left to engage in its own
untying – and there are already signs of it (the large demonstrations all

around Europe in 2010, from Greece to France and the UK, where the student demonstrations against university fees unexpectedly turned violent). In asserting the threat of "abstract negativity" to the existing order as a permanent feature which cannot ever be *aufgehoben*, Hegel is here more materialist than Marx: in his theory of war (and of madness), he is aware of the repetitive return of the "abstract negativity" which violently unbinds social links. Marx re-binds violence into a process of the rise of a New Order (violence as the "midwife" of a new society), while in Hegel, this unbinding remains non-sublated.

One cannot emphasize enough how these "militaristic" ruminations are directly grounded in Hegel's fundamental ontological insights and matrixes. When Hegel writes that the state's negative relation to itself (i.e., its self-assertion as an autonomous agent whose freedom is demonstrated through its readiness to distance itself from all its particular content) "is embodied in the world as the relation of one state to another and as if the negative were something external," he evokes a precise dialectical figure of the unity of contingency and necessity: the coincidence of external (contingent) opposition and immanent-necessary self-negativity – one's own innermost essence, the negative relation-to-oneself, has to appear as a contingent external obstacle or intrusion. This is why, for Hegel, the "truth" of the external contingent opposition is the necessity of negative self-relating. And this direct coincidence of the opposites, this direct overlapping (or short-circuit) between extreme internality (the innermost autonomy of the Self) and the extreme externality of an accidental encounter, cannot be "overcome," the two poles cannot be "mediated" into a stable complex unity. This is why Hegel surprisingly evokes the "solemn cycles of history," making it clear that there is no final *Aufhebung* here: the entire complex edifice of the particular forms of social life has to be put at risk again and again – a reminder that the social edifice is a fragile virtual entity which can disintegrate at any moment not because of contingent external threats, but because of its innermost essence. This regenerating passage through radical negativity cannot ever be "sublated" in a stable social edifice – a proof, if one is needed, of Hegel's ultimate *materialism*. That is to say, the persisting threat that the radical self-relating negativity will put at risk and dissolve any organic social structure points toward the *finite* status of all such structures: their status is virtual-ideal, lacking any ultimate ontological guarantee, always exposed to the danger disintegration when, triggered by an accidental external intrusion, their grounding negativity explodes. The identity of the opposites does not mean here that, in an idealist way, the inner spirit "generates" external obstacles which appear as accidental: external accidents which cause wars are genuinely accidental, the point is that, as such, they "echo" the innermost negativity that is the core of subjectivity.

Notes

1 Quoted from http://london.sonoma.edu/Writings/MartinEden/.

2 All passages from Hegel's *Philosophy of Right* are quoted from http://www.marxists.org/reference/archive/hegel/prindex.htm.

3 Quoted from http://marxists.catbull.com/archive/marx/works/1843/critique-hpr/index.htm.

4 G. K.Chesterton, *Orthodoxy*, San Francisco: Ignatius Press 1995, p. 116.

5 Jean-Pierre Dupuy, *La marque du sacre*, Paris: Carnets Nord 2008.

6 See Claude Lefort, *Essais sur le politique*, Paris: Editions du Seuil 1986.

7 See Slavoj Žižek, *Looking Awry*, Cambridge (Ma): MIT Press 1991.

8 Quoted from Stathis Gourgouris, *Does Literature Think?*, Stanford: Stanford University Press 2003, p. 179.

9 I am here fully solidary with Benjamin Noys who, in his *The Persistence of the Negative* (Edinburgh: Edinburgh University Press 2010), emphasizes and deploys the link between the vicissitudes of the "purely philosophical" notion of negativity and the shifts and impasses of the radical politics: when one talks on negativity, politics is never far behind.

10 One can even establish a link between Hegel's residual anti-Semitism and his inability to think pure repetition: when he gives way to his displeasure with the Jews who stubbornly stick to their identity, instead of "moving forward" and, like other nations, allowing their identity to be sublated /aufgehoben/ in historical progress, is his displeasure not caused by the perception that Jews remain caught in the repetition of the same?

11 I rely here on Frank Ruda's *Hegel's Rabble. An Investigation into Hegel's Philosophy of Right*, New York: Continuum 2011.

12 I owe this formulation to Mladen Dolar.

13 Jacques Lacan, "Le troisieme," *Lettres d'Ecole freudienne de Paris*, No 16 (1975), p. 187.

14 Quoted from Hegel, op.cit.

15 Ruda, op.cit., p. 132.

16 Op.cit., ibid.

17 Rebecca Comay, *Mourning Sickness. Hegel and the French Revolution*, Stanford: Stanford University Press 2011, p. 141. Numbers in brackets refer to the pages of this book.

18 G. W. F. Hegel, *Lectures on the Philosophy of World History*, p. 26–27.
19 See Elisabeth Lloyd, *The Case of the Female Orgasm*, Cambridge: Harvard University Press 2006.
20 Hegel died a year after the French revolution of 1830.
21 Quoted from Howard Zinn, *A People's History of the United States*, New York: HarperCollins 2001, p. 95.

Index